THE DESIGN
OF SOCIAL POLICY
RESEARCH

robert r. mayer / ernest greenwood

Bryn Mawr College   *University of California*

THE DESIGN
OF SOCIAL POLICY
RESEARCH

PRENTICE-HALL, INC., Englewood Cliffs, New Jersey 07632

Library of Congress Cataloging in Publication Data

Mayer, Robert R (date)
    The design of social policy research.

    (Prentice-Hall series in social work practice)
    Bibliography: p.

    Includes index.
    1.–Policy sciences–Research–United States.
    2.–Social science research–United States. I.–Greenwood,
    Ernest (date), joint author. II.–Title.
    H62.M328   309.1'73'0926   79–12905
    ISBN 0–13–201558–7

H 62
. M 328

Editorial/production supervision and interior
    design by Marina Harrison and Linda Schuman
Cover design by Wanda Lubelska
Manufacturing buyer: Ray Keating

PRENTICE-HALL SERIES IN SOCIAL WORK PRACTICE
Neil Gilbert and Harry Specht, Editors

Printed in the United States of America

10 9 8 7 6 5 4 3 2 1

PRENTICE-HALL INTERNATIONAL, INC., *London*
PRENTICE-HALL OF AUSTRALIA PTY. LIMITED, *Sydney*
PRENTICE-HALL OF CANADA, LTD., *Toronto*
PRENTICE-HALL OF INDIA PRIVATE LIMITED, *New Delhi*
PRENTICE-HALL OF JAPAN, INC., *Tokyo*
PRENTICE-HALL OF SOUTHEAST ASIA PTE. LTD., *Singapore*
WHITEHALL BOOKS LIMITED, *Wellington, New Zealand*

contents

preface

Since the 1960s interest has burgeoned in public policy as the object of scientific study as well as the outcome of a deliberate social process. This interest emerged from the more active stance taken by the federal government in dealing with social and environmental problems requiring public intervention, and from the introduction into government operations of techniques for systematic planning and management. This development has been followed on university campuses by a veritable eruption of academic programs designed to increase understanding of the policy-making process and to train persons who would function in policy-making positions. Almost all graduate professional schools in the social policy area—social work, education, public health, city planning and related human services—have created policy tracks or concentrations in their curricula. Schools and departments of policy analysis or public administration have been established to study policy making and to train professionals to assist in the formulation and analysis of policy alternatives. Two approaches have characterized these academic programs. On the one hand, social scientists have offered their theoretical perspectives and methodologies in an effort to demonstrate the usefulness of social science to policy making. Their results have often been disappointing because, though their analyses may have been theoretically and methodologically sound, they did not always have relevance for policy making. On the other hand, practitioners of the art of policy analysis have hastened to invent new methodologies in an effort to meet the lack of relevance. Their results constitute a confusing array of procedures differing from those of the social sciences more in name than in substance. Our book is an attempt to bring some order to this scene. We present models of the policy-making or planning process, of the empirical research process, and of the relation between the two. An understanding of this relation should enable the policy analyst or planner to design studies that have relevance for policy making.

The primary aim of this book is to provide a guide for designing policy investigations prior to their undertaking, a subject in which the existing literature is deficient. The focus is the design of an investigation and not the techniques whereby it is executed. For the latter the reader is directed at each design stage to the existing relevant literature. Our primary concern is with the formulation of the problem for investigation, its conceptualization, and the selection of the appropriate procedures for investigating it. A mastery of this design process is essential for all empirical studies but particularly for those dependent upon special funding sources. Without it the investigator cannot guarantee that the investigation will produce the findings expected. Current effort to introduce research methods into the analysis of social policy has focused on the evaluation of programs or of policies already operating. Important as this is, it ignores the potential contribution of empirical research to the earlier stages of policy making. We contend that the analyst should not be confined to analyzing decisions already implemented but should also be employed in the design of alternative policies and programs and in the selection of the one to be implemented. This view of the role of the analyst is reflected in the design instructions set down in this volume.

The book is divided into two parts. Part 1 describes the basic processes of policy research and the assumptions that underlie them. Chapters 1 and 2 discuss the nature of policy making and the scientific method, respectively, and Chapter 3 brings these two together in a description of social policy research. Chapter 4 is an overview of the research design process, the subject of the book.

Part 2 describes the nine stages in designing policy research, with a chapter devoted to each: (1) justification of the research, (2) history of the policy problem, (3) conceptual framework of the policy problem, (4) specification of the research objective(s), (5) determination of the study population, (6) specification of data to be collected, (7) selection of procedures for data collection, (8) specification of analyses to be performed, and (9) administration of the research. Each chapter discusses the decisions to be made in designing that particular stage and the factors to be considered by the analyst in reaching them. Examples clarifying each stage are drawn from various areas of social policy.

This book, then, provides both a conceptual framework for the understanding of social research in planning and policy making and some practical guides for its design. It should enable the policy analyst to utilize the research process and the behavioral scientist to adapt that process to policy making. However, the utility of this volume is not limited to those engaged in policy research. The nine stages of research design are applicable to any investigation. We therefore offer this book as a contribution to the literature on research methodology.

In this joint endeavor the four chapters of Part 1 and the first four chapters of Part 2, eight in all, were the product of the collaborative efforts of both authors. The remaining chapters (9 through 13 of Part 2), dealing with the technical stages of research design, were the responsibility of the senior author, who benefited in their preparation from the criticism and suggestions of the junior author.

The authors acknowledge their debt to those who facilitated this endeavor: their students at the University of North Carolina (Chapel Hill), the University of Texas (Austin), and the University of California (Berkeley) whose learning experiences shaped this book; Harry Specht and Neil Gilbert who encouraged their efforts; Angell Beza and David Kleinbaum who reviewed the technical sections; and Denise Thomas and Jane Rynning who invested many hours of clerical labor in the manuscript.

ROBERT R. MAYER
Bryn Mawr, Pennsylvania

ERNEST GREENWOOD
Berkeley, California

THE DESIGN
OF SOCIAL POLICY
RESEARCH

PART 1 / THE NATURE
OF SOCIAL
POLICY RESEARCH

chapter 1 / the policy-making process

The purpose of this chapter is to present an overview of the policy-making process. With this background in hand, the reader should be able to put into perspective the principal subject of this book, the design of policy research. We shall proceed by setting forth some basic definitions that should help to distinguish policy making as a unique social process. We then follow up with a delineation of the stages of policy making as we understand them, and of policy analysis as it fits into this process. The chapter concludes with a list of assumptions about the role of the policy analyst, our protagonist in this book, and the kinds of settings that are germane to such a role.

THE NATURE OF THE POLICY-MAKING PROCESS

The literature reflects numerous attempts in recent years to conceptualize and define policy, policy making, and policy analysis. As is true of any newly created field, there is often considerable variation, and even some disagreement, among these attempts. From among the several formulations of each concept we will select those elements that are most distinctive of the policy process and also seem to have the widest consensus.

Bauer (1968), whose writings are among the earliest, refers to policy as a decision involving some impending or intended action, as distinct from a decision regarding some cognitive or evaluative state (such as, "That is a pretty sunset," or "I really like blue better than green"). However, he goes on to distinguish three different levels of decisions based on the breadth of their implications. At level one are the *trivial and repetitive decisions* about routine actions that are made almost daily. They would be exemplified by the decision a bureaucrat might make, using an operations manual, regarding the eligibility of an applicant for a service. At the second level are more complex decisions that have wider ramifications and require some degree of thought or analysis. Such decisions are called *tactics*. An example would be decisions entering into the design of a community health center or into the planning of a neighborhood recreation program. It is for the third level of decisions that the term *policy* is reserved: "Those which have the widest ramifications, the longest time perspective, and which generally require the most information and contemplation" (Bauer 1968, p. 2). An example of such a decision would be whether to provide some form of tax-supported health insurance or to require relatives to be financially responsible for the medical care of the indigent.

This definition identifies three characteristics of a policy decision: (1) it involves an intended course of action, (2) it occurs at the highest or most inclusive level of decision making relative to the action to be taken, and (3) it incorporates consideration of complex implications anticipated from the proposed action.

Such a definition of policy is a bit open-ended; it contains no criterion by which to distinguish the highest level of decision (policy) from the middle level of decision (tactics). Bauer acknowledges that the distinction is relative to the level of social organization at which the decision is made. That is to say, a decision made at one level of an organization may constitute policy for the level below it, but tactics for the level above it. For example, if the president decides to submit a balanced budget to Congress, that decision clearly represents a policy of the executive branch of government, since no higher level of decision making exists in the federal structure. The decision of the president's Office of Management and Budget (OMB) to reach a balanced budget by means of an across-the-board cut of all budgets submitted to it by executive departments of government is clearly a tactical decision with respect to that made by the president. The OMB could have decided upon differential cuts in the proposed expenditures of those departments. However, with respect to any specific department, for example, Health, Education and Welfare (HEW), the OMB decision represents a policy. In order to stay within this reduced budget figure, the secretary of HEW might decide to place a freeze on all new program proposals. With respect to OMB such a decision is tactical, but with respect to the several divisions of services within HEW it represents policy.

Added clarity is imparted by Lowi (1972), who defines policy as "a general statement by some governmental authority defining an intention to influence the behavior of citizens by use of positive or negative sanctions" (p. 27). We do, however, disagree with Lowi in his restriction of policy to governmental decisions. The decision of the National Association for the Advancement of Colored People, a voluntary organization, to place a higher priority on legislative lobbying than on the provision of social services represents policy with respect to its constituency. Similarly, a decision of General Motors to compete in a certain segment of the automobile market represents policy with respect to the actors in that entrepreneurial organization. The distinction reflected in Lowi's definition which clarifies our viewpoint is that policy is a decision of a corporate body, be it a government, an enterprise, or a voluntary organization, with respect to resources at its disposal. Thus we shall be concerned with policy making as a collective rather than an individual act.

A further clarifying point in Lowi's definition is the recognition that policy represents an intent to constrain or to coerce the constituents of some collective. Thus the decision to spend money for a neighborhood playground is indeed coercive in the sense that it forecloses the spending of limited tax dollars for some competing alternative. Policies may vary with respect to the degree and form of coercion they imply, yet the *fact of coercion* makes the formulation of collective policy an act that generates complex ramifications. Policy making need not always involve the degree of separation between government and the citizenry implied in Lowi's statement. A policy can represent a decision resulting from the consensus of an entire collective, as in an Israeli kibbutz or in a Quaker meeting. However, once made, whether by collective deliberation or delegated authority, a policy acts on individuals, and some members of the group are affected more favorably than others.

We will summarize this discussion by defining policy as a *decision to act which is made in the name of a particular social group, which has complex implications, and which constitutes an intent to influence the group members by the provision of sanctions.* Accordingly, policy making can be defined as the social process in which multiple actors, aided with technical information, interact to formulate policy. It is the function of policy-oriented research to facilitate that process by providing relevant technical information, without which an analysis of implications would be impaired.

It will be helpful to pause a moment to consider the nature of two quite similar concepts: policy making and planning. Because the field of policy analysis is still in the early stages of development, whatever distinguishes policy making from planning has yet to be defined. Some writers differentiate between these processes by equating policy making with collective decision making at the highest level (after Bauer) and planning with decision making at the middle level (Bauer's tactical decision making). In other words, policy making is thought of as the selection of the goals of collective action, while planning becomes synonymous with the selection of means for attaining those goals. From this distinction it follows that policy making is characterized by value choices and political bargaining, while planning is characterized by technical or rational analysis.

We reject this distinction on two grounds. First, although since World War II the field of public planning has tended more in the direction of technical or rational decision making, there have been periods in its history when the formulation or selection of ideal ends was a dominant theme (Mumford 1938, Tugwell 1954, Wright 1943, Manuel 1966). It may be, therefore, that the distinction is more historical than substantive; planning may simply be an older term for essentially the same process. Second, the need to choose between competing values is not an exclusive characteristic of the selection of goals; it also characterizes the selection of means, as most practitioners can readily attest. Nor is resort to rational analysis an exclusive characteristic of the selection of means; it is also involved in the examination of the relative merits of alternative ends. Our position is that the relative emphasis on ends over means and on values over efficiency is characteristic of the level at which collective decision making occurs, and of the degree of value conflict involved in the choices to be made. Such emphases do not distinguish policy making from planning, for there is no inherent difference between them. *We choose, therefore, to use the terms* policy making *and* planning *interchangeably.* When the occasion requires it, we will use the term *policy planning* to refer to the higher level and *program planning* to refer to the lower level of decision making. The research process as we conceive it in this book is equally valid at both levels, though it may vary in its method. Hence, in discussing the role of research in public decision making, we shall have occasion to refer to all levels of that process.

Now we are faced with the task of clarifying the terms *goal, objective,* and *program.* Planners usually speak of a *goal* as the intention to attain some end state that is fairly broad in scope and relatively long in duration. A goal lends direction or purpose to the planning process but is usually not attainable within the scope of time allowed to a specific plan. As an expression of an intention to act, a goal is always stated as an infinitive—for example, to equalize educational opportunity; to provide decent housing for every American; to achieve a full employment economy; to make quality medical care available to all irrespective of income. The term *objective* refers to a specific end which can be attained by means of a specific plan or policy. An objective must meet four criteria. It must specify (1) an observable condition that is to be attained or changed, (2) a finite population of which that condition is a characteristic, (3) an amount of change which the policy maker seeks to attain with respect to that condition, and (4) a time period in which the change is to take place. Examples of objectives are:

> to reduce inequality among school district expenditures in the state of Texas to within 10 percentage points by 1978
>
> to increase the number of American families living in standard housing by 20 percent by 1980
>
> to reduce the rate of unemployment among heads of households in Raleigh, North Carolina, by 50 percent by 1977

It should be noted that objectives are *not* the means by which goals are attained, they are the operational expressions of goals. A *program* is a specific sequence of activities which the plan or policy is intended to set in motion to achieve an objective. Examples of programs that are relevant to the preceding objectives are (1) the adoption of a statewide educational tax system, (2) the provision of federal subsidies for low-cost housing construction, and (3) the provision of manpower training. Thus programs are the means by which goals are attained, and objectives are the concrete criteria by which programs are evaluated.

Planning in relation to human services has often been devoid of objectives. Health, education, and social services have been proposed as means of reducing illness, increasing the productivity of the labor force, or preserving family life. However, in the absence of specified objectives the decision maker is left with no alternative but to conclude that any increase in expenditures for such services would enhance the attainment of their respective social goals.

The designation of a goal as an element apart from an objective is not academic. The importance rests on whether one conceives of policy making or planning as a goal-attainment process (sometimes referred to as developmental planning) or as a problem-solving process (sometimes referred to as adaptive planning or disjointed incrementalism) (Ackoff 1973, Friedmann 1967); on whether one views public decision making as motivated by the desire to serve broad, long-range purposes or to avoid an immediate discomfort or undesirable condition. In both cases objectives are specified; however, in developmental planning the objective is deduced from some ultimate goal the decision maker wants to achieve; in adaptive planning it is derived from the necessity of avoiding some existing state of affairs. Goal-oriented planning, in contrast to a problem-solving approach, is likely to result not only in a different set of objectives but also in a different range of actions. A school system that seeks to create equality of educational experience among ethnic groups is likely to produce a different desegregation plan from one which seeks to avoid court litigation (Mayer, et al., 1974). A government which seeks to achieve an equitable distribution of income will formulate a different welfare policy from one which seeks to mitigate poverty.

The difference in objectives arises from the fact that goal-oriented policy making forces the decision maker to think explicitly about desired end states; it requires him or her to confront basic values and to think in a future time perspective. Planning under these conditions tends to be more innovative, broader in scope, and evolutionary. By contrast, problem-solving planning focuses on present situations, looks to the past for confirmation of progress, and is more opportunistic in the sense that any departure from present conditions will suffice. Problem-solving planning can often be a more satisfying activity. In evaluating his or her efforts, the policy maker is comparing an objective with some existing, known situation; hence progress is more easily demonstrable. In goal-oriented planning, on the other hand, one is always comparing an objective with a future state that has never been experienced. In this instance progress is bound to be more difficult to demonstrate.

The research process to be discussed in Part II of this book is equally applicable to goal-oriented and to problem-solving forms of planning. However, both the analyst and the policy maker should be aware of the distinction between these two forms of decision making; they should realize that, whichever form they choose to pursue, the choice will be determined not by the research design process but by their own interests and values.

It should be obvious from this discussion that values do function in the policy-making process. The formulation of a goal can be considered an expression of the policy maker's value preference. The selection of objectives as well as the strategies to reach them are highly influenced by values. A commitment to the creation of more jobs, rather than to income redistribution, reflects a value preference for gainful employment as a more acceptable means of reducing poverty. Similarly, the use of public agencies to operate school systems, as opposed to proprietary management, expresses a preference for government rather than for private enterprise as the provider of tax-supported services. Therefore, the normative nature of policy making must be taken into consideration in designing policy research. Of this we will have more to say in Chapter 3.

STEPS IN THE POLICY-MAKING PROCESS

Having described in some detail the nature of policy making, or planning, we are now in a position to identify the steps in the policy-making process. An understanding of the components of this process is necessary in order to see how and where research fits into it.

Numerous treatments of this subject, whether in the literature on policy making or on planning, are essentially similar (Meyerson and Banfield 1955, pp. 312–322; Braybrooke and Lindblom 1963, pp. 37–41; Dror 1968, p. 132; Parker 1974). What variation appears stems from the writers' conceptions of the extensiveness of the decision-making process and of the role of the policy analyst or planner. We will present what we regard to be the most comprehensive set of steps as reflected in these treatments. We are referring, of course, to the rational model of planning, sometimes referred to as comprehensive or synoptic. These steps are: (1) determination of goals, (2) needs assessment, (3) specification of objectives, (4) design of alternative courses of action, (5) estimation of the consequences of alternative actions, (6) selection of a course(s) of action, (7) implementation of the action(s), (8) evaluation of outcomes, (9) modification of goals, objectives, and courses of action based on feedback (see Figure 1-1).

1. *The determination of goals* refers to the selection of broad, long-range purposes which the policy or plan is to promote by reaching its objectives. Goals are broad in nature so as to provide a context within which to evaluate the significance or relevance of the specific conditions reflected in an objective. As such, goals cannot be measured directly nor attained within the time frame of a

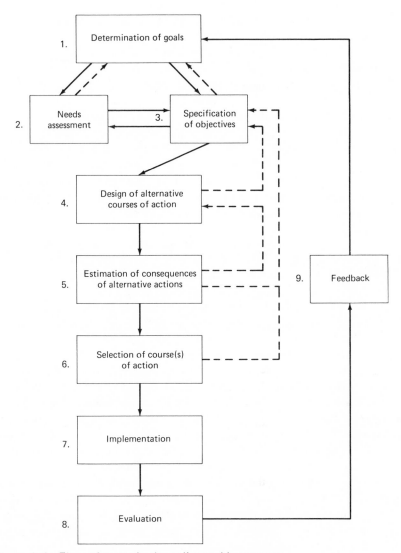

Figure 1-1 Flow of stages in the policy-making process.

given policy or plan. Goals are direct expressions of the value system of a social group and therefore have meaning only in the context of the group espousing them. In short-range or problem-solving planning this phase may be omitted, since objectives are derived directly from some assessment of an existing condition.

2. *Needs assessment* represents an elaboration of the rational planning model that has received increased attention with the advent of human services

planning. It refers to the determination, through some fact-finding procedure, of the extent of some undesirable condition or the degree of departure from some desired state of affairs as reflected in the policy objective. Needs assessment is seen as a step parallel to the specification of objectives. One cannot know what needs to assess until one has determined the observable conditions to be dealt with, which is part of the specification of objectives. Conversely, one cannot determine the amount of change aimed for in the policy objective until one knows the extent of the condition involved, which is the function of needs assessment. It should be noted that needs assessment in this model refers to the condition to be changed rather than the strategy to be used or the program to be provided. Current practice in the planning of social services often ignores the former and considers only a specific program, thereby eliminating from the process any statement of objectives that can later be used to evaluate that program.

3. *The specification of objectives* refers to the setting of specific targets that can be expressed in operational, usually quantitative terms, and can be reached within the time perspective and resources of a given policy or plan. The specification of objectives includes identifying (1) the condition to be remedied or the state to be achieved, (2) a finite population in which that condition exists, (3) a time frame in which change is to occur, and (4) the amount and direction of change sought in the condition. It is at this point that constraints surrounding the policy-making process enter. The limitation of funds, the rate of social change acceptable to the public, and the technical knowledge available to deal with the condition will all affect the setting of specific targets embodied in the policy objective. The identification of constraints may be considered as a separate stage. However, since it rarely involves empirical research, we have treated it as an integral part of the specification of objectives.

It should be noted that these first three stages do not necessarily follow this order in a given policy-making process. For example, when goals are formally given, as in the case of federal or state legislation, the planning process proceeds from the declaration of those goals to needs assessment and the specification of objectives. When relevant current reporting systems are available, as in the case of vital statistics and the U.S. Census, needs assessment may be unnecessary, and the process may go directly from the statement of goals to specification of objectives. On the other hand, needs assessment may initiate the policy-making process in the absence of any public discussion of goals or objectives. It can be argued that the War on Poverty of the 1960s grew out of the extensive documentation and articulation of this problem during the 1950s. Likewise, epidemiological research on lung cancer and heart disease produced a widespread awareness of these problems among the general public. Needs assessment may trigger off public debate and the enunciation of goals, or it may lead directly to the specification of objectives. When policy making is short-range or ad hoc in perspective, the specification of objectives is usually derived from the assessment of needs without reference to goals. In long-range planning any attempt to specify objectives is usually set in the context of an explicit statement of goals. Regardless of whether planning begins with the determination of goals or the assessment of needs, objectives must be specified before the process can proceed.

4. *The design of alternative courses of action* refers to the development or identification of various means by which the objectives of policy can be achieved. This stage represents the creative aspect of the planning process. Sometimes these alternatives are predetermined at the outset of the policy-making process and must simply be identified to the decision maker. In more goal-oriented or long-range planning, analysis goes beyond the consideration of actions that are already known to the development of new alternatives. The appropriate range of alternatives to be considered is still a moot issue in planning theory and need not concern us here.

5. *Estimation of the consequences of alternative actions* refers to an analysis of the effects, positive and negative, to be derived from each alternative course of action. These effects can be measured both directly (that is, in terms of the "amount" of objective achieved) and indirectly (in terms of the effects upon other objectives, such as the growth of the local economy or the support of a political constituency). Consequences are always estimated on the basis of existing knowledge about the phenomenon, or reasonable assumptions thereof. At this stage in the policy-making process there is rarely time to undertake studies to verify the presumed causal relations between alternative actions and their objectives, hence the reliance on reasoned judgment. Sometimes this stage is referred to as the "evaluation of alternative courses of action." However, because the term "evaluation" has a special meaning in the literature on research methodology, we will reserve it for a later stage in the policy-making process.

6. *Selection of a course(s) of action* refers to the policy maker's determination of a course of action seen as most desirable for achieving the objectives. This selection may consist of a combination of two or more of the alternatives analyzed in stage 5 and often involves the introduction of special criteria such as cost or feasibility of implementation, which become constraints on the selection of what otherwise would be ideal solutions. In dealing with policy alternatives in relatively cut-and-dried areas, for example, the construction of physical facilities, such constraints may become evident at stage 3, so that they may already be incorporated in the design of alternative courses of action. In human resources planning such definitiveness is unlikely, and the decision maker often makes constraints explicit only after alternatives and their consequences have been examined. However, in either case there is increasing insistence, even in such highly technical fields as transportation planning, on some form of social process in which citizens as well as decision makers can participate in the final selection after all the technical analyses have been completed. This step may involve special selection procedures such as public hearings, voting, or referenda.

7. *Implementation* refers to carrying out the courses of action selected in stage 6. Implementation involves its own sequence of actions and may thus require its own planning process. For example, let us assume that the objective under consideration is the expansion of medical care to low-income families. The alternative courses of action under consideration may be the provision of voucher payments by the government to private practitioners and the establishment of public clinics with a sliding fee schedule. Selection of either alternative would then require the decision maker to lay out a series of alternative actions designed to implement each decision. Of course, he or she must then examine the consequences of these various means and select the optimal one. This brief description of implementation points up the difference between program planning and policy planning discussed earlier. Planning with respect to the implementation of a given policy we refer to as program or administrative planning. Planning with respect to the policy itself we refer to as policy planning.

8. *The evaluation of outcomes* refers to the determination of the actual results achieved by having implemented the chosen course(s) of action. The results may include both those reflected in the policy objective as well as secondary results accruing to other objectives held by the policy maker. Since research plays a major role in this stage, the nature of evaluation in the policy-making process will be discussed in more detail in Chapter 3.

9. Finally, the evaluation of policy outcomes sets in motion a *feedback* process in which the results or outcomes are, so to speak, recycled in the planning process: to see to what extent the original goals have been fulfilled, to determine if any new objectives or any alterations in the original ones are called for, and to see if any new alternative courses of action or changes in their implementation are required. It should be noted that the evaluation of policy outcomes involves their inherent comparison with objectives, since the latter are always expressed in terms of intended outcomes. Therefore, the results of evaluation can be fed directly to the original statement of goals. Thus the feedback loop makes of policy making a reiterative process that can be repeated on an annual or program cycle basis.

It should be noted that the policy-making process is not always unidirectional. There are very likely to be internal feedback loops between certain stages (see Figure 1-1). For example, estimates in stage 5 of the consequences of proposed actions may be so marginal or even negative as to cause the analyst and decision maker to return to stage 4 to reconsider additional policy alternatives. Similarly, if all possible alternatives have been found wanting in stage 5, the process may have to revert to stage 3 in order to specify new objectives. Sometimes alternatives that have been deemed technically feasible in stage 5 are found to run counter to unexpressed but implicit value constraints in the selection process in stage 6, sending the analyst "back to the drawing boards" in stage 4. Ultimately, the process must pass through all nine stages before it is complete.

POLICY ANALYSIS

Policy analysis is a general term which refers to the multi-faceted process of ascertaining, measuring, and evaluating the ends and means of a policy, as well as their interrelationship. Such analysis may involve the identification and advocacy of particular ends to be sought by public policy, or it may focus on specifying or designing particular programs to meet those ends. Then again, it may be more concerned with evaluating the relationship between those means and those ends.

Policy analysis can also be applied to either of the levels of decision making we discussed earlier. It can examine the relationship between objectives and alternative actions (policy planning) or that between an action and its implementation (program planning). The focus of analysis will tend to vary with the audience for whom it is designed. The general public and elected decision makers will be more interested in the relationship between an objective and a course of action. They are inclined to ask the question, "Does the policy or program work?" Administrators and service providers, on the other hand, tend to be interested in the relationship between a course of action and its implementation. They are more prone to ask the question, "How does the policy or program work?"

Despite the fact that policy analysis remains a nascent discipline, we can readily identify four models, each with its unique methodology. These models are formulated around the concepts of efficiency, effectiveness, feasibility, and ethics. The model of *efficiency* focuses on the relationship between the cost of resources employed to implement a policy and the extent of the benefits it delivers. Its evaluative yardstick might be phrased as, "Do the benefits derived from the objective outweigh the costs of attaining it?" or "Which of several alternatives has the lowest cost per unit of benefit attained?" Efficiency models usually take into account several objectives; that is, they measure the cost not only of obtaining the primary objective but of obtaining secondary results that may also be of interest to the policy maker.* For this reason, we say that efficiency is measured in benefit-cost and cost-effectiveness ratios. This methodology holds the promise of being the most comprehensive model of policy analysis. However, its use requires us to assume that we can accurately predict the effects of a given policy and that a methodology exists for measuring the effect of the means on the desired ends. The efficiency model further assumes the desirability of the ends to which policy making is directed.

The model of *effectiveness* provides a methodology for determining the

---

*Because of their consideration of both direct and indirect benefits, such analyses are sometimes referred to in the literature of economics as "effectiveness" measures to distinguish them from the engineering model of efficiency involving the "least cost" evaluation of a single objective.

effects of a given policy. It focuses on the utility of the relationship between the means and the ends, that is, on the substantive effects that are achieved by the means employed. Such a model poses the question, "To what extent does the course of action employed result in the desired objective?" Even if progress toward a desired end is achieved, the decision maker cannot be sure what part of that progress can be attributed to the policy itself and what part is owing to other factors in the environment. In other words, progress may have been serendipitous—the result of forces other than the intervention of the policy maker. Evaluations based on effectiveness are particularly appropriate in social planning, where the knowledge needed to predict effects is less well developed. Measures of effectiveness are based on the techniques of causal analysis employed in the behavioral sciences. However, as a model of policy analysis, the strategy of effectiveness remains incomplete. Measures of effectiveness must be combined with cost information into a measure of efficiency for a complete evaluation of the means-ends relationship.

A third approach to evaluation deals with the *feasibility* of the means for achieving the desired ends. Feasibility in this sense refers to a special kind of cost, namely, political cost. It deals with the effect of the policy on the political constituency whose support is necessary for its successful implementation. Political cost also refers to the effect of the means employed and/or of the ends to be achieved on constituencies whose support the policy maker may need for other ends that he or she desires to achieve. A feasibility evaluation seeks to answer the questions, "Is there sufficient political support for the means contemplated?" or "Will the utilization of these means consume scarce political capital needed to attain other ends?" The model is reflected in the efforts of political scientists to analyze partisan politics and the voting behavior of legislative bodies.

Our fourth model, a more recent one, attempts to evaluate policy on *ethical grounds*. The ethical model focuses more on the goals and objectives of policy rather than on its outcomes. It deals with the relationship of a particular policy goal to the values, either explicit or implicit, of the policy-making system. Here the question to be answered is, "Do the ends to be sought and/or the means to be employed in achieving them enhance or conflict with values important to the policy maker and to his or her constituency?" The method of ethical analysis, though less well developed, rests essentially on logic as that process is employed in philosophical inquiry. Ethical analysis involves a number of activities: explicating the values underlying a particular policy problem; examining the consistency of a set of policy goals with the societal value system; determining whether the goals are consistent among themselves; and finally, reconstructing the logic by which a given set of objectives was derived from a given set of goals. The purpose of this last activity is to determine if the stated objectives represent an adequate operational expression of the goals.

It is impossible to do justice to all four methodologies here, and we shall not attempt to do so. A considerable body of literature already exists on the effectiveness (Suchman 1967, Weiss 1972) and efficiency (Margolis 1970, Merewitz and Sosnick 1971, Aldine-Atherton, Industrial Relations Centre 1970) models, to which the reader is advised to turn. Newly developed work is also appearing on the methodologies for analyzing the feasibility (Morris and Binstock 1966, Lindblom 1968, Lowi 1972, MacRae 1970) and the ethics (MacRae 1971) of the means-ends relationship. The focus of this book is on the empirical research process as it is used in policy making. Empirical research is a basic element in three of the models discussed above: It is essential to determining the outcomes or effects associated with a given policy, a prerequisite for calculating measures of efficiency; and it is also the central method used for deriving measures of effectiveness and feasibility. It goes without saying that any complete effort at policy analysis should incorporate all four perspectives.

THE ROLE OF THE ANALYST

So far we have simply taken for granted certain terms that refer to various actors in the policy-making process: policy maker, decision maker, analyst, and planner. The time has come to clarify these terms. We conceptualize the participants as performing two parallel but interacting roles throughout the process: One involves making decisions that lead to action, and the other involves carrying out analyses that lead to those decisions.

We have defined policy as a decision of intent on behalf of a collective to influence the behavior of its members. It follows, therefore, that the policy maker is some person or group authorized by a collective to make such a decision, or it may be the collective acting as a body. The policy literature uses the terms *policy maker* and *decision maker* synonymously. The terms usually connote elected or appointed officials or the governing board of a governmental agency. However, the terms can also apply, as we have noted earlier, to comparable actors in voluntary organizations, such as labor unions or community associations. Sometimes governmental agencies or voluntary organizations hire ad hoc consultants to assist them in policy analysis, in which case they have a contractual rather than an administrative relationship to the person performing the analytical role. In such a relationship the decision makers may be referred to as clients. *Hence, we will use the terms* policy maker, decision maker, *and* client, *interchangeably to refer to persons empowered to make policy or adopt plans on behalf of a collective.*

The other participant in the policy-making process, and the one of primary interest to us in this text, is the person who assumes responsibility for performing the analyses that lead to policy decisions. Sometimes the policy maker himself plays this role. But usually this task is delegated to another person, both because the policy maker's task is a more than full-time occupation and because the nature of policy analysis is often quite complex and technical. The analyst may be a permanent staff member of the policy maker's agency, an outside consultant hired temporarily for a specific task, or a volunteer member of the organization who donates his or her services.

Because of the increasing demand for policy analysis in government and in other large organizations, and because of the increasing sophistication of the procedures entailed, this function has become institutionalized. Sometimes the person performing it is called a policy analyst, sometimes a planner, sometimes a researcher, and sometimes a program evaluator. Each term tends to reflect a particular professional discipline in which its user has been trained. Some terms, such as *planner,* connote other functions or roles in addition to analysis, for example, statesman, designer, advocate, mediator. However, there is a common denominator for all of them, and that is a preoccupation with a rational examination of policy making. *In the material that follows, we shall use the term* analyst *to refer to anyone, regardless of his or her professional background, who performs the analytical function in policy making.*

•This book is written primarily to clarify the tasks performed by the policy analyst. A word is in order, therefore, regarding the role of the analyst vis-à-vis that of the policy maker. The efforts of the analyst are inextricably linked to the interests and actions of some decision maker. That decision maker may be an elected official or administrator under whose supervisory control the analyst works, or a voluntary interest group with which the analyst has contracted to provide a specific service.

Given the analyst's lack of independence, there is an understandable tendency to conceive of his or her role as a dependent, unimaginative one. According to this view the analyst is a "technician," one who has expertise in some specialized technical process, usually quantitative in nature, and who applies this expertise to measurement problems defined by the policy maker or client. From this it follows that the analyst is confined to participating at only two points in the policy-making process, namely, in estimating consequences of alternative courses of action and/or evaluating outcomes of policy interventions.

Our conception of the policy analyst's role is much broader. Since we consider policy analysis as a process of reasoning about and of verifying means-ends relations, it is applicable at all stages of the policy-making process—in the determination of goals and objectives to be achieved, in the design of alternative courses of action to achieve those objectives, and in the evaluation of those actions, both proposed and implemented. We view the analyst as an activist rather than a technician, as one who not only evaluates policy options in terms of technical procedures, but who also questions the policy maker's initial conception of the policy problem and the alternative courses of action for dealing with it. *In short, the analyst is one who is actively engaged in an intellectual partnership with the decision maker throughout the policy-making process.*

The role we have just projected for the analyst, as expert in the reasoning process, contrasts with another view of the policy analyst as a substantive expert. To be sure, some policy analysts are identified with a specialized field—perhaps education, housing, criminal justice, health, or welfare—because their expertise is based on knowledge about the relevant variables and their interrelations in that field. By contrast, we view the role of the policy analyst as cutting across substantive fields. This does not require, however, that the analyst be a generalist. Rather, he or she is one who specializes in methodologies for verifying policy-relevant relationships within substantive fields. We do not mean to imply by this position that substantive knowledge is incompatible with methodological expertise. Both are needed in policy making. Our position is based on the recognition that both types of expertise are rarely found in the same person, and that both functions need not be performed by the same actor. This book is designed to facilitate the methodological rather than the substantive role in policy analysis.

SUMMARY

We have defined policy as a decision of intent made on behalf of a collective to influence the behavior of its members through the use of positive or negative sanctions. We have described a nine-step model of the policy-making process, in which policy making and planning are treated interchangeably. Policy analysis is a process for making a rational choice among goals, objectives, and the means for their attainment. Four models of policy analysis were identified based on efficiency, effectiveness, feasibility, and ethics. Empirical research is an important basis for the analysis of particular policy alternatives. The policy analyst is one who works in partnership with a policy maker by bringing relevant information to bear on the value choices confronted in decision making.

REFERENCES

ACKOFF, RUSSELL L., "Science in the Systems Age: Beyond IE, OR and MS," *Operations Research* (May/June, 1973), 661–671.

BAUER, RAYMOND A. "The Study of Policy Formation: An Introduction," in *The Study of Policy Formation,* ed. Raymond A. Bauer and Kenneth J. Gergen. New York: Free Press, 1968.

Benefit-Cost Analysis, an Aldine Annual. Chicago: Aldine-Atherton.

BRAYBROOKE, DAVID., and CHARLES E. LINDBLOM. *A Strategy of Decision: Policy Evaluation as a Social Process.* New York: Free Press, 1963.

Cost-Benefit Analysis and the Economics of Investment in Human Resources, an Annotated Bibliography. Kingston, Ontario (Canada): Industrial Relations Centre, Queens University, 1970.

DROR, YEHEZKEL. *Public Policymaking Reexamined.* San Francisco: Chandler Publishing Co., 1968.

FRIEDMANN, JOHN. "A Conceptual Model for the Analysis of Planning Behavior," *Administrative Science Quarterly, 12* (September, 1967), 345–370.

HAVEMAN, ROBERT H., and JULIUS MARGOLIS, eds. *Public Expenditures and Policy Analysis.* Chicago: Markham Publishing Co., 1970.

LINDBLOM, CHARLES E. *The Policy-Making Process.* Englewood Cliffs, N.J.: Prentice-Hall, Inc., 1968.

LOWI, THEODORE J. "Population Policies and the American Political System," in *Political Science in Population Studies,* eds. Richard L. Clinton, William S. Flash, and R. Kenneth Godwin. Lexington, Mass.: D. C. Heath, 1972.

MacRAE, DUNCAN, JR. *Issues and Parties in Legislative Voting: Methods of Statistical Analysis.* New York: Harper & Row, 1970.

MacRAE, DUNCAN, JR. "Scientific Communications, Ethical Argument, and Public Policy," *American Political Science Review, 65* (March, 1971), 38–50

MANUEL, FRANK E., ed. *Utopias and Utopian Thought.* Boston: Houghton Mifflin Co., 1966.

MAYER, ROBERT R., CHARLES E. KING, ANNE BORDERS-PATTERSON, and JAMES S. McCULLOUGH. *The Impact of School Desegregation in a Southern City.* Lexington, Mass.: D. C. Heath, 1974.

MEREWITZ, LEONARD, and STEPHEN H. SOSNICK. *The Budget's New Clothes.* Chicago: Markham Publishing Co., 1971.

MEYERSON, MARTIN, and EDWARD C. BANFIELD. *Politics, Planning and the Public Interest.* New York: Free Press, 1955.

MORRIS, ROBERT, and ROBERT H. BINSTOCK. *Feasible Planning for Social Change.* New York: Columbia University Press, 1966.

MUMFORD, LEWIS. *The Culture of Cities.* New York: Harcourt, Brace & World, 1938.

PARKER, FRANCIS H. "Social Policy and Social Planning," in *The Field of Social Work* (6th ed.), ed. Arthur E. Fink. New York: Holt, Rinehart and Winston, 1974.

SUCHMAN, EDWARD. *Evaluative Research.* New York: Russell Sage Foundation, 1967.

TUGWELL, REXFORD. *The Place of Planning in Society.* San Juan: Puerto Rico Planning Board, 1954.

WEISS, CAROL H. *Evaluation Research.* Englewood Cliffs, N.J.: Prentice-Hall, Inc., 1972.

WRIGHT, FRANK LLOYD. *An Autobiography.* New York: Duell, Sloan and Pearce, 1943.

chapter 2 / the nature of scientific research

The subject of this book is the design of empirical research to facilitate policy making. Empirical research is inquiry conducted according to rules that collectively constitute the scientific method. It follows, therefore, that the basic elements and processes the policy analyst must bring to bear in the design of policy research are those of science. As a consequence, we will devote our attention in this chapter to the nature of scientific research, the understanding of which is a necessary underpinning to our discussion of the nature of policy research in Chapter 3.

Although this book is not an exposition of scientific methodology, a brief review of its tenets is highly advisable. The more one understands the elements and processes of science, the greater command one will have over research methodology and the greater skill one will develop in the design of research. The elements of the scientific method include *concepts,* the components of any statement about the nature of reality; *propositions,* statements by which concepts are linked into relationships that depict reality; and *theories,* bodies of propositions that explain those relationships. The processes of science consist of those procedures that guide the formulation and validation of these concepts, propositions, and theories. However, before turning to their examination let us define the nature of research.

THE NATURE OF RESEARCH

Research is any inquiry or investigation undertaken with the aid of standardized procedures in order to obtain information that will augment a shared body of knowledge. The terms *standardized* and *knowledge* merit elaboration. By standardized is meant systematic, communicable, and repeatable. The procedure employed by an investigator to obtain information must have a predetermined order and system. As such, it can be described to others who can thus visualize it. These investigators can then repeat the procedure in order to verify the new information in terms of both its validity and its reliability. Procedures that share these three characteristics are the hallmark of acceptable research in any discipline. Knowledge generated by this type of research is regarded as public because the findings upon which it rests are verifiable. By contrast, investigations conducted by individuals to inform themselves on a particular subject are not considered research. For while such effort may well remedy personal ignorance, it does not enhance public knowledge by generating new information (Macdonald 1960). Research has as its function, and sole justification, to uncover hitherto unavailable information.

The term *research* often elicits the picture of a scientist conducting experiments in a laboratory; however, this conception seems unduly to restrict the meaning of the term. Scientists do not have sole monopoly over research. Investigations can be conducted in any field of intellectual endeavor—thus we speak of legal research, literary research, and historical research, to name a few. Research, in other words, is the medium whereby any and every intellectual community expands its own unique body of knowledge. In this book we will be concerned with scientific research, more specifically, with social research.

Scientific Research

What are the distinguishing characteristics of scientific research? First, it is *empirical.* The term is of Greek origin and translates literally as "experiential"; its more common meaning is "observational." In scientific research the primary data consist of the investigator's experiences with the persons, objects, or events of the natural world. In other words, the raw materials from which scientific knowledge is derived are systematic observations of reality.* Hence, when an investigator engaging in scientific research collects data by whatever procedure, that person is said to be conducting observations. So characteristic is this feature that "empirical research" has become a synonym for scientific research (Tripodi, Fellin, and Meyer 1969).

The second and equally distinct feature of scientific research is the mental process whereby observations are converted into meaningful information. From the observations, generalizations are derived to describe the phenomenon under study; from the generalizations a theory is formulated; and from the theory hypotheses are derived to predict future occurrences of the phenomenon. The hypotheses are then tested for accuracy by reobserving the phenomenon.

---

*It should be obvious that the expression "empirical observations" is a redundancy. If a datum is empirical, it is ipso facto observational.

This cycle of reasoning (from observation to observation) is governed at every step by the canons of deduction and induction. This process and these canons are referred to collectively as the *scientific method,* and we will discuss them in greater detail later in this chapter.

A third distinctive characteristic of scientific investigation is that it invariably possesses a structure or *design.* The design may vary from inquiry to inquiry, but it is inherent in all scientific investigations. This structure is essentially a set of written directives outlining the sequence of operations that the investigator will undertake. It is for the researcher what a blue print is for an architect. In no other intellectual discipline does the investigator invest so much time, thought, and effort in planning his or her research prior to undertaking it.

Social Research

Social research is the term used to designate investigations designed to augment the body of knowledge of a social science or of a social practice. There are thus two types of social science research: pure research, the intent of which is to expand our understanding of social processes, and applied research, the intent of which is to make us capable of influencing these processes. Most importantly, however, both types rely on the same methods and techniques and depend on the same rules of evidence and inference—in other words, they share the same "language of social research" (Lazarsfeld and Rosenberg 1955). Because social research is modeled after scientific research, it shares many of the techniques common to the physical sciences. To be sure, there is a great difference between the aspects of the natural world studied by physical scientists and those studied by social scientists and social practitioners. But this difference aside, social research is essentially empirical research grounded in the scientific method. However, when social scientists refer to a piece of research as "empirical," they are using the word somewhat more loosely than would a chemist or physicist, for example. If the reader is not to be left confused by some sections of Part II, we must clarify this particular connotation of "empirical."

Empirical social research in its purest form occurs when the investigator himself, either as a participant or a nonparticipant observer, witnesses the phenomenon under investigation. However, if students of the social sciences had to depend exclusively on firsthand observation, social research would be seriously hampered; not infrequently they find themselves separated by time and space from the phenomenon to be investigated. In these instances, the researcher must resort to vicarious observation—that is, to interviewing those who have actually witnessed the phenomenon. By controlling the content of questions and the manner of questioning, the researcher may gain from the responses of informants an indirect view of the remote events. If face-to-face contact with prospective informants should prove impossible, the investigator can of course solicit their responses by means of a mailed questionnaire.

In all this the investigator is once removed from the phenomenon that he or she would wish to but cannot observe. Nonetheless such research is regarded as empirical, because the investigator is collecting his or her own raw data. In fact, the term *empirical* is elastic enough to include an inquiry wherein the investigator derives information by *reanalyzing* observational data that had been previously collected by another researcher to serve an entirely different purpose (a procedure called secondary analysis). And if the original data were not obtained firsthand, but indirectly from informants, our investigator is now twice removed from the phenomenon under study.

Thus far we have been considering inquiries in which information was extracted from data collected for some research project. However, social researchers have stretched the "empirical" label to cover inquiries involving the analysis of written materials that were generated for purposes far removed from research. Thus, the content analysis of social service records, legislation, transcripts of public hearings, newspaper articles, and organizational minutes is classed as empirical research. And so we see that while empirical literally means "experiential," in the language of social research it does not imply that the investigator must personally experience the phenomenon that he or she wishes to study.

ELEMENTS OF SCIENCE

We turn now to a discussion of the elements that constitute the scientific method, namely concepts, propositions, and theories.

Concepts

Concepts are the building blocks of science. Every investigation begins and ends with concepts. Concepts are the means by which experiences about the real world are organized into mental images that can be communicated by the researcher in the course of investigating or testing a particular proposition describing that experience. They are also the vehicle by which the results or findings of an investigation are translated into mental images for the larger public. In order properly to design a research project, one must therefore fully understand the nature of concepts.

Concepts are ideas, or mental images, about the real world. They can be graphically portrayed, as in Figure 2-1, in terms of a *triangle of reference* (Ogden and Richards 1948, p. 11). The structure of a concept consists of three parts: (1) *the idea* or mental image one has of some phenomenon in the outside world; (2) *the referent,* that is, the actual phenomenon to which this idea refers; and (3) *the term* or the symbol whereby the idea is communicated to others. Thus, the idea refers to some aspect of reality embodied in a referent; the idea

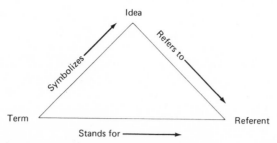

Figure 2-1 Concepts as a triangle of reference. *Source:* C. K. Ogden and I. A. Richards, *The Meaning of Meaning* (New York: Harcourt, Brace Jovanovich, Inc., 1948), p. 11.

is symbolized by a term, a language form; and the term stands for the referent. We can say that a concept is an idea linked to a referent by means of a term.

The triangle of reference makes clear that neither the term nor the idea is identical with the actual phenomenon that it represents. To think otherwise is to commit the fallacy of reification. Concepts are public, because they have referents which are observable by many persons and because they are given symbols which permit their communication to others. It is this public quality of concepts that makes possible the practice of science, which is a social enterprise.

An understanding of the way in which concepts are formed, or the *conceptualizing process,* is crucial to the design of research. The ability to conceptualize is essential to the formulation of research objectives. For this purpose the triangle of reference can be expanded to a parallelogram as shown in Figure 2-2. The conceptualizing process begins with sensory stimulations produced by referents or objects in the real world which generate *perceptions.* These perceptions are then processed by the mind for their common characteristics. Dissimilarities among the perceptions are ignored, and similarities are retained. This mental process results in an *abstraction,* or idea. For example, one may look around a crowded room and observe that people are sitting on variously shaped objects. Some of these objects are four-legged (chair or sofa, for example), some

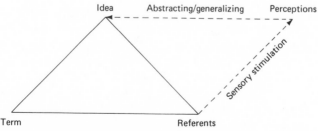

Figure 2-2 The conceptualizing process

are three-legged (stool), some two-legged (bench). Some have backs for supports, others do not. Some are high, others are low. But they all have one thing in common: Their legs support a surface which is sufficiently raised off the floor to allow people to sit comfortably in an upright position. Immediately the idea of "object to sit on" emerges in the mind. Once this abstraction has been formulated, a generalizing process is initiated. From a series of experiences, or set of perceptions, one projects the existence of a hypothetical class of objects to which a label or term is attached: seating furniture. The class encompasses a wide variety of objects, all having a set of common characteristics. It is this commonality which enables one to distinguish and keep mentally separate chairs from tables (although both have four legs) or benches from tables (although both have long surfaces).

Thus, the conceptualizing process consists of abstracting from a set of perceptions certain common elements, and then on the basis of these elements generalizing to a hypothetical class, even though all members of the class have not been perceived. One has only to watch the children's television series *Sesame Street* to see this process at work. Children are confronted with a series of objects accompanied by the familiar jingle, "Which of these things is not like the others?" By constant repetition of sets of objects with similar and dissimilar characteristics the child is taught to form concepts of shapes, colors, and even purposes or uses.

Concepts can and have been classified in a variety of ways. Any classification makes good sense if it serves the perspective and purpose of the classifier. We shall not burden the reader with the varying distinctions among concepts that have been drawn by logicians. However, for purposes of policy research the distinction between *class* concepts and *property* concepts is relevant (Hempel 1952).

A class concept has as its referent a collection of persons, objects, or events that share one or more common characteristics and thus belong to a single entity distinct from all others. Examples are working women, clinic patients, social agencies, depressed neighborhoods. Note that the units which comprise a class may be either of two kinds, individuals or collectives. Thus, each clinic patient is a single individual, whereas each social agency is itself a collection of individuals who interact as a unit. This distinction is quite relevant to our purposes, for social policy research deals not only with individuals whose welfare is at issue, but also with the organizations responsible for enhancing that welfare. With respect to a class concept, the idea has a one-to-one correspondence with some aggregation of individuals or collectives in the real world.

A property concept may be thought of as a more abstract version of a class concept. Its referent is some *characteristic* exhibited by a series of persons, objects, or events; for example those property concepts that correspond to the class concepts mentioned above are marital status (working women), health (clinic patients), auspices (social agencies), and location (depressed neighborhoods). Lazarsfeld and Barton further distinguish between two types of property concepts—relational properties and individual or personal properties (1951, p. 189). An individual property is a characteristic pertaining to a particular individual, whereas a relational property exists only with reference or in relation to someone else. Thus when we categorize members of a group according to their height or weight, we do so on the basis of standard characteristics that do not derive from interpersonal comparisons. But when we categroize those same individuals as leaders or followers, as conformers or deviants, or as equals or unequals, we can do so only by taking into account the corresponding characteristics of others who form a social context for the individuals in question. Relational properties serve a useful function in policy research. They focus attention on the social milieu as the subject of analysis. They draw attention to the fact that the phenomenon under investigation may have its origin in the relations *between* individuals rather than in the characteristics *of* individuals.

Since discourse between two persons involves the exchange of concepts, the efficiency of communication depends on the degree of agreement between them regarding the meaning of those concepts. A term used by the speaker should symbolize the same idea in the listener's mind, and should in turn designate the same referent for both. Such agreement is established by means of a definition. A commonly accepted definition imparts to the concept a fixed and standardized meaning. The process of defining a concept can be more easily understood by keeping in mind the triangle of reference. A definition tightens the mental links holding together the three points of the triangle. Essentially there are only two ways of defining a concept, *connotatively* and *operationally*.

A connotative definition defines a concept in terms of other concepts. It links the concept to other less abstract concepts and thereby enables the listener to grasp the more complex term. Any one of the following, for example, might serve as a connotative definition of poverty: a state of living in substandard conditions; the absence of any means of earning a livelihood; a psychological state of despair or deprivation. A word of caution is in order, however: If the concepts that comprise the definition are as abstract as the one being defined—and hence as difficult to comprehend—each of them will in turn require its own definition. Then the connotative definition will fall short of its intent. A certain amount of ambiguity is bound to arise in any discussion over a subject of common interest between two persons, even when both are working in the same discipline and presumably speak the same technical language. Accordingly, when the listener asks the speaker to define his or her terms, the speaker will invariably respond by giving some connotative definitions of the ambiguous terms so that the discussion can proceed.

In contrast to the connotative, the operational definition is *denotative* in that it points to the phenomenon itself to which the idea refers and from which it was abstracted. To be more specific, an operational definition states the conditions, the materials, and the procedures needed either to identify or to reproduce one or more referents of the concept being defined. Thus, to borrow a phrase from Lundberg, a recipe for sponge cake is an operational definition of it (Lundberg 1942, p. 89). The definition derives its name from the fact that it specifies the mental and/or physical operations to be engaged in, so as to arrive at the referents of the concept. According to Ackoff, the operational definition is directive (1953, p. 352). The operations enable us to bring the concept down from the abstract level of idea to the concrete level of reality, so that the phenomenon referred to may be clearly recognized. Thus an operational definition of poverty may be "existence for a family of four on an annual income below $5,000."*

Operational definitions are indispensable for the conduct of research. As the reader will shortly see, concepts function in the research process as guides to observation. Without clear specification of the referents of a guiding concept, which operational definitions furnish, the researcher is unsure *what to observe.* The scientific method requires that the investigator specify his or her observational procedures so that others will be able to replicate the study and thereby verify its findings. Operational definitions of the guiding concepts fulfill this requirement better than connotative ones. In actual practice, both types of definition are used to define highly abstract concepts. Such concepts are first defined connotatively, so as to relate them to less abstract concepts, and then these are operationalized. The entire process, known as *conceptual clarification,* will be treated in detail in Part II.

Propositions

Concepts of course do not exist in isolation; they are linked together into propositions, or statements about the nature of reality. Propositions are simply problem statements that the researcher seeks to verify, and that once proven, constitute the building blocks of theory. It is necessary to distinguish among four different types of proposition that one encounters in the research process: (1) value assumptions, (2) presuppositions, (3) empirical generalizations, and (4) hypotheses. *Value assumptions* are assertions about the way things ought to be, in other words, positive or negative valuations of objects or events. Such propositions as "all persons should work in order to receive an income," or "children should be raised by their mothers" are value assumptions. Such propositions are neither theoretical nor empirical. Their validity is not subject to empirical verification and therefore they do not constitute appropriate subject matter for research. However, because they are implicit in every research task and thereby constrain one's view of the policy problem or of potential solutions to it, such valuations need to be made explicit early in the process.

*The 1975 estimate of the President's Council of Economic Advisors.

Presuppositions are assumptions of a causal nature.* They are state-ments about the nature of reality which are assumed to be true within a given context, but not actually known to be true. Therefore, unlike value assumptions, they are potentially subject to empirical verification. Presuppositions are used as an underpinning so that the investigator can move to those propositions (hy-potheses) that are the focus of the inquiry. In this sense presuppositions are affirmed so as to enable us to test their consequents.

Empirical generalizations are propositions enunciating observable uni-formities about any class of persons, objects, or events, about their properties, or about relations between classes or properties. They are true by virtue of the fact that they are empirically affirmed. Any two persons can observe the same uni-formity in reality and arrive at the same generalization about it. Generalizations conform to the canons of science—they are communicable, replicable, and verifi-able. They are generated by the process of induction.

Hypotheses, on the other hand, are conjectures about uniformities, be-cause they have not yet been verified by observations. They are deduced from some set of propositions which are known to be true (empirical generalizations or theory) or accepted as though true (presuppositions).** When such a set of propositions is part of a formally expressed theory, the deduced hypotheses are said to be "theoretic." Thus, hypotheses are propositions which have a theoreti-cal or deductive basis but do not yet have an empirical basis. They are generated by the process of deduction.

Theory

The nature of these different types of propositions and their relationship to the research process can be better understood in the context of theory. Theory can be defined as the linking together of two or more empirical generalizations by one or more explanatory propositions. Thus a theory constitutes an explanation of empirical generalizations. It should be noted that theories are based on veri-fied propositions, not on conjectures. However, a theory in turn generates hypotheses which, when verified, constitute a test of the theory; that is, this second wave of hypotheses demonstrates the theory's ability to explain phenom-ena that lie beyond the original ones the theory was designed to explain. Clearly, theory building is a cyclical process; it begins with empirical generalizations from

---

*Kaplan refers to presuppositions, suppositions, and assumptions as fulfilling the same general function (1964, p. 86–89). The only way in which they differ seems to be in their level of abstraction. For purposes of our summary treatment here, this difference will be ignored.

** This view may tend to glorify the bases of hypotheses. Often hypotheses grow out of personal experiences, which can be thought of as unrigorous or unsystematic empiri-cal generalizations; or out of hunches, which are implicit or unsystematized "private the-ories"—explanations of the world that derive from individual experiences of it—reflected in the familiar remark, "I have a theory . . ."

which it is constructed, and ends with new generalizations resulting from the verification of the hypotheses by which the theory is tested. This process will be examined in greater detail later in this chapter.

Theory differs from empirical generalizations and hypotheses in two important respects. In the first place empirical generalizations and hypotheses are descriptive while theory is explanatory. Empirical generalizations and hypotheses state observable uniformities, for example, "persons who are unemployed or underemployed have a higher rate of participation in criminal activity," or "cities decrease in density from the center outward toward the suburbs." Theory, on the other hand, explains why and how the facts asserted in these propositions occur. Secondly, because empirical generalizations and hypotheses have a one-to-one correspondence to the world of observable events, they can be verified by reference to those events through observation. In this sense they are factual. By contrast, theories can be tested only by means of deducible hypotheses that assert uniformities among observable events. Thus, while it can be empirically demonstrated that the hypotheses are either consistent or inconsistent with such events, the theories themselves can be proved correct only in a logical sense.

Because of this relationship between theory and facts, it is inappropriate to think of theories as true or false in the conventional sense of those terms. They are better described as correct or incorrect. We will use the term *testing* to refer to determining the correctness or adequacy of a theory. By this we mean its logic—consistency, clarity, generality, and falsifiability. We will use the term *verifying* to refer to determining the conformity of a proposition or hypothesis (which may be deduced from a theory) with the facts. By this we mean the empirical fidelity or truth of the proposition.*

The correctness of a theory can be determined by reference to four criteria: (1) *exhaustiveness*—Does it link up all of the empirical generalizations about a given phenomenon? (2) *internal consistency*—Are the explanatory statements in the theory consistent with each other, or does the theory generate conflicting hypotheses? (3) *external consistency*—Is the theory consistent with related theory? (4) *falsifiability*—Is a set of empirical conditions (an hypothesis) conceivable that is inconsistent with the theory (Kaplan 1964, pp. 311–322; Popper 1965, pp. 84–92)? This last criterion refers to the fact that it is never possible to test a theory in an absolute sense—it is humanly impossible to conceive of or anticipate all the possible empirical conditions to which the theory might apply. The best one can do is attempt to falsify it, that is, generate hypotheses that are *not* consistent with the theory and then attempt to verify them.

In the world of science, theory never conforms neatly to these criteria.

*In making this distinction between testing and verifying we are adopting the position of Popper that, to be valid, it is not enough that a proposition be consistent with observable facts; it also must be compared with events which have the potential of falsifying the proposition (1965, pp. 32–42).

Existing theory in any discipline is characterized much more by incompleteness, competition, and dynamic succession. It is impossible for any theory to be complete or correct for all time. All the relevant facts are never known, new facts constantly emerge, and alternative theories based on radically different premises are formulated. Sometimes the response to such inconsistencies is a revision of an established theory to conform to new facts, or its incorporation into a more encompassing theory, thereby yielding a more comprehensive explanation. When the discrepancy between new facts and an existing theory is severe, or when a rival theory is more suited to changing social values, the old theory is discarded for a new one and we speak of a "scientific revolution" as occurring.* However, such a succession does not mean that the superseded theory is incorrect with respect to the set of facts upon which it was based. The theory merely becomes incorrect or obsolete with respect to new facts that are discovered or new social purposes that emerge.

An Example of Theorizing

We will illustrate the relationship between the basic elements of science—concepts, propositions, and theory—through a simple hypothetical example of theorizing taken from the field of heath care. The example is diagramed in Figure 2-3. One of the means most frequently adopted to improve the quality of health services has been to increase the participation of consumer groups in the work of public health planning agencies at the local level. Let us assume, for purposes of illustration, that we are interested in determining what effect consumer participation has had on the work of such agencies. Toward this end we undertake an investigation that involves our attending meetings of the boards of directors of health planning agencies to observe consumer representatives in action. Our observations lead us to recognize three distinct classes of board members: (1) *providers,* those persons who provide a professional health service or represent an agency which does so; (2) *consumers selected by the health planning agency,* members of subgroups in the target population who were selected for membership on the board by the health planning agency; and (3) *consumers selected by consumer organizations,* members of subgroups in the target population who were selected by organizations comprised of consumers, such as labor unions and neighborhood action groups.

Further observation of such meetings leads us to the conclusion that differences characterize the behavior of board members: Some attend meetings more regularly than others and some offer vocal opposition to proposals more frequently than do others. In order to understand this matter more fully we interview board members after each meeting to ascertain their attitudes toward

---

*Such conflicts are resolved not on factual grounds but on the basis of preferences for new explanations that presumably serve different social purposes (Kuhn 1962).

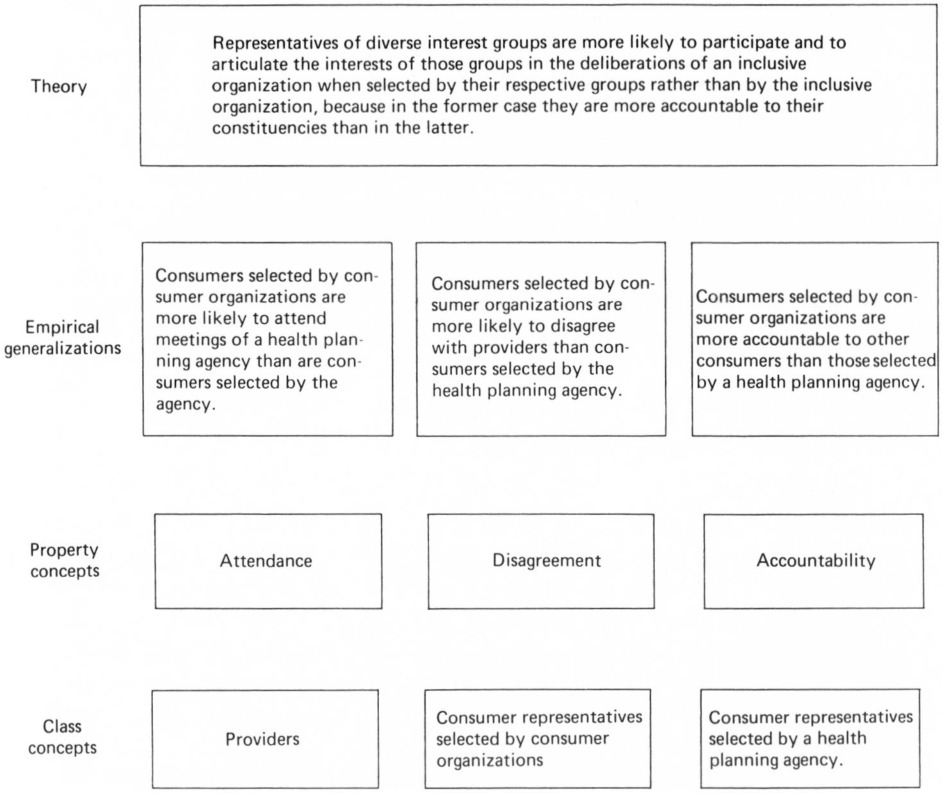

Figure 2-3 An example of the theorizing process

and perceptions of the agency's work. In so doing we discover a difference that characterizes the behavior of consumer board members: Some consult frequently with (are accountable to) other consumers between one board meeting and the next, while others rarely do. Thus our observations have led us to the identification of three property concepts: (1) attendance at meetings, (2) disagreement in the discussion of proposals, and (3) accountability to other consumers (see Figure 2-3).

We are now in a position to put these three class concepts and three property concepts together into a series of propositions that describe their interrelatedness. After reviewing all of our observations, and checking out our hunches through further observations at board meetings, we formulate the following empirical generalizations:

1. Consumer board members selected by consumer organizations are more regular in their attendance at board meetings than consumer members selected by the health planning agency.

2. Consumer board members selected by a consumer organization express verbal disagreement with providers more often than do consumer members selected by the health planning agency.
3. Consumer board members selected by consumer organizations consult with (are accountable to) other consumers more frequently than do consumer members selected by the health planning agency.

At this point we have a series of propositions that describe uniformities between two or more classes or properties but that do not constitute an explanation of consumer participation. To accomplish the latter objective we need to bring the propositions together into a system in which one empirical generalization is accounted for by reference to another empirical generalization. We can explain the first and second empirical generalizations in our series by reference to the third empirical generalization:

> Consumer board members selected by consumer organizations are more likely to attend board meetings and to disagree with provider board members than are consumer members selected by the health planning agency, because the former are more accountable to other consumers than are the latter.

Now we have an explanation but not a theory, because the system of propositions applies to only a single class of events, consumer participation in health planning agencies. To constitute a theory the explanation must be stated at a level of abstraction high enough to permit the derivation of hypotheses about a new class of events, and thereby permit the theory to be tested. This can be done by converting each of the concepts in our system to a higher level of abstraction. Thus:

> Members of an inclusive decision-making organization who are representative of diverse interest groups are more likely to participate and to articulate the interests of their respective groups in the deliberations of the inclusive organization when they are selected by their group rather than by the inclusive organization, because the former are more accountable to their constituencies than are the latter.

As should be expected, this "theory of consumer participation" raises as many questions as it answers. How do we account for the high level of participation of providers? Is accountability the only way in which consumers can become more active? Under what conditions might providers advocate the interests of consumers? A given theorizing process necessarily leaves some links incomplete and generates new questions, so that the investigator must make fresh observations and from these do some additional theorizing. And so the process continues. We shall now go on to examine at greater depth the very important connection between concepts, empirical generalizations, theory, and hypotheses that constitute this feedback loop.

PROCESSES OF SCIENCE

In discussing the basic elements of science—concepts, propositions, and theory—we touched only briefly upon the processes whereby these elements are brought together to generate scientific knowledge. Now we will discuss them more systematically in order to round out our picture of the scientific method that underlies all research. The basic processes of theory building in science are usually summarized as description, explanation, and prediction.

Description, as has been already noted, is simply the detailing of uniformities among a series of persons, objects, or events. The literature distinguishes between two types of description: *qualitative* and *quantitative.* Qualitative description refers merely to identification of the distinguishing properties or characteristics of a group of persons, objects, or events. It involves essentially the process of conceptualizing and results in the formation of classification schemes. Such description typifies the initial stage of development of any given discipline. Quantitative description, on the other hand, represents a more advanced stage of observation. In possession of a set of such classificatory schemes, the investigator now proceeds to measure the size or distribution of those properties among members of a particular class. It is at this point that such statistical techniques as frequency distributions and measures of central tendency and dispersion come into play. Descriptions of either type (qualitative or quantitive) can deal with uniformities involving a single variable, two or three or more variables. These three types are known as univariate, bivariate, and multivariate description, respectively. Bivariate and multivariate descriptions can be expressed in the form of either typologies or statistical correlations. In order for a science to achieve explanatory power, that is, to develop theory, it must move from univariate to multivariate descriptions.

The process of *explanation* may be thought of as an extension of description, but the "object" of the description is now the *relationship* between two or more classes or two or more properties. Rather than simply describing their covariation, however, explanation accounts for the occurrence of one class in terms of the other class(es) of variables. In essence explanation is an inference about the causal relationship between two or more phenomena.

Sometimes it is difficult to draw a distinction between description and explanation. In the course of describing the sequence of events leading up to a phenomenon, one may virtually explain "why" it happened. For example, with the increasing sophistication of statistical techniques, it is possible to use correlational and regression analysis to separate out the relative contribution of individual variables to a criterion or dependent variable, and thus lay the groundwork for explanation. On the other hand, scientists use the experimental method to establish causation, but the use of the latter is always subject to the precondition that all relevant variables have been controlled. For most practical purposes it is impossible to control all relevant variables, so perfect explanation is rarely achieved. This state of affairs has led Cohen (1931) to conclude that as a field of science becomes more sophisticated, its subject matter is expressed less in causal terms and more in terms of invariant relations, which are essentially descriptive propositions.

Kaplan takes issue with the distinction between description and explanation when he observes that causal analysis essentially involves placing an empirical generalization in the context of other facts or empirical generalizations (1964, p. 329). A proposition is "explained" only in the sense that it is located logically in a larger set of propositions that lend it plausibility. This form of explanation he calls *concatenated description*. The example of theorizing we presented in Figure 2-3 may be thought of in these terms, for our "explanation" of one empirical generalization was merely a description of its relationship to other empirical generalizations. Concatenated description is probably a more accurate depiction of the process of science in that no phenomenon can be explained in an ultimate sense; it can only be located in relation to the necessary or sufficient conditions for its occurrence.

Nonetheless, the distinction between description and explanation has operational meaning in the design of research. If explanation is an objective, certain procedures must be built into the research design to enable the analysis of data to move beyond the description of uniformities to the testing of causal assumptions which account for those uniformities. A causal assumption is tested by verifying the following three conditions: (1) *time order*—the presumed causal agent, or change in the independent variable, occurs prior in time to the occurrence of the presumed effect, or change in the dependent variable; (2) *covariation*—the presumed causal agent always occurs (or occurs more often than not) with the occurrence of the presumed effect; (3) *elimination of rival hypotheses*—at least one other presumed causal agent, or variation in an independent variable, does *not* occur with the occurrence of the presumed effect. Each of these three conditions can be verified by empirical research. The design of a descriptive study may permit the verification of the first two conditions, but not the third. It is the inclusion of procedures for verifying all three conditions that distinguishes explanatory from descriptive research.

The ultimate process in the development of science is *prediction*. Once a theory has been developed, predictions (or hypotheses) can be deduced from it about future events or relationships that transcend those already observed. Prediction should be distinguished from a projection or forecast, a process frequently used in planning and policy studies. Projections are simply extrapolations of future trends based on past uniformities without understanding them. They are sometimes referred to as mechanical predictions, since they are based on description rather than on explanation. Estimates of the size of future populations based on past trends in birth and death rates are a case in point. Inclusion of the estimations of factors that influence such rates (urbanization, level of income, industrialization, medical care) can yield more accurate predictions. The accurate prediction of future events is the ultimate test of a theory. Thus, the status of a given science lies not so much in the ability of its practitioners to manipulate their environment in testing their theories, as in their ability to predict the course of events in that environment based on those theories. Astronomy is no less a science because of the inability of astronomers to control the movement of the stars. This characteristic is particularly important to social scientists who cannot test their theories under laboratory conditions.

Types of Scientific Reasoning

To arrive at correct inferences about causal relationships (explanation), we may employ two contrasting but complementary types of reasoning, *induction* and *deduction.* The two processes differ both in their starting points and in the way they lead to their conclusions. In induction we start with a series of observations about a phenomenon in the real world and from them conclude the existence of some uniformity or relation in that phenomenon. The conclusion of an inductive process is, therefore, a generalization about a set of observed facts. The inductive process is outlined in the classical model of the experimental method as formulated by John Stuart Mill in his now famous four canons or rules.

In deduction we start with propositions that we can assume to be true either by prior observation or "reason," and using them as premises derive a conclusion. The conclusion of a deductive process thus consists of the implications contained in the starting propositions. The Aristotelian syllogism is the prototype of deduction. The correctness of a conclusion reached by induction depends upon the accuracy of our observations. By contrast, the correctness of a conclusion reached by deduction depends upon the truth of the propositions that we use as premises. If these premises are true, then the conclusion is logically valid.

The processes of induction and deduction are employed interdependently in science. Thus, it is by engaging in induction that scientists derive generalizations they can subsequently use as premises to engage in deduction. And it is by the process of induction that they test the factual truth of conclusions arrived at by deduction. The interdependence of these two processes is illustrated by our previous discussion. In our hypothetical example of theorizing we arrived at generalizations about the behaviors of consumers and providers by induction. But we arrived at a theory to explain these behaviors by deduction. To continue the inferential process we would, again by deduction, derive some hypotheses from this theory; and we would test the factual correctness of these hypotheses inductively through observation.

Induction of a causal nature is the logic that underlies most research designs that attempt to be explanatory. Therefore we shall discuss this form of reasoning in greater detail. The canons of causal induction formulated by Mill have also been known as the canons of experimental inquiry because the experimental method was assumed identical to the scientific method. Mill formulated four basic canons of which only two are relevant here—the canon of agreement and the canon of difference.* The canon of agreement is as follows:

> If two or more instances of a phenomenon under investigation have only one circumstance in common, the circumstance in which alone all the instances agree, is the cause (or the effect) of the given phenomenon (Cohen and Nagel 1934, p. 251).

Thus if we are interested in the problem of mongolism (the effect), we may examine a series of mongoloid births and find that the mothers involved vary with respect to race, income, and body type, but that they are all of a similar age, that is, 40 and over. According to the canon we could argue that the mother's age at the time of an infant's birth may be the causal factor in producing mongolism in offspring.

Although the canon of agreement may be adequate for discovering possible causes, it is inadequate for testing their truth. According to Mill, if we are to prove that a hypothesized factor (for example, age at birthing) is the cause C of a presumed effect E (for example, mongolism), we must show that C is present every time E is present and that C is absent every time E is absent. This may be symbolized as CE and $\overline{CE}$. In other words, to demonstrate causation, we must establish both CE and $\overline{CE}$. The canon of agreement, while it enables us to establish CE, does not enable us to establish $\overline{CE}$. For this latter purpose it is necessary to invoke the canon of difference:

> If an instance in which the phenomenon under investigation occurs, and an instance in which it does not occur have every circumstance in common save one, that one occurring in the former; the circumstance(s) in which alone the two instances differ is the effect or the cause . . . of the phenomenon (Cohen and Nagel 1934, p. 256).

In this repect the canon of difference requires the opposite combination of units of observation from that required by the canon of agreement. The reader will note that whereas the first canon calls for two (or more) units which *resemble* each other in that they all exhibit the phenomenon under study, the second canon calls for (at least) two units which *differ* from each other in this regard. Hence, this time we would proceed by comparing a series of mongoloid births with a series of normal births. If, in examining the mothers involved, we found

---

*Mill's other two canons are the canons of concomitant variation and of residues. Cohen and Nagel refer to the last two canons as quantitative methods, because their application requires the aid of prior measurement of the data to which they are applied (1934, p. 262). The first two canons, which call for no such prerequisite, they refer to as qualitative methods. Because of this distinction the first two of Mill's canons are the more frequently discussed and illustrated in the methodological literature.

that they were all of the same race, income group, body type, but that members of the first group were all 40 years of age or older, while those in the second group were all younger than 40, we could establish the fact that the mother's age at birthing may be the cause of mongolism. The reader will recognize in this canon the basis of that method which is commonly known as the experimental method.

Thus we may define the experimental method as follows:

> An experiment is the proof of an hypothesis which seeks to hook up two factors into a causal relationship through the study of contrasting situations which have been controlled on all factors except the one of interest, the latter being either the hypothetical cause or the hypothetical effect (Greenwood 1945, p. 28).

It will be noted that this description of the process of induction involves reasoning either from the effect to the cause, or from the cause to the effect. In actual practice, analyses that proceed from effect to cause often yield biased or invalid conclusions for two reasons. In the first place, cases are selected for examination after the fact; that is, after "the experiment" has been completed. Even if we were able to study all those cases in which the effect occurs, we would have no assurance that all the persons originally exposed to the presumed causal variable (that is, those who began the experiment) actually made it through to the end of the exposure period so as to register the effect or its absence. Thus, in our hypothetical example of mongolism, an undeterminable number of births may not have been reported, either because the mothers may have moved out of the study area or because the pregnancies may have resulted in stillbirths, or for whatever reason the health of the newborn may not have been known. Some of the unreported births may well have been mongoloid, and if so, we have no way of knowing whether any or how many of the mothers were over age. In other words, we have no way of insuring that we have examined an adequate sample of cases where the effect appears.

However, there is a more fundamental reason why this line of induction may be invalid. Most social phenomena are not universally prevalent, that is, causal relationships rarely take the invariant form; they are more likely to be probabilistic in nature. Inferences about such relationships are based on the relative distribution of factors in comparison groups rather than on their universal presence or absence. It is absolutely essential, therefore, to observe a sample of cases that are representative or matched on the basis of the causal variable rather than on the effect variable. For example, it is necessary to know what proportion of women over 40 produce mongoloid births compared to the proportion under 40 who do so. If, in our hypothetical example, we picked a small sample of women 40 and over, and an equal sample of women under 40, we might find several cases of mongolism in the first group but none in the second. This finding would indicate some relationship between age and mongolism, but hardly the definitive one implied in our earlier example. To draw our cases solely on the basis of the presence or absence of mongolism ignores those women over 40 who did not produce mongoloid children. In the absence of this latter figure we cannot calculate the proportion of such women exhibiting the effect to the total number of women giving birth. Hence, we cannot calculate the probability of the occurrence of the effect.

We may summarize this discussion as follows: when undertaking an inductive inquiry, it is possible to discover potential causal relationships through effect-to-cause analyses, but it is then necessary to verify such relationships through cause-to-effect analyses.*

INTERRELATIONSHIP BETWEEN ELEMENTS AND PROCESSES

Previously, we referred to the scientific method as being cyclical, in that its elements and processes constitute a feedback loop that leads to a progressive refinement of a given body of knowledge. The elements and the transformations through which they pass can be represented as a system, following a model developed by Wallace (1971, pp. 16–25) (see Figure 2-4). In this model the elements are represented by boxes and the transformations (subprocesses) by circles. As a system, it can be entered at any point, there being no beginning and no end. Since in our example of theorizing we began with the observation of discrete events, let us enter the diagram at that point (lower right-hand corner of the figure).

The model shows that the process of observation results in the formation of concepts of classes and properties, which in turn is followed by observation that yields data about relations between those classes and/or properties. From these observations are derived empirical generalizations, which in turn are transformed into theory by the formulation of explanatory propositions that bring them together into a causal system. From theories hypotheses are generated by the process of syllogizing. These inferences are then subjected to verification through the observation of the discrete phenomena and the relations whereby they are operationalized. This second set of observations yields new empirical generalizations that are compared with the original hypothesis for consistency and that form the basis for a decision to accept or reject it. Acceptance leads to confirming or elaborating the theory; rejection leads to its modification

---

*Epidemiologists use the term "case histories" to refer to investigations involving two comparison groups, one exhibiting the illness in question (the effect) and the other not. The groups are compared to determine what other factors distinguish them. Working from effect-to-cause is considered more efficient for discovering a probable causal agent. Once such a variable has been identified, the reverse process is adopted, called "analytic epidemiology," to verify the causal relationship. Two groups are selected, one which has been exposed to the causal agent, and one which has not, in order to determine the relative incidence of the illness (the effect) in the two groups (MacMahon and Pugh 1970).

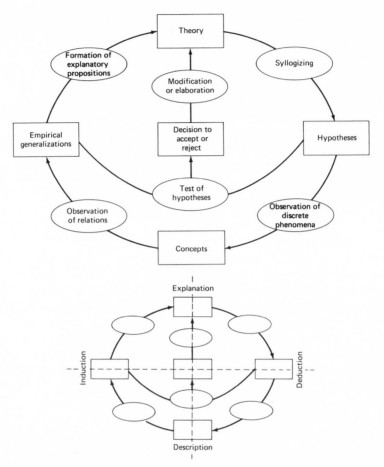

Figure 2–4 Interrelationship between the elements and processes of science. Adapted with permission from Walter L. Wallace, *The Logic of Science in Sociology* (New York: Aldine Publishing Company) Copyright © 1971 by Walter L. Wallace, pp. 18, 23.

or abandonment. In actual practice, the scientific method may be more appropriately viewed as a spiral than as a closed circle. When investigating a phenomenon the scientist goes through the cycle from concepts to generalizations, to theory, to hypotheses, and back again to concepts repeatedly. But each time the scientist returns to the point of entry, he or she is at a higher level of abstraction, because more is known about the phenomenon being investigated.

Figure 2–4 also explicates the respective processes of science in the scientific method. The bottom half of the system involves the process of description, while the upper half reflects the process of explanation. Similarly, the left half of the system involves induction, while the right half involves deduction. This summarization is an obvious oversimplification, for, as we noted earlier, induction and deduction often intertwine in any given stage. The point being conveyed is that reasoning in the left half of the system is essentially inductive, that is, inferences can be traced ultimately to observations that have been rigorously conducted. By contrast, reasoning in the right half of the system originates from a deductive stance, that is, inferences are based on premises which are known or assumed to be true.

This graphic depiction serves to summarize the essential characteristics of the scientific method. It illustrates the fact that theory is linked to the world of fact by empirical generalizations and hypotheses; that empirical generalizations are distinguishable from hypotheses by their relationship to observations; and that both the processes of induction and deduction are essential to the exercise of the scientific method.

REFERENCES

ACKOFF, RUSSELL L. *The Design of Social Research.* Chicago: University of Chicago Press, 1953.

COHEN, MORRIS R. *Reason and Nature, An Essay on the Meaning of Scientific Method.* New York: Harcourt, Brace and Company, 1931.

COHEN, MORRIS R., and ERNEST NAGEL. *An Introduction to Logic and Scientific Method.* New York: Harcourt, Brace and Co., 1934.

GREENWOOD, ERNEST. *Experimental Sociology.* New York: Kings Crown Press, 1945.

HEMPEL, CARL G. "Fundamentals of Concept Formation in Empirical Science", in *International Encyclopedia of Unified Science,* Vol. II, Chicago: University of Chicago Press, 1952.

KAPLAN, ABRAHAM. *The Conduct of Inquiry.* San Francisco: Chandler Publishing Co., 1964.

KUHN, THOMAS S. *The Structure of Scientific Revolutions.* Chicago: University of Chicago Press, 1962.

LAZARSFELD, PAUL F., and ALLEN H. BARTON. "Qualitative Measurement in the Social Sciences: Classification Typologies and Indices," in *Policy Sciences,* Harold D. Lasswell and Daniel Lerner eds. Stanford, Calif.: Stanford University Press, 1951.

LAZARSFELD, PAUL F., and MORRIS ROSENBERG. *The Language of Social Research.* New York: The Free Press, 1955.

LUNDBERG, GEORGE A. *Social Research, A Study in Methods of Gathering Data.* New York: Longmans, Green & Co., Inc., 1942.

MACDONALD, MARY E. "Social Work Research: A Perspective," in *Social Work Research,* Norman A. Polansky ed. Chicago: University of Chicago Press, 1960.

MacMAHON, BRIAN, and THOMAS F. PUGH. *Epidemiology: Principles and Methods.* Boston: Little, Brown and Co., 1970.

OGDEN, C. K. and I. A. RICHARDS. *The Meaning of Meaning.* New York: Harcourt, Brace and Company, 1948.

POPPER, KARL R. *The Logic of Scientific Discovery.* New York: Harper and Row Publishers, 1965.

TRIPODI, TONY, PHILIP FELLIN, and HENRY J. MEYER. *The Assessment of Social Research.* Itasca, Ill: F. E. Peacock, 1969.

WALLACE, WALTER L. *The Logic of Science in Sociology.* Chicago: Aldine Atherton, Inc., 1971.

chapter 3/ the nature
of policy research

In Chapter 1 we discussed the nature of the policy-making or planning process, and in Chapter 2 we discussed the nature of scientific or empirical research. In this chapter we bring these two themes together in a discussion of the nature of policy research. We begin with a definition of policy research and a description of its general characteristics. This involves us, necessarily, in an examination of the role of values in policy investigations. Next, we turn to a description of the three research methods that enter into the design of policy research. The chapter concludes with a brief discussion of some of the ethical problems encountered in conducting policy studies that must be anticipated in their design.

POLICY RESEARCH DEFINED

We have defined policy as a decision outlining the most effective and efficient means for achieving a collectively determined objective, and policy making as the process whereby that decision is reached. In a policy decision two elements are joined. One consists of the values of the policy maker and of the collective in whose behalf he or she acts. As we have seen, values define the goals of policy as worthy of attainment. The other element consists of factual information which determines the most effective means for attaining these ends. Without values there is no motive to action; without information there is no basis for effective action. It is the function of policy research to generate the relevant technical information needed to render policy making effective. To define it more precisely, *policy research is empirical research undertaken to verify propositions about some aspect of the means-ends relationship in policy making.*

Policy research may be thought of as applied social research because it shares with the latter a primary focus on practical problem solving. However, in policy research the analyst does not approach problem solving by applying some established body of social theory; rather by focusing on taking actions, whatever their derivation, toward the attainment of a goal. For this reason policy research is as concerned with the process of achieving a given solution as it is with the solution itself. It is not incorrect to state that policy research is a relatively new and different kind of applied social research that has yet to be satisfactorily defined in the literature. We turn now to a discussion of those characteristics by which it can be distinguished.

General Characteristics

As is true in any emerging field for which the intellectual foundations are still under construction, the characteristics that define policy research are only partially known. However, a number of general characteristics have been identified that serve to set it apart from other types of research (Etzioni 1971, Gans 1971, Gouldner 1965). These characteristics will not apply to all policy studies, but when taken together they provide a framework for formulating research problems in a policy context.

Policy research is *goal-oriented,* that is, it tends to focus on the goals as well as the means involved in a proposed course of action. This goal orientation leads the analyst to question not only the actions a policy maker proposes to attain a given set of objectives, but also the objectives themselves in relation to the expressed goals of the policy maker. In short, the analyst is actively involved in defining the policy problem itself. Since goals are values expressed as intentions to act, this orientation also places policy research in the context of explicit value debates. Thus, such research cannot ignore the relationship between facts and values, between what is possible and what is desirable, for values will influence the way a policy problem is conceptualized as well as the function of research in its resolution.

Policy research has a *system perspective,* that is, one in which attention is paid to the goals of the entire social unit affected by the proposed policy as well as to the interests of a given decision maker in that unit. Public affairs take place within a specific social context or system, be it a unit of government, a formal organization, or a voluntary group of citizens pursuing a common interest. Invariably, policy is formulated and executed by a subset of the members of that system, rather than by the entire system acting in a consensual manner. It is not uncommon that in their perception of the public interest policy makers actually mask their own self-interest. In policy research, therefore, an attempt is made to view the proposed goals and actions from the vantage point of every relevant subset within that system, not just from the perspective of its leadership. In this manner research can inform about the systemic effects of a proposed course of action. For example, a board of education may request assistance in evaluating the effects on academic performance of a new curriculum. A system perspective would take into account the effects of such a curriculum change on the teaching staff who must carry it out, on the parents of students involved, on the adult population who provide the tax base and legitimize the board of education, and so on. A system perspective is also relevant in research dealing with a policy advocated by a subset that is not the leadership. With such a perspective one cannot only identify points of possible support or opposition elsewhere in the system, but also suggest ways of modifying the original proposal so as to maximize support or minimize opposition.

Policy research is *focused on action.* Its ultimate function is not simply to generate predictors or descriptors of conditions or of needs to which policy making should be addressed, but also to generate and validate actions to meet those needs. While the assessment of needs is often necessary to initiate policy making, research must eventually focus on the nature of proposed policies or programs to fully inform that process. Furthermore, in being action-focused, policy research cannot deal solely with the relationship of a given set of actions to a given set of objectives, but must also give consideration to the processes by which those actions will be carried out. For this reason such research is as concerned with the implementation of a policy in a given institutional context, as with the substance of the policy itself.

Policy research involves *manipulable* variables. This means that the independent variables in such research constitute factors over which the policy maker has some control within the policy-making context under investigation. We speak of such variables as policies, programs, or interventions. Because of its pragmatic orientation, policy research eschews historical or global investigations of the conditions to which policy making is addressed and searches instead for factors which are currently operating to maintain those conditions or to block progress toward their alleviation. For example, a social scientist may find the process of urbanization an adequate framework for investigating current housing patterns. But urbanization is too long-term and global a process to be useful as a basis for intervention. The policy analyst would be more interested in financial lending practices, construction technology, or labor market factors that perpetuate housing patterns. About these something immediate can be done.

In policy research the analyst cannot confine his or her attention to a simple cause-effect chain. Public interventions take place in contexts shaped by many forces. Therefore, policy research must strive to be *comprehensive* in studying the effects of a given action on achieving some objective. It must consider latent or unintended consequences that may flow from either the adoption of a particular policy or from the achievement of a policy objective. Such consequences may result in feedback loops that undermine public support for the policy or have long-term effects which undo short-term positive results. Policy research must also consider implementation and adjunct variables, that is, organizational structures and processes by which the policy or program is to operate, or with which it must contend.

It follows from the characteristics already enumerated that policy research is *multidisciplinary*. Focused as it is on goals and actions, policy research cannot be conceptualized within the theoretical bounds of any one discipline or profession as we presently know them. Human problems are by nature multifaceted. Policy research may draw on any one of the social sciences or relate to any field of social policy. The mark of such research is its analytical approach and its system perspective, not its substantive content. This characteristic sets policy analysis apart from applied social science, which tends to formulate both the policy problem (the substance of the mean-ends relationship) and the research problem (the verification of that relationship) in terms of the analytical concepts and research techniques of a particular discipline.

A characteristic of all forms of action-oriented research is *uncertainty*. Decisions dependent on such research must be made within a time frame established by public events—they cannot wait until all of the necessary data have been gathered or until the ideal verification procedures have been performed. Even under ideal conditions it is impossible to predict with certainty the course of future events. Unforeseen factors can and do emerge to offset the most competent calculations. The findings of policy research, therefore, must be treated as partial or imperfect. Two types of safeguards should be taken. One involves a full recognition, in reporting research findings, of the limitations of the information and of the analyses upon which those findings are based. A second is the introduction into the analysis itself of techniques for reflecting the degree of uncertainty characteristic of the events under consideration and/or of their observation. Considerable work has been done in this respect in the field of statistical decision theory which lies beyond the scope of this book (Mack 1971).

Finally, because policy research explicitly deals with value-based social action, the analyst must assume a commitment to consider the *ethical implications* of his or her research. Any course of action in the service of a particular value is bound to conflict or interfere with the attainment of other values. For example, confining manpower training to skills that are marketable conflicts with providing the unemployed the freedom to choose those skills they might wish to learn. In addition, action in pursuit of a particular value will have a differential impact throughout a population, producing beneficial effects upon some members, but harmful effects upon others. As in the case of any normative enterprise, criteria must be adopted for judging the ethical acceptability of a particular research. We shall take up such criteria later in this chapter.

Earlier we noted that values play a considerable role in policy making. However, in Chapter 2 we also noted that values are set aside from facts in the scientific method. How, then, can the role of values be rationalized in policy research?

At the outset let us dispel the myth that the assertion of values and the conduct of science are mutually exclusive. In the first place, the very enterprise of science rests on certain assumptions that can only be asserted as preferences rather than as objective truths. For example, science rests on a preference for knowledge based on empirical evidence rather than on mysticism or other extrasensory forms of knowledge; it also rests on a preference for pragmatism rather than for authority as a criterion of truth. In the second place, the practice of science is inextricably related to values by the choice of subject matter with which it deals, although these values often are not made explicit. For example, during World War II important theoretical and methodological advances were made in sociology as a result of research conducted on the effects of saturation bombings in Germany and on similar attempts to facilitate the war effort (Stouffer 1949, Hyman 1955, p. 87ff.). In the ideological climate of the 1970s such investigations seem highly questionable in their value implications. Furthermore, the formulation of alternative solutions to public problems is constrained by values. For example, during the 1960s most of the research conducted into ways and means of reducing poverty focused on changing the characteristics of poor persons through social services, rather than on instituting political changes in society at large or on redistributing income (Rose 1972). The latter strategies were ignored largely by virtue of their implicit conflict with publicly espoused values.

In the policy-making process, some way must be found purposefully to link value assumptions so crucial to policy making to propositions that are verifiable by the rules of the scientific method. Among the policy-oriented disciplines this relationship has come to be expressed in the concept of *normative theory* (Zeckhauser and Schaefer 1968). Normative theory can be thought of as a system of propositions which explicitly combines value assumptions and causal assumptions. In contrast, *positivist theory* consists solely of propositions that conform to the rules of science.

The process of explicitly incorporating value assumptions into the conduct of science can be depicted graphically by revising our earlier model of the scientific method (Figure 2-4). Figure 3-1 shows the convergence of propositions derived from positivist theory and propositions derived from value assumptions so as to form normative theory. It is from normative theory, by means of syllogisms, that we derive proposals for public policy. These proposals to act are analogous to hypotheses in that they are deductively generated. And like hypotheses, they are verified by observation. That is, when the proposals are actually implemented as policy, their validity is put to the test. Observations of the

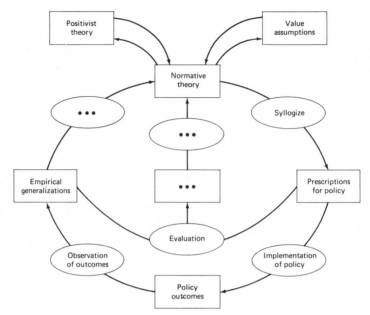

Figure 3-1 Incorporation of value assumptions and positivist theory into normative theory.

outcomes of policy are transformed into empirical generalizations which provide a basis for evaluating the original prescriptions, resulting in turn in elaboration or modification of normative theory. The diagram also indicates that revisions of normative theory based on empirical generalizations regarding public interventions can in some cases lead to revisions of positivist theory, and, when the evidence is overwhelming, revisions in value assumptions as well (Mayer, Moroney, and Morris 1974, p. 203).

The interrelatedness of value assumptions and research problems should not obscure the fact that the *conduct* of research must be value free. That is, once the researcher has formulated the subject of inquiry or the proposition to be verified, he or she must not let personal values determine what to observe and what to ignore. In other words, to employ the scientific method, the researcher must be free of values that operate during the process of observation, what we normally term *biases*. It is in this sense that the scientific method is value free or unbiased.

The important point to remember is that value assumptions cannot be eliminated from the *design* of a research effort, only from its *execution*. Value assumptions must be made explicit in the research design so that the analyst is clear about which propositions are open to question and which must remain sacrosanct. However, once the analyst is engaged in verifying a given proposition, he or she must follow a strictly unbiased or value-free course, exposing the proposition to the facts as they are observed, not distorting them to substantiate the proposition. As Kaplan has observed, "freedom from bias means having an open mind, not an empty one" (1964, p. 375).

If value assumptions are to play an explicit role in formulating problems for policy research, we must have a criterion by which to distinguish them from other types of assumptions (referred to as presuppositions) which frame a research problem, but which are amenable to empirical verification. Kaplan offers such a criterion in his distinction between an *instrumental value* and an *inherent value* (1964, pp. 393–396; Lindblom 1968, pp. 16ff.). An instrumental value is a value that is believed to lead eventually to something else which is desired and prized. An inherent value, however, is a value that is believed to be desirable and worthy in and of itself. Phrased in terms of the familiar means-ends scheme, the first is valued as a means to some end, whereas the second is valued as an end in itself. For example, progressive taxation is valued in our society because it leads to a certain amount of equity in income distribution. However, equity in income distribution is usually valued as an end in itself. An assertion regarding the validity of an instrumental value is verifiable because it can be linked causally to an implied end. It is verifiable as any means is, namely, against the criterion of efficiency: Is the instrument the only or the least costly means to the desired end? On the other hand, an assertion regarding the validity of an inherent value is not verifiable because it involves an end which is its own justification. It is susceptible to analysis and criticism on logical grounds only.

However, some preferences may possess either instrumental or inherent value depending on the policy-making context in which they are considered. In our previous example, the goal of achieving equity in income distribution features as an inherent value if its proponents were to appeal to no other higher value in its defense, that is, if income equity is considered good in and of itself. If, however, its proponents were to value income equity because they believed that it would create social stability, then income equity features in their rationale as an instrumental value. What was originally an end has been converted into a means in the service of some still higher end, thereby making the preference for income equity susceptible to empirical verification. We will discuss this distinction further in Part II in connection with the process by which the analyst identifies the researchable aspects of a particular policy problem.

THE METHODS OF POLICY RESEARCH

We have defined policy research as empirical research undertaken to verify some aspect of the means-ends relationship in policy making. At this point we will describe the various research methods available to the analyst for use in policy studies and will indicate at what stage in the policy-making process each is appropriate. This should serve as a background for the discussion of designing policy investigations employing these methods, which is the focus of Part II.

In the previous chapter we described the nature of the scientific method from a generic perspective, regardless of the scientific discipline in which it is applied. In actuality, investigators working in the various scientific fields must utilize very different research methods to accord with the differing nature of the reality they study and with the differing circumstances under which they study it. Hence, the research methods employed in the natural sciences differ markedly from those employed in the social sciences. Even within the social sciences the methods vary with the subjects investigated. Thus, the procedures employed in a behavioral science such as psychology are quite different from those used in economics. But different though these special procedures may be, they all must and do conform to the basic canons or rules which govern scientific activity. The research called for by the policy-making process is research about human goals and about human actions for achieving them. It is, therefore, quite appropriate for us to adopt the logic and the methods of social research as the guiding framework of this book. Because, as we have pointed out, policy research is multidisciplinary, the policy analyst can and should utilize the methods employed in all of the social sciences, thereby taking advantage of a more inclusive array than exists in any single social science.

Even the seasoned social researcher may at times be a bit confused by the veritable plethora of terms current to designate the variety of research methods used in the social sciences. A recent perusal of the methodological literature uncovered mention of over thirty different research methods available to social scientists.* To be sure, the count includes some duplicates, i.e., the same method by different names, which only augments the confusion. Despite the latter, the terms do serve a function. As an adjective describing the procedure to which it is appended, each is a handy identifying label in that it imparts specificity to the "method" which it modifies. The same may be said for the labels used to describe the various procedures employed in policy studies, viz., needs assessment, process evaluation, monitoring, summative evaluation, impact study, formative evaluation, just to name a few. However, what should be pointed out is that so many of the labels current are ad hoc, that is, not derived from any classification scheme. Labeling is fine; but it is not ipso facto classifying. Thus, to label a research method as "observational" or "longitudinal" or "survey," tells us what the method does, but fails to relate it to other research methods. This only a classification scheme can do.

---

*The methods mentioned included: case study, clinical, cohort, comparative, content analysis, cross-sectional, descriptive, diagnostic, documentary, evaluative, ex post facto, experimental, exploratory, field, historical, hypothetico-deductive, idiographic, interview, longitudinal, nomothetic, observational, panel, projective, qualitative, quantitative, quasi-experimental, questionnaire, retrospective, sociometric, statistical, survey.

There have been numerous attempts to impose some sort of system upon the wide array of research procedures in vogue in the social sciences. Virtually every writer on methodological issues has, at one time or another, tried to formulate a classification for them. Even a cursory review of such efforts will indicate the lack of any substantial agreement among them. Certainly one factor contributing importantly to this state of affairs is the tendency on the part of writers to confuse research method with research technique. Methodological textbooks tend to employ the two terms interchangeably. What should be called technique is often referred to as method, and vice versa. Ackoff (1953, vii) has already drawn attention to this improper usage. Inasmuch as we will be using these two terms frequently throughout Part II, it is imperative that we pause to distinguish between them.

Method may be defined as an orderly arrangement, a systematic procedure, an overall plan. A research method is a general approach toward the phenomenon that the researcher has chosen to investigate and is, thus, a kind of logic that guides the investigation. A technique, on the other hand, is any discrete operation performed to achieve some sub-objective of the plan. A research technique is a specific physical or mental manipulation employed by the researcher for collecting or processing the data called for by the plan of the investigation. To employ an analogy, method is to technique as strategy is to tactic. Accordingly, it is more appropriate to refer to controlled observation or interviewing or quantitative analysis as techniques rather than as methods, because they are specific and discrete, and each focuses upon some relatively narrow objective of the study wherein they are utilized. By contrast, the case study or the survey or the experiment are methods, because each refers to a plan or strategy toward the phenomenon under study. Thus, the case study involves the intensive examination of only a few cases selected purposively and investigated by a multiplicity of observational techniques which are relatively unstructured. The survey method involves probability sampling, schedule construction, interviewing, coding, and multivariate analysis. The experimental method involves purposive sampling, matching, controlled observation, and significance testing.

There is, therefore, a hierarchical relation between research method and technique in that the latter is auxiliary and subordinate to the former. The objective of the investigation, once defined, determines the selection of the research method best suited for it. But it is the method which determines the selection of the research techniques needed for the specifics of the investigation. For method consists of a certain sequence of interrelated techniques linked together by the study plan. Hence, having chosen the method to be employed as an approach to the study phenomenon, the investigator next proceeds to put together the proper combination of auxiliary techniques whereby he or she operationalizes the method. This is done, as we will see, in the technical stages of the research design. Employing a terminology only slightly different from ours, Kornhauser and Lazarsfeld (1955) long ago made the same distinction between method and technique and attributed the same hierarchical relation to them.*

In conclusion, the confusion of method with technique may well have frustrated the development of a single classification for the research procedures in social science. It would, therefore, be advisable to separate the methods from the techniques, and to construct a scheme for each.

One such scheme about which some agreement exists is the aforementioned threefold classification consisting of the case study or field method, the survey, and the experiment (Babbie 1975, Simmons 1969, Black and Champion 1976). This scheme does have the virtue of bringing some order to the large variety of existing techniques in that each method groups together those techniques that facilitate a distinct type of research objective. However we believe that research objectives are distinguished by the process of science required for their achievement, as discussed in Chapter 2, namely qualitative description, quantitative description, and explanation. In this respect the scheme is deficient, for these methods do not have an exclusive correspondence with those processes. For example, the case study method, though it is uniquely suited to qualitative description, can also be used to explain relations between variables (McCall and Simmons 1969, Glaser and Strauss 1967). Similarly, the survey, though it is the preferred method for quantitative description, can also be used to achieve research objectives that are explanatory in nature (Hyman 1955).

For this reason we have adopted a scheme which both rests on the technical requirements of the three processes for developing scientific knowledge and encompasses the variety of informational needs of policy making, as well. We justify this scheme on pragmatic grounds. After all, any set of entities can be classified in more ways than one, depending on the classificatory principle employed as being of significance to the classifier. Essentially, a classification is simply a conceptual device for imposing some sort of order on seemingly disparate reality, so that it can be communicated for use by others. Hence, the validity of a scheme rests largely on its utility, that is, the extent to which it makes good sense to and serves the needs of those who must operate with it. The scheme we have adopted was borrowed from another context and adapted to our needs. In the subsequent paragraphs we will describe its rationale and its adaptation to our use.

The Exploratory-Descriptive-Explanatory Typology

In a pioneering methodological treatise Jahoda and her associates called attention to the crucial importance of one's prior knowledge about the subject to be

---

*The authors cited above differentiate between what they call "master techniques" (our "research methods") and "servant techniques" (our "research techniques"). They assert that the former are involved in research planning and go far in determining the latter which are involved in research operations.

investigated, in determining the focus of the investigation (Selltiz, Wrightsman, and Cook 1976). Thus, in a social science, the function of which is to develop explanatory theories for its empirical generalizations, the objective of a given research is conditioned by the degree of familiarity with which the scientist approaches the phenomenon for research. The investigator's degree of understanding of his subject is reflected in the very questions that he or she addresses to the study phenomenon; the greater is the former, the more penetrating can be the latter. Jahoda et al. suggested that the scientist's knowledge about a phenomenon progresses through three stages. Hence his or her objective and approach may assume one of three possible forms, which they have labeled as the *exploratory*, the *descriptive*, and the *explanatory*.*

The first stage of inquiry typically occurs when an investigator confronts a novel phenomenon about which he or she has only the barest comprehension; the information that can be brought to bear is quite minimal. Given this fact, the data that are to be collected in the inquiry cannot be precisely specified prior to their collection. Under such circumstances, the only choice open to the investigator is to assume a probing or exploratory approach to the subject. The objective of the study undertaken at this stage must be primarily that of formulating the basic concepts about the study phenomenon. To be specific, the objective must cover the following: to conceptualize the properties distinguishing the phenomenon from other phenomena; to formulate operational definitions for these concepts, thereby converting them into variables about which data may be gathered; to differentiate between independent and dependent variables; and to develop crude scales for ordering and measuring variables, so that variations in the properties of the phenomenon may be noted later.

On acquiring the above information, the investigator has attained the second stage of knowledge. By now he or she knows the variables to be observed and which is independent and which is dependent; he or she can define precisely the data that must be collected about the phenomenon, and having established appropriate classes, categories, scales, and units of count, he or she knows clearly how to order the data once collected. Therefore, the objective of research at this stage is to achieve a quantitative description of the phenomenon. Specifically, the description covers the following: the size and distribution of the major variables in the population manifesting the phenomenon or, if the latter is too large, in a sample of it; and the size and direction of relations, if any, among the variables. All of these are described quantitatively in the form of frequency distributions, measures of central tendency and dispersion, and of association and

---

*The above formulation was initially suggested by Jahoda, Deutsch, and Cook, in *Research Methods in Social Relations* (Dryden, 1951). Originally they employed the terms "exploratory-formulative, descriptive-diagnostic, and experimental-causal." The formulation was refined and may be found in the third edition of that work (Selltiz, Wrightsman, and Cook 1976). The formulation was applied to research designs by Black and Champion (1976, 77–84).

covariation. In short, the objective is to identify regularities in the phenomenon around which generalizations may be formulated.

On acquiring such information about the phenomenon, the investigator has attained the third stage of knowledge. By now he or she has at hand a series of generalizations regarding the sizes, distributions, and interrelations of the major variables characterizing the study phenomenon. The objective of the investigation now undertaken is to account for these generalizations, i.e., to explain the how and the why of the facts thus far uncovered. This the investigator does by establishing (a) that two specific variables are indeed strongly related (covariation), (b) that one precedes the other (time order), and (c) that no third variable has influenced the relation (elimination of rival hypotheses).

Although the typology just described was formulated by Jahoda et al. in order to classify studies in terms of their objectives, the scheme may be extended to classify them in terms of the research methods whereby these objectives are achieved (Simon 1969). It is in this last meaning that we will employ the terms exploratory, descriptive and explanatory. Such extension of the terms merits justification. In the first place, Jahoda et al. refer to these terms as designating varying approaches or strategies toward the phenomenon on the investigator's part. As strategies, they match well our earlier definition of what is a research method. Secondly, the typology reflects faithfully the scientific processes we described in the previous chapter. Note that the investigator discovers the basic concepts about the phenomenon under study and their interrelatedness through the exploratory study (qualitative description); he/she develops generalizations about them through the descriptive study (quantitative description); and he/she tests theories about them through the explanatory study. Third, the typology is most applicable to studies in social policy because it addresses the range of informational needs that arise in the course of policy making. In fact, a scheme closely approximating it is already in use in epidemiology (MacMahon and Pugh 1970). Accordingly, henceforth in this volume, the exploratory-descriptive-explanatory typology will be used to classify the study undertaken according to the objective pursued, and the method employed.

Design Implications of the Typology

In view of the foregoing discussion, we can say that the level of information required to solve the policy problem determines the objective of the research to be undertaken. The objective of the research determines the research method to be selected, and the method selected determines the techniques needed to carry out the latter. Hence, upon the research method of the study depends a number of technical details which must be considered when designing a study. The more important of these are: how the units of observation are to be selected from the population exhibiting the policy problem; what kind of data will be collected about them; how the data are to be collected; and, once collected, how they are to be analyzed. The selection of the method has the effect of narrowing the range of auxiliary techniques to be employed in executing that method. Inasmuch as we will discuss in detail the design characteristics of the three methods in Part II, at this juncture we will provide the reader only with a quick overview.

The kind of research objective for which the *exploratory method* is suitable is exemplified in the following questions:

> What are the effects of a rent subsidy program as a means of providing low cost housing?
> What type of clients are most successful in manpower training programs?
> What factors lead to successful school desegregation?

The exploratory method does not require a large number of cases for observation; a few purposively chosen ones, if intensively observed, will suffice. The cases must be so selected as to permit the analyst to apply to them either one of the inductive canons of Mill discussed in the previous chapter. The canon of agreement calls for at least two cases of the phenomenon under investigation to permit the analyst to identify what properties they share in common. On the other hand, the canon of difference calls for at least two cases, one wherein the phenomenon is present to some degree and another wherein it is absent (or present in minute degree). In this manner the analyst can identify what properties distinguish the phenomenon by being present in the former and not in the latter. It is preferable that the analyst employ both inductive canons, in which case the minimum number of cases observed will have to be at least three. Since the units of observation are few in number and selected purposively, they will not be representative of their population. The cases are observed in their native setting intensively and comprehensively by means of a variety of unstructured and unrefined data collection techniques. The collected data are analyzed qualitatively, permitting inferences about the existence of certain properties as characteristic of the phenomenon. These inferences constitute operational definitions of the properties that distinguish the phenomenon under study. They are expressed either as categories of a classification scheme, or as values by which a measurement scale can be constructed. However, since the observed cases are not representative, no inference can be made about the size or distribution of these properties in the population for which the prospective policy is intended.

Because the exploratory method involves the intensive observation of both comparable and contrasting cases in the field setting, synonyms for it that are to be found in the methodological literature are "case study," "comparative method," "participant observation," "field study," and "qualitative method." Each of these terms focuses on only one feature of the exploratory method; hence, none captures comprehensively the nature of the procedure.

The kind of research objective for which the *descriptive method* is appropriate is reflected in the following examples:

> How many families receiving rent subsidies live in above standard housing?
>
> What is the rate of employment among graduates of manpower training programs by age and prior education?
>
> What is the degree of variation in the racial and ethnic composition of public school systems?

These questions reflect sufficient familiarity with the phenomenon to be studied to permit quantitative measurement of its properties. For example, the first question suggests that the analyst already knows how many and which families receive rent subsidies, and that he or she has developed an operational definition of the concept of standard housing and a scale to differentiate housing above from that below standard. Should this basic information be lacking, the analyst must undertake exploratory research to obtain it.

The relation between the exploratory and the descriptive research methods may be further illustrated. Let us suppose that the analyst is interested in ascertaining the factors that distinguish schools that are considered to have been successfully desegregated from those that are considered to have been unsuccessful in that effort. An exploratory study is undertaken using as informants school administrators, teachers, and parents. As a result, the analyst finds that the racial composition of the faculty, in-service training, the diversity of racial and ethnic content in the curriculum, and the presence of strong student governance were associated with successful desegregation. Now the analyst knows the range of factors that make for success in desegregation, but he or she does not know their distribution among the various schools. For this descriptive research must be undertaken wherein schools are surveyed regarding the presence or absence of each of the factors uncovered by exploratory research.*

In contrast to the exploratory, the descriptive method is much more rigorous. With its emphasis on quantitative precision it calls for more structured data collection and analysis procedures. Hence, its design requirements are more exacting and detailed than those of the exploratory method. The introduction of greater rigor is, of course, rendered possible, because the variables have by now been specifically defined. Since the aim is to ascertain the size, distribution and interrelations of these variables, the method calls for the observation of large numbers of units. It may, however, also involve a few cases whenever the phenomenon studied manifests itself in very large units, such as organizations or

---

*On the basis of our earlier distinction between positivist and normative theory, all three research methods are essentially descriptive, because they purport to depict the nature of reality as is. The analytical methods of business, politics, and the human service professions are, by contrast, prescriptive or normative, because they purport to depict reality as it ought to be.

communities. The data are capable of precategorization to permit analysis of their distribution. Hence, while the findings yielded by the exploratory method are qualitative in form, those yielded by the descriptive method are quantitative in form. In policy research, studies utilizing the descriptive method are either univariate or multivariate. The former describes the distribution of a single property or variable, which is usually the condition reflected in the policy objective. The latter describes the simultaneous distribution of two or more properties or variables, which are usually the policy objective and one or more of the alternative courses of action under consideration. Because the descriptive method involves the collection of precategorized data obtained from large samples, it is often referred to as the "survey" method. However, it is not strictly correct to equate the two. Not every survey is descriptive; as we have noted, some surveys are explanatory. And not every descriptive study is a survey in the sense of involving large samples; as we have noted, the descriptive method may involve a few cases when the latter are very large units.

And lastly, the kind of research objective for which the *explanatory method* is appropriate is exemplified in the following:

> Does the provision of rent subsidies to low income families result in upgrading the quality of their housing, given a sufficient vacancy rate in the housing market?
>
> Does manpower training increase the entry of unemployed persons into full-time employment, given a low rate of unemployment?
>
> Was the rise in the number of families whose income exceeds the poverty line the result of changes introduced into the tax structure, or the result of an increase in the availability of employment?

Note that each of these questions raises the likelihood of a causal relation between the policy intervention, here the independent variable, and the policy objective, here the dependent variable.* To ascertain the answer to these questions the descriptive method is inadequate. From a study using the descriptive method one can draw conclusions about the size, distributions, and interrelations of variables in a population, but no conclusions about the causal character of these interrelations based solely on their measures of correlation. For this, the analyst must invoke the explanatory method.

The relation between the descriptive and explanatory methods may be illustrated by the earlier example regarding the success of desegregation uncovered in certain schools. Assume that a majority of the administrators in success-

---

*We will subsequently show (in Part II, Chapter 4) that in the actual design of a study involving the explanatory method, the likelihood of a causal relation between two variables is not raised as a question, but asserted as an hypothesis to be accepted or rejected by the analyst. In the actual conduct of research causality is posited in the form of a declarative statement, which is then affirmed or refuted by the findings produced by the explanatory method.

fully desegregated schools report having student-faculty governing bodies. From this association we cannot conclude that it is just such a governing structure which accounts for the success. For such an inference we need the kind of information which only the explanatory method can furnish.

As we have already noted, determining causality between two variables requires ascertaining whether or not their relation is accountable in terms of some third variable. Thus, to infer that success in desegregation is due to the schools' having student-faculty governing bodies, we would have to examine them for the presence of other possible explanatory variables, such as the sizes or the social compositions of their student bodies. If the successful schools are also similar with respect to these other variables, also called control variables, this would raise some doubt as to whether school governing structure alone produces successful desegregation. It is through the explanatory method that we can resolve that doubt.

To permit the testing of causality, the study population should be divisible into at least two comparison groups, both similar with respect to the explanatory or control variables, but different with respect to the independent variable that is presumed to be the causal agent, the latter being present in one group and absent in the other. A study population purposively selected to pose this contrast will not be representative of the one for which the policy is intended. Obviously the larger the population observed, the more reliable will be the findings. Also, the larger the population, the more groups into which it can be subdivided, thus permitting more explanatory variables to be controlled and thereby allowing more causal hypotheses to be verified. At the same time, the method can also involve only a few cases if the phenomenon studied is complex and is manifested in large organizations or communities. Of this more will be said later.

Explanatory studies assume three subtypes, differing in the way they are designed. They are the *pure,* the *natural,* and the *ex post facto experiment;* the last two are sometimes referred to as quasi-experiments. The design of a *pure experiment* permits the analyst to create the comparison groups himself; that is, to determine before-hand who will and who will not be exposed to the independent variable, the presumed cause. Since the analyst is on hand before the causal agent is introduced into the setting, he or she is in position to observe as it produces its effect and thereby witness the time order of events. This degree of control over the situation enables the analyst to verify the widest range of alternative hypotheses, as we shall later see (Part II, Chapter 5).

The design of a *natural experiment* also enables the analyst to observe the unfolding of events and thus establish their time order. But unlike the pure experiment, it allows him or her no control over who are to be and who are not to be exposed to the presumed cause. Exposure occurs via the natural course of events, which the analyst can observe but cannot influence. The subjects, in a sense, expose themselves to the presumed cause. Consequently, the study population must be so selected that it contains two comparison subgroups, which are similar with respect to all explanatory variables, but also different in that one subgroup does while the other does not expose itself to the causal agent. Both the pure and the natural experiments are prospective in that they are designed before the presumed cause produces its effect and the analyst looks forward to the events he will observe.

By contrast, the *ex post facto experiment* is retrospective. It is designed after the presumed cause has produced its effect and the analyst must work backward in time. Here the analyst neither has control over who are the exposed and the unexposed, nor is able to observe the sequence of events which comprised the causal relation. Hence, the study must be so designed as to enable the reconstruction of past events in a manner permitting him or her either to affirm or to refute the causal hypothesis. As in the natural experiment, the study population is so selected as to be similar with respect to all explanatory variables, but different in that one portion has already been, while the other portion has not been exposed to the independent variable. However, in attempting to establish time order, he must take special care to ascertain that the effect was not already present among the exposed even before their exposure.

The Typology and the Policy-Making Process

We can now consider the ways in which the three research methods enter into the policy-making process, which was described in Chapter 1. The focal means-ends relation in policy-making is that between the objective(s) of the policy (the ends) and the course(s) of action proposed to achieve the former (the means). The appropriateness of a given research method depends on the level of information required to solve a policy problem. Consequently, any one of the methods might come into play at any stage in the policy-making process depending on the information that is lacking but required. However, the level of the information characteristically varies with the stages of policy-making. Thus, in the early stages of the process, knowledge about the policy problem is invariably much less than it is in the latter stages. As a consequence, there is a tendency for the three research methods to be associated with particular stages of policy making. The most characteristic way in which methods and stages are related is shown in Figure 3-2.

Empirical research enters the policy-making process at stage 2, needs assessment, which precedes the specification of objectives. Since objectives express the amount of change in existing conditions sought by the policy-maker, information about the current state of affairs is required so as to set realistic objectives. What is desired, here, is documentation of the extent of the undesirable condition (in the case of problem-oriented planning) or the extent of the need (in the case of goal-oriented planning). A typical question confronting the analyst at this stage is exemplified by, "How many families have incomes

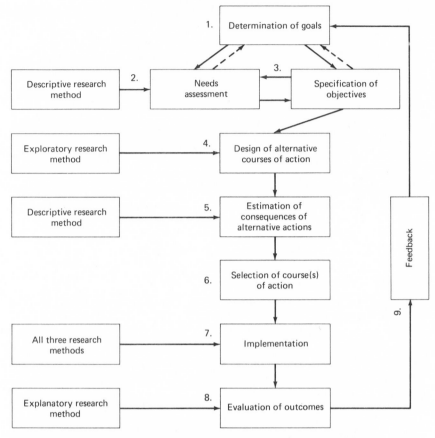

Figure 3-2 Relation of research methods to stages of policy making

falling below the poverty line?" Hence, for this stage of policy-making the descriptive research method is most appropriate.

The policy objective(s) having been specified, the analyst must next design alternative courses of action when the means of achieving the objective(s) are unknown or if known, unspecified. Research at this stage has as its objective to identify policy alternatives. A typical question that may arise here, is exemplified by "What conditions amenable to public intervention characterize communities with a high number of families living in poverty?" Hence for this stage of policy-making the exploratory research method is most appropriate.

By stage 5 the analyst has drafted for the policy maker a list of policy options in the form of possible actions that he or she can take. Hence the policy maker must engage in a rational selection among them. However, wise selection requires prior estimates of the likely consequences of each option. For such estimates the analyst must build a model or conceptual framework of the many factors which are thought to precipitate the condition (the desirable state) that is to be the objective of policy, since it is a truism that the conditions addressed by policy making contain many facets or dimensions. The model should depict how each of the contemplated policy alternatives relates to these precipitating factors. To construct such a model, information is needed on the amount of change in the precipitating factors that is predictable for a given level of intervention. Such information, based on correlation or regression analysis, is derived from previous studies, presumably explanatory in method. Once such a model has been constructed, policy making depends on information regarding the distribution of those precipitating factors in the (target) population to whom policy is to apply. To obtain this information, research is required. A typical question that may arise in this connection, is exemplified in the following: "How many families would have their incomes raised above the poverty line by means of a negative income tax compared to a children's allowance?" Hence, for this stage of policy-making the descriptive method is most appropriate. The findings yielded by studies using this method are presented to the policy maker as an estimate of the relative contribution toward the policy objective that may be expected from each of the policy options.

The next stage in the policy-making process that calls for research is that of implementation. As we noted earlier, the implementation stage itself involves a sequence of actions about which the level of knowledge may vary. It follows, therefore, that this stage may involve any one of the three research methods. When the factors in the implementation of a policy have been specified in a formal plan, analysis is usually concerned with determining the extent to which the policy was carried out according to that plan, a form of study referred to as "monitoring" (Weiss 1972, 16f.). For such analysis the descriptive method is appropriate in that the analyst seeks to determine the extent of the specified activities conducted and/or the amount of the resources expended while the policy was in force. Lacking a plan of implementation, so frequently the case in human services planning, analysis may focus on identifying the steps by which the policy or program was implemented, in order either to document program success or to identify sources of program failure. Such analysis is often referred to as "process evaluation," and for it the exploratory method is proper (Suchman 1967, 66-68). And finally, when the policy maker is committed to a given policy or program, the efficacy of its implementation becomes the focus of analysis and decision making; in essence, the policy problem is reformulated as one in program planning. Decision making may require a test of the success of a particular implementation strategy, assuming, of course, that the decision maker is unwilling to question the validity of the policy or program itself. Such a study calls for the explanatory method, and is sometimes referred to as a "formative evaluation" (Scriven 1967, Rieken and Boruch 1974).

The last stage in the policy-making process calling for research is that of evaluation of outcomes. By now the policy has been in effect for some time and the policy maker needs an assessment of its effectiveness, a process sometimes referred to as "summative evaluation" (Scriven 1967, Rieken and Boruch 1974). This requires evidence that the policy has produced (or is producing) its anticipated consequences. A study undertaken for this purpose must focus on causality inherent in the means-ends relation between policy and objective; it must account for the attainment of the objective (the ends) in terms of the policy (the means). For such a study the explanatory method is the more appropriate. However, policy evaluation does not always call for the explanatory method (Suchman 1967). There are two exceptions to the rule.

Planners have traditionally conceived of evaluation as a comparison of outcome achieved against the objective intended. Studies conceived thus are referred to as "impact evaluations." They are typically undertaken when causality is not an issue (e.g., in engineering projects involving the construction of a highway or dam) or when large scale public interventions prevent the isolation of cause-effect linkages (e.g., in environmental public health measures or in manipulations of the income tax structure). Here the descriptive method is much more appropriate. Planners also speak of policy evaluation as identifying the unintended consequences of a proposed action. Thus, for example, before approving the construction of a major public facility, the federal government requires an environmental impact assessment to identify the potential social and economic effects of the project. An investigation for identifying such unknown variables calls for the exploratory method.

Henceforth in this volume studies which employ the exploratory, the descriptive, and the explanatory methods will be referred to as the exploratory study, the descriptive study and the explanatory study, respectively.

ETHICAL IMPLICATIONS OF POLICY RESEARCH

In our earlier discussion of the characteristics of policy research we noted the creation of ethical problems for the policy maker and for the analyst. Because its effects are systemwide and involve the values of individuals, a given policy is likely to harm some while it helps others. Given this conflictual nature, it behooves the analyst to proceed in the investigation of policy alternatives in a manner that will increase the likelihood that those benefits and costs are equitably shared. We will first discuss certain practices in the conduct of research which generate problems in this regard, before proceeding to a brief discussion of steps that can be taken to resolve them (Rieken and Boruch 1974).

Ethical Problems

The gathering of information about a given segment of the population without the knowledge or consent of the members of that population violates the values of an open, democratic society and increases the potential for manipulation.

Obviously, actions taken on the basis of such information may well be contrary to the best interests of that population, which lacks the knowledge necessary to protect its rights. There are various ways in which data collection can *lack openness.* One is through the outright failure to secure the permission of the subjects involved. Any kind of covert research, such as the use of false identities in participant observation or in the securing of data from public records, is of this sort. Another means is through misrepresenting the purposes of an inquiry when eliciting information from subjects who are assumed to be noncooperative or whose answers are assumed to be biased by knowledge of the true purpose of the study. Such a practice is frequent in studies of attitudes or behaviors against which there is strong social disapproval. Still another form of spurious openness is securing the voluntary consent of the subjects under conditions of implicit or explicit coercion. Prisoners who are asked to volunteer for experiments, or applicants for public welfare who are required to give information before they can receive assistance, are susceptible to this kind of manipulation.

It is not always possible to achieve openness in policy research. Sometimes other social values may be overriding. For instance, in the interest of protecting citizens against victimization, secret surveillance of criminal activity may be justified; or in order to protect clients against the abuse of public power, covert studies of public bureaucracies may be required. However, if the government decides to propose punitive legislation against welfare families without cause, the use of family case records to determine the basis for such legislation without the clients' knowledge and/or consent would be hard to justify on moral grounds. Of course, some public decisions are sufficiently complex, or the process by which they are made so intricate, that to inform all those affected and to obtain their consent would inordinately delay any positive effects. Such cases do not necessarily carry the potential for manipulation. For example, national legislation dealing with the health needs of the elderly may depend on information obtained through the social security system about the number and distribution of such persons. It may be unfeasible to meet the informational needs of the legislators if obtaining the consent of all elderly social security recipients were required. The ethics of utilizing information under such conditions must rest on an assumption that the interests of the subjects is thereby served. A simple test of whether or not such use leads to manipulation is to ask the question, "Would the average or "rational" subject have voluntarily provided that information if he or she had known the purpose for which it is to be used?"

When the evaluation of a public program is being conducted along the lines of a pure experiment, it may inadvertently produce *harmful effects* if certain benefits of the program are by design denied to individuals comprising a control group. A particularly tragic example is provided by the U.S. Public Health Service's experiment with syphilis treatment among 400 black males in Tuskegee, Alabama (*N.Y. Times* 1972). As a result of the natural course of that disease a number of men died whose lives might have been saved had they been given the treatments afforded the experimental group. One way of minimizing such consequences is to provide alternative benefits to the control group, rather than no benefits. The income maintenance experiments sponsored by the U.S. Office of Economic Opportunity in New Jersey and elsewhere provided the normal public assistance to a control group of eligible families, and various levels of income support based on a negative income tax to an experimental group of comparably poor families (Watts 1972). In this case nobody in need was denied financial assistance from the government. When the prevailing level of service is provided the control group, at least no one will suffer the effects of being deprived of all assistance. In addition to these assurances, all potential subjects should be advised of the nature and extent of the experiment so that they can exercise choice over whether or not to expose themselves to the risks involved.

Sometimes the policy being analyzed has *effects unintended* by the policy maker. For example, the use of television as an instructional medium may increase the reading skills of children but may in turn reduce the amount of socializing they experience from direct interaction with others. The analyst has an ethical responsibility for anticipating such effects and making their potential known to the client or the public.

A final consideration is the amount of *confidentiality* accorded to the personal information obtained from individuals in a study. If their identification with such information were to fall into the hands of others, neither the analyst nor the subjects have any assurance that the disclosure would not be used adversely.

This brief look at the ethical problems involved in policy making is not meant to be exhaustive nor to imply that ethical problems can be avoided. One or more of them will be present to some degree in any research activity. The analyst must evaluate these problems in light of the purposes of the study to determine that the benefits to be achieved justify the ethical risks taken, and that every effort has been and/or will be made to minimize these risks when they cannot be avoided.

Preventive Measures

Since it is not always possible to anticipate the ethical consequences of a particular research effort, it may be useful to identify in advance some research contexts in which ethical problems are likely to arise. Then it may be possible to introduce preventive measures into the research design or, failing that, at least to anticipate remedial actions (Kelman 1968).

When a research effort is designed to satisfy two or more *conflicting interests,* it is almost certain that the researcher will become embroiled in one or another of the ethical problems we have just outlined. One set of inherent values is almost certain to be violated, resulting in the manipulation of a subgroup in the population. For example, in researching the effectiveness of a particular public program favored by a political party, the analyst may find him or herself under subtle pressure to ignore evidence of program failure, or even to suppress negative results in order to enhance the party's chances for election. Hence, before tackling such an assignment, the analyst should assess the likelihood that he or she will be able to conduct the inquiry without bias, and that the results will be disseminated, regardless of their implications, within a reasonable period of time. If these conditions cannot be assured, the analyst should seriously consider rejecting the project; to proceed is to invite a moral risk.

A second general caveat is to avoid those research contexts in which it is not possible to anticipate with reasonable certainty the immediate outcomes or the unintended side effects of a given intervention when there is *reason to believe that such outcomes and side effects could be injurious.* In the absence of clear-cut cause-effect linkages, it is impossible to guard against the likelihood of harmful effects flowing from a study. The classic example is the case of the widespread use of thalidomide, a sedative first introduced in Sweden and only later found to cause congenital defects in human fetuses (*Britannica* 1966).

The *requirement of secrecy* within the research context is still another precursor of ethical problems. Such a requirement implies that certain groups within the social unit must be deprived knowledge of the research being carried on and must, therefore, remain unable to express their disapproval or to act to protect their rights. Since no decision maker can be fully aware of the needs and interests of all those affected, there is no guarantee that the research to be undertaken will be in their best interest. This difficulty often arises in research conducted under the guise of national security and accounts for much of the aversion of social scientists to such efforts. Secrecy also creates a potential for mischief in that the research may be appropriated for purposes other than that for which it was designed. Third parties may become aware of its existence and make false claims about its implications which cannot be refuted precisely because of the secrecy of the endeavor. For example, the secrecy surrounding the Moynihan report on black families was responsible for a veritable bureaucratic war over its alleged policy implications based on rumored perceptions of the report which took on a life of their own (Rainwater and Yancey 1970). The issue of secrecy should not be confused with that of anonymity. One can protect the anonymity of subjects involved while being open about the purposes of the research and the dissemination of its findings.

The fourth contextual safeguard against violating ethical principles is to insist upon *consistency between the larger goals of the decision makers and the objectives of the policy research* being proposed. No matter how ethically valid the analyst's role may be in a given research project, his/her work is open to challenge on moral grounds if the project itself is to be used to further ends that are morally questionable (Kelman 1968, pp. 34–57). This dilemma is well illustrated by Project Camelot, the objective of which was to achieve understanding of the sources of revolutionary discontent in underdeveloped countries

(Horowitz 1970, pp. 157-183). The research was deemed morally defensible by the social scientists involved on the grounds that violence is a dehumanizing phenomenon. However, since the research was commissioned by the United States Army as part of its larger goal of controlling counter-insurgency movements, the ultimate aim was in effect to violate the rights of disadvantaged groups to act on the basis of their self-interests.

A fifth caveat is that the context of policy research provide the analyst with *sufficient independence* to examine the research question from all perspectives of the social unit affected. This may be thought of as a "law of symmetry." If the sponsors of research into a particular social problem inhibit the analyst from investigating the issue from the perspective of other subgroups, the analysis is bound to generate an ethical dilemma. For example, if an all-white board of education seeks to ascertain the most feasible plan for school desegregation, the analyst should be free to consider the attitudes of teachers as well as of students, of black families as well as of white families. To examine the proposal solely from the perspective of the board of education not only violates the interests of other actors in the system but may ultimately undermine the interests of the leadership itself by failing to bring to light the complex ramifications of such an issue.

No matter how much care is taken to conduct a study ethically, research that forms the basis for collective decision making inevitably affects the lives of some people in adverse ways. In this respect it is manipulative even though the subjects affected are informed of the research and its results. To minimize this impact, the policy analyst should endeavor to *increase the range of alternative courses of action,* that is, to expand the decision maker's array of options, in order to generate interventions which may be less adverse. The ethically committed analyst will avoid research problems that implicitly restrict the scope of potential actions or prevent the contribution of various subgroups to the research.

As in any human endeavor, it is impossible for the analyst to foresee all possible consequences, or to control his or her actions entirely. In the final analysis, ethical quality of policy research will depend on the sensitivity that the analyst brings to the task and on his/her willingness to accept honestly and openly responsibility for personal decisions in the face of social criticism.

SUMMARY

Policy research is defined as empirical research, the purpose of which is to verify a proposition about some aspect of the means-ends relationship in policy making. There are three types of research methods: Exploratory research leads to the identification or specification of properties of a given phenomenon; descriptive research results in quantitative measures of the size, distribution, or covariation of properties in a given population; and explanatory research seeks to verify the conditions of causality in relations among properties. Policy research is characterized by explicit attention to those value assumptions that underlie the formulation of a policy problem. This intermingling of social values and analysis inevitably places the conduct of such research in a context of social conflict. We have identified some of the forms this ethical conflict can take and also some of the measures the policy analyst can adopt to minimize it.

REFERENCES

ACKOFF, RUSSELL L. *The Design of Social Research.* Chicago: The University of Chicago Press, 1953.

BLACK, JAMES A., and DEAN J. CHAMPION. *Methods and Issues in Social Research.* New York: John Wiley and Sons, Inc., 1976.

BABBIE, EARL R. *The Practice of Social Research.* Belmont, Calif.: Wadsworth Publishing Company, Inc., 1975.

"Doctor Says He Was Told Not to Treat Men in V.D. Experiment," *New York Times,* August 8, 1972, p. 16:4.

ETZIONI, AMITAI. "Policy Research," The American Sociologist, *6* (June 1971), 8-12.

GANS, HERBERT J. "Social Science for Social Policy," in *The Use and Abuse of Social Science,* ed. Irving Louis Horowitz. New Brunswick, N.J.: Transaction Books, 1971, pp. 13-34.

GLASER, BARNEY G., and ANSELM L. STRAUSS. *The Discovery of Grounded Theory.* Chicago: Aldine Publishing Co., 1967.

GOULDNER, ALVIN W. "Explorations in Applied Social Science," in *Applied Sociology,* eds. Alvin W. Gouldner and S. M. Miller. New York: Free Press, 1965, pp. 5-22.

HOROWITZ, IRVING LOUIS. "The Life and Death of Project Camelot," in *The Values of Social Science,* ed. Norman K. Denzin. Chicago: Aldine Publishing Co., 1970, pp. 157-183.

HYMAN, HERBERT. *Survey Design and Analysis.* New York: The Free Press, 1955.

KAPLAN, ABRAHAM. *The Conduct of Inquiry,* San Francisco: Chandler Publishing Company, 1964.

KELMAN, HERBERT C. *A Time to Speak: On Human Values and Social Research.* San Francisco: Jossey-Bass, Inc., Publishers, 1968.

KORNHAUSER, ARTHUR, and PAUL F. LAZARSFELD. "The Analysis of Consumer Actions," in *The Language of Social Research,* eds. Paul F. Lazarsfeld and Morris Rosenberg. New York: Free Press, 1955.

LINDBLOM, CHARLES E. *The Policy-Making Process.* Englewood Cliffs, N.J.: Prentice-Hall, Inc., 1968.

MACK, RUTH. *Planning on Uncertainty.* New York: Wiley-Interscience, 1971.

MacMAHON, BRIAN, and THOMAS F. PUGH. *Epidemiology: Principles and Methods.* Boston: Little, Brown and Co., 1970.

MAYER, ROBERT, ROBERT MORONEY, and ROBERT MORRIS. *Centrally Planned Change, A Reexamination of Theory and Experience.* Urbana, Ill.: University of Illinois Press, 1974.

McCALL, GEORGE J., and J. L. SIMMONS. *Issues in Participation Observation.* Reading, Mass.: Addison-Wesley Publishing Co., 1969.

"Pharmacology," *Britanica Book of the Year,* 1966, 605.

RAINWATER, LEE, and WILLIAM L. YANCEY. "Black Families and the White House," in *The Values of Social Science,* ed. Norman K. Denzin. Chicago: Aldine Publishing Co., 1970, pp. 127–157.

RIEKEN, HENRY W., and ROBERT F. BORUCH, eds. *Social Experimentation, A Method for Planning and Evaluating Social Intervention.* New York: Academic Press, 1974.

ROSE, STEVEN M. *The Betrayal of the Poor.* Cambridge, Mass.: Schenkman Publishing Company, 1972.

ROSSI, PETER H., and WALTER WILLIAMS. *Evaluating Social Programs.* New York: Seminar Press, 1972.

SCRIVEN, MICHAEL. "The Mythodology of Evaluation," in *Perspectives of Curriculum Evaluation,* eds. Ralph W. Tyler, Robert M. Gagne, Michael Scriven. Chicago: Rand McNally and Co., 1967.

SELLTIZ, CLAIRE, LAWRENCE S. WRIGHTSMAN, and STUART W. COOK. *Research Methods in Social Relations* (3rd ed.). New York: Holt Rinehart and Winston, 1976.

SUCHMAN, EDWARD. *Evaluative Research.* New York: Russell Sage Foundation, 1967.

SIMON, JULIAN L. *Basic Research Methods in Social Science.* New York: Random House, 1969.

STOUFFER, SAMUEL A., LOUIS GUTTMAN, EDWARD A. SUCHMAN, PAUL F. LAZARSFELD, SHIRLEY A. STAR, and JOHN A. CLAUSEN. *The American Soldier.* Princeton, N.J.: Princeton University Press, 1949.

WATTS, HAROLD W. "The Graduated Work Incentive Experiments: Current Progress," *The American Economic Review, 61* (May 1971), 15–21.

WEISS, CAROL H. *Evaluation Research.* Englewood Cliffs, N.J.: Prentice-Hall Inc., 1972.

ZECKHAUSER, RICHARD and ELMER SCHAEFER. "Public Policy and Normative Economic Theory," in *The Study of Policy Formation,* eds. Raymond A. Bauer and Kenneth J. Gergen. New York: Free Press, 1968, pp. 27–97.

chapter 4 / an overview of the research design process

As we noted in Chapter 3, problems often arise in the course of policy making or planning, which can only be resolved through empirical research. Such problems occur in connection with specifying policy objectives, designing policy alternatives, estimating their consequences, and evaluating the effects of the implementation of policy. The conduct of such research involves its own sequence of activities which must be carefully designed prior to its execution. It is the job of the policy analyst to prepare such a design and to demonstrate how the proposed investigation can contribute to the policy-making process.

In this chapter we will provide an overview of the research design process. First, we attempt to convey the nature of research design and to justify the need for it; we then proceed to describe the stages that constitute the process and how these stages are interrelated as a sequence of operations carried out by the analyst. This chapter serves as an introduction to Part II of this book. It should be read carefully before undertaking the individual chapters that follow, each of which deals with one of the stages in research design.

THE RESEARCH DESIGN

A research design is a comprehensive plan of the sequence of operations that an analyst intends to execute to achieve a given set of research objectives. As such, it may be thought of as an operational expression of the scientific method. The design specifies the research method and techniques the analyst has chosen to employ, together with the rationale underlying the investigation and any administrative details requisite to the design's execution. The drafting of a design involves anticipating the alternative ways in which each operation might be executed and making a choice as to which alternative is best suited for achieving the given objective(s). The design is thus a detailed outline of the analyst's decisions, along with the reasons for each, based on scientific norms

One may question whether the considerable amount of time and resources required to plan a research project is warranted. Cannot one simply identify a research problem, plunge into research by collecting data on that problem, and subsequently try to find the best fit between the data and the problem? Experience shows that partially planned or unplanned research efforts often suffer on two counts. They either end up with irrelevant data or with data that are indeed pertinent but so numerous as to obfuscate the analysis. One of the most frequent complaints voiced by inexperienced researchers is, "I have all these data but I don't know what to do with them." The design guide offered in this book is intended to avoid such pitfalls.

One might also question the basic value of the entire design process. Does not adherence to a formal design stifle the research process, prevent the discovery of facts which may turn out to be more useful than those the analyst anticipates prior to the investigation, and thereby eliminate the possibility of discovering unsuspected relationships? Premature closure is certainly a danger in any designed task. The analyst must be open to the need for making adaptations in the research design during its execution. However, the assumption underlying this book is that, with opportunity for feedback, a well-designed research effort will more likely achieve its primary objectives than an undesigned one.

Finally, a word may be necessary about the very concept of research design. It could be argued that the whole process of evolving research designs is esentially a nonrational one which does not lend itself to exposition. Being noncommunicable, it must be learned, like any art, primarily through personal experience. If the design process is indeed an art, then each of us can acquire it only by observing some skilled practitioner at work, and through reiterative practice develop our own capacity for it. Such a view, however, overlooks the substantial element of rationality and technical knowledge involved in designing anything. Architects receive formal instruction in the process of designing houses. To design a house requires knowledge of the relevant properties of the building materials to be used and of the spatial structure that will result from the way they are combined. This fact in no way stifles the architect's creativity in achieving the final product. Similarly, the designing of research is a rational process involving technical knowledge. Problems for research can be investigated via alternative approaches. Hence it is possible to identify the steps involved in these alternatives and to spell out the criteria for preferring one alternative to another. This is not to deny that a large measure of creativity enters into both the conceptualization of alternatives and the development of techniques for their execution. Despite these objections, we will endeavor to expose the rational procedures that the analyst can utilize to design a research endeavor which, rather than inhibiting, will actually maximize whatever creativity he or she may bring to this task.

As we conceive it, the process of preparing a research design consists of nine stages. The analyst must take a definitive stand on each of these nine issues with respect to the specific policy problem under investigation:

1. the justification of research as a resolution of the policy problem
2. the history of the policy problem
3. the conceptual framework of the policy problem
4. the objective(s) of the research
5. the population to be studied
6. the data to be collected
7. the procedures of data collection
8. the analyses of data to be performed
9. the administration of the research

How the analyst responds to each of these issues in his/her written research proposal comprises the research design.

We have referred to these issues as stages because they constitute a progression. As a rule, they represent the actual working sequence that an analyst follows in drafting the design, for decisions made in the early stages of the design shape those made in the later stages. However, when the analyst presents the design to others in the form of a written research proposal, he or she may wish to depart from this sequence. For example, the research objective is usually presented first, even though it does not occur in that order in the design process. In addition, investigations differ in the degree of emphasis they place on the various stages. It is conceivable that in drafting the design of one investigation minimal attention needs to be paid to the historical framework, for example, whereas in another, understanding this background may be crucial to resolving the problem. For our purposes, however, it is preferable to retain the original sequence of presentation and to treat each stage with thoroughness.

STAGES OF THE RESEARCH DESIGN

1. *Justification.* The design process begins with the analyst's establishing the relevance of the proposed investigation to the policy-making process; that is, with an analysis of the policy problem. Research that does not begin with this focus cannot result in guides for policy making, except perhaps as an accidental or indirect outcome. The analyst's task at this stage is thus to determine whether the research requested is indeed necessary to resolve the problem faced by the policy maker. The investigator must ascertain the stage of policy

making at which the problem occurs and the nature of the information required to resolve that problem. The information may be an assessment of needs that leads to the specification of objectives; or it may be the identification of alternative courses of action, the estimation of the probable consequences of each alternative, or the evaluation of the outcomes of an implemented policy. The justification stage of the design process is intended as a precaution against embarking upon an investigation which has no potential for problem solving or for the attainment of goals, and which is not motivated by an intent to take action toward attaining a given objective.

2. *History.* Next in the design process the analyst reviews past attempts to deal with the policy objective at issue. Such a review should cover the following: time-series data that reveal trends in the state or condition that the policy attempts to influence; past efforts to conceptualize the policy objective and the means for achieving it; and the results of others' research to evaluate previously employed means to achieve such policy ends. The historical review informs the analyst of everything known to date about the policy objective and about the ways of dealing with it. Such a review serves to protect the analyst from undertaking research on questions for which answers are already available and/or which do not necessitate research. The information thereby collected also provides the analyst with an experiential background or basis for approaching the remaining stages of the design.

3. *Conceptual Framework.* Equipped with the perspective gained in the first two stages of the research design, the analyst must construct a logical framework for the prospective investigation. Such a framework should include both propositions that are taken as "givens" or "knowns" (and thus represent the assumptions on which the prospective investigation is to rest) and those that are taken as "unknowns" (and hence require substantiation by research). The framework will specify (1) the dependent variable(s)—that comprising the end of policy; (2) the independent variables—those comprising the means for achieving the end(s); and (3) the causal linkages connecting these two sets of variables to each other and to related policy variables that are part of the analysis. The conceptual framework defines the logical boundaries for the investigation and serves as a guide whereby the analyst can judge what is relevant and what is irrelevant to study.

4. *Research Objective(s).* The conceptual framework enables the analyst to formulate the objective(s) of the planned investigation. By the term *research objective(s)* is meant the specific proposition(s) that are the subject of investigation, as well as the research method suited to carrying out the investigation. These propositions are statements about the means-ends relationship of policy making and follow directly from the conceptual framework. They take the form either of questions to be answered or of hypotheses to be verified, and they impart direction to the research. Research objectives indicate the units that should be observed, what to observe about those units, and how the process of

observation should be structured and implemented in order to achieve those objectives. These decisions are elaborated in the remaining stages of research design.

5. *Study Population.* The design of the study population involves four decisions: (1) specifying the unit of observation, (2) designating the population of units to be observed, (3) adopting a procedure for selecting or arranging units for observation, and (4) determining the number of units to be observed. In executing this stage the analyst must distinguish between the *study population,* the actual collection of persons, objects, or events subject to observation, and the *target population,* to which one or more of the policy alternatives will be applied by the policy maker. Often the two are the same, but just as often they are not. In the latter case, it is the degree of similarity between them that determines the extent to which findings from the observation of the study population can be applied to the target population. The design of the study population is the principal means by which the method of research is operationalized. In explanatory studies it is known as "experimental design." We have adopted the more general term *study population,* which encompasses the design requirements of exploratory and descriptive studies as well.

6. *The Data.* The analyst must next specify the data that are to be collected about the study population. Data are specified by identifying the major concepts that comprise the statement of the research objective(s) and then developing operational definitions for these concepts. These operational definitions take the form of variables, which in turn point to the data to be collected. This set of detailed specifications serves to guard the analyst against collecting data that will turn out to be irrelevant and unnecessary.

7. *Data Collection.* Having specified what data should be collected, the analyst must next decide upon the proper procedures for data gathering, given the constraints of the research setting. He or she must describe in detail the techniques to be used, the instruments to be employed, and the sequence of steps to be followed in using those instruments. If original instruments are to be employed, the procedure for their construction must be described. The design of data collection procedures will in large measure determine the reliability and validity of the data that will be collected.

8. *Data Analysis.* When the data to be collected are specified, the analyst must simultaneously consider the appropriate procedures for their analysis. Specifically, he or she must decide how the data are to be classified or ordered into measures of the respective variables, and how the presence and degree of relationship among the variables are to be ascertained. To make these decisions, the analyst anticipates the kinds of findings that the research objective(s) requires, and on that basis selects the procedures that will most probably generate them. In fact, this stage of data analysis is a substantive test of the research design that also requires the analyst to anticipate any limitations that may apply to the inferences he or she draws.

9. *Administration*. Once the analyst knows the population to be studied, the nature of the data to be collected, and the kinds of procedures to be employed in collecting and analyzing these data, he or she has a basis for making a series of administrative decisions. The analyst must estimate the money, the time, the personnel, and the organization that the prospective investigation will require. Ultimately it is the character of these decisions that will determine whether the investigation is feasible. The benefits to be derived from the planned investigation consist of policy choices that are more "rational" than would be achieved otherwise. These benefits must more than offset the administrative "costs" of conducting the study in order to warrant its undertaking. Sometimes the research findings will result in a choice among policy alternatives that has only a marginal impact on the policy objective. Sometimes the cost of obtaining the research findings is very large in relation to the benefits to be derived from the policy or program. In either case to undertake the investigation would be an "irrational" decision.

The actual number of design stages that we have identified may be regarded as somewhat arbitrary. In this respect experienced analysts and funding agencies do differ among themselves. Thus, for example, some may combine stages 3 and 4, conceptual framework and research objectives, into one. Others may combine stages 7 and 8, data collection and data analysis, into one. Similarly, analysts differ with respect to the relative emphasis they place upon various stages. Virtually all consider stages 4 through 9 (research objectives, study population, specification of data, data collection, data analysis, and administration), the more technical aspects of the research, as essential to its design. Many actually omit the first three stages (justification, history, and conceptual framework). This last practice, we believe, is a serious mistake. It is our view that these first three stages of the research design are particularly important for policy investigations. To fail to establish a justification for the research is to jeopardize the potential utility of the proposed investigation. To omit an examination of the history of the policy problem may result in the analyst's "rediscovering" an already existing practice. And to embark on the research without a conceptual framework is to operate without a criterion of validity, which will make it ultimately impossible for the analyst to differentiate between those research findings that are valid for the attainment of policy objectives and those that are invalid.

As indicated earlier, the order in which we have presented the design stages frequently differs from the order in which they are presented in a formalized research proposal. The sequence we have employed is the actual working sequence followed in planning the investigation. When the analyst writes up the research proposal, he or she may rearrange the stages to suit the dictates of the funding agency to which it will be submitted or to meet self-imposed standards of comprehensibility. For purposes of instruction, it makes more sense to follow the sequence in which the analyst will actually operate when faced with having to plan an investigation, rather than the one he or she might employ to present the final research proposal.

THE DESIGN AS PROCESS

The stages described in this book are intended to represent discrete tasks which the analyst carries out in developing a research design. Each of the chapters of Part II describes one of those stages and discusses the decisions the analyst must make to complete it. The conclusion of each stage results in a written statement detailing those decisions, and the cumulation of such statements represents the research design. Each chapter, therefore, serves as a guide to the analyst in preparing the respective segment of the research design.

Although the design process is usually presented as a series of cumulative steps, it is in actuality a dynamic process in which there is considerable interplay or feedback between stages (see Figure 4-1). For example, the first three stages—justification, history, and conceptual framework—logically follow one another and build the foundation for the specification of the research objective(s) in stage 4. However, in actual practice there are important feedback processes. For example, a review of the history of prior attempts to deal with a problem inevitably results in a modification of the policy alternatives specified in stage 1; similarly, when one attempts to elaborate the conceptual framework, one's understanding of the policy problem (stage 1) will inevitably undergo some modification. It is useful, therefore, to consider these three stages as a subset and to execute them, in terms of proposal writing, as a unitary subprocess. Thus the analyst may make only some rough notes on the justification for the research based on his/her exploration of the feasible action alternatives, and instead go on to examine the history of attempts to deal with the problem and the presumed causal linkages involved, before beginning to write the justification statement, the history statement, and the conceptual framework in their final form.

Similarly, there are important feedback loops that create subprocesses among the stages in the second half of the design process. The specification of the research objective(s) in stage 4 indicates the units which are the subject of the investigation, the characteristics of those units which are to be observed, and the way in which those observations are to be made in order to carry out the method of the study. Thus, the statement of the research objective(s) (stage 4) generates guidelines for the study population (stage 5), data to be collected (stage 6), procedures for collecting data (stage 7), and analyses of the data (stage 8), all of which tasks are usually thought of as the "formal" research design. But here again, each of these subsequent stages has the effect of further refining or modifying the statement of research objective(s) in stage 4. For example, in de-

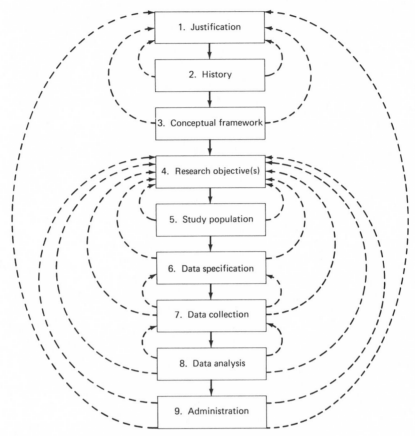

Figure 4-1 Interrelatedness of stages in the design process

fining the study population, the analyst must find a collection of units of observation that are actually accessible to observation. This accessible population may differ in certain respects from the one intended in the statement of the research objective(s). Since it is the accessible population to which the findings will apply, these differences should be fed back to stage 4 and the statement of the research objective(s) modified accordingly. Similarly, in stage 6, when the concepts contained in the statement of the research objective(s) are operationalized in terms of variables that can be measured (observed), they take on more precise and sometimes different meanings than those implied in their original form. These differences should be fed back to stage 4, and the statement of the research objective(s) modified accordingly. Again, when in stage 7 procedures are designed for collecting data, certain conditions, such as the characteristics of the units being observed, may require the adoption of observational procedures which further delimit the population to be observed and the data to be collected. Again, these refinements should be fed back to stage 4, and the statement of the research objective(s) modified accordingly.

Stages 6, 7, and 8 have a special interrelatedness. The operational definition of the concepts to be measured, which takes place in stage 6, depends in large part on the procedures to be used for collecting those data, decisions that are made in stage 7. Similarly, decisions reached in stage 8 (data analysis) will affect the form in which data will be collected (stage 7). These constitute refinements in the instruments to be used, and should be fed back to stage 7 where modifications can be made accordingly. To summarize, although the analyst may deal with the three decision stages in order, yet his or her conclusions must be considered tentative until all decisions in the subprocess have been finalized. Thus, it may be advisable to execute stages 6, 7, and 8 as a subset.

Stage 9 generally stands as a conclusion to the research design process, dependent on the cumulative decisions made in all the prior stages. Even here, however, there is an exception: When resources available to conduct the research are fixed and known at the outset, this fact must be fed into stage 4 so that the operational aspects of the research design in stages 5, 6, 7, and 8 can be made within that financial constraint. In any event, after the cost of conducting the research is estimated in stage 9, this estimate should be fed back to stage 1 for one final test of the justification of the proposed research, to determine if its costs are warranted by the benefits expected from the policy choice.

It is important, therefore, for the analyst to keep the design flexible at each stage of the process. Rather than preparing a finished statement for each stage of the process, the novice analyst should try to limit him- or herself to a rough sketch of each section. Then, from the perspective of the final stage, he or she can return to specific decisions and modify them to fit into a final integrated design. Because we have found this kind of tentative approach so useful in research design, we recommend essentially the same approach in reading this book for the first time. By reading through Part II in its entirety before undertaking to use it chapter by chapter in the design of proposed research, the reader can form some idea of the research process as an art as well as a technique.

The reader should keep in mind that, because they are intended as universal guides, the nine stages have been stated in general terms, meant to fit most, if not all, policy researches. Although Part II contains numerous illustrations, it is ultimately the reader's task to translate them into specifics as called for by the peculiarities of the policy problem to be investigated. Because both the nature of these problems and the conditions for their investigation vary greatly, no two research designs, as written statements, will be identical in content; only in format will they resemble each other.

In drafting a research design, the analyst is compelled to anticipate the actual conditions he or she will in all likelihood confront at each stage of the investigation. Hence, the research design is, in essence, a statement setting forth these many decisions *before* the respective conditions have been encountered.

However, even the most experienced analyst cannot possibly foresee every single contingency likely to arise in the course of a planned investigation. That is the reason for pilot studies, small-scale "rehearsals" of the research design whereby the investigator identifies the obstacles that have eluded his or her foresight. The information provided by the pilot study enables the analyst to revise the research design. Even so, when the investigation proper is finally under way, he or she may still be compelled to make some ad hoc decisions which, despite maximum care, could not be foreseen.

A well-written research design is the product of a great amount of observing, reading, conferring, and thinking about the policy problem to be investigated and about the mode of its investigation. This fact should become quite apparent as the reader progresses through the book. To transform the policy problem into researchable objectives, to provide it with a conceptual framework, to plan a sequence of research operations for it, all this is no small task. Hence, it is no exaggeration to state that the preparation that must precede the investigation proper can consume as much as one-third of the life of the entire research project.

PART 2 / THE RESEARCH
DESIGN PROCESS

chapter 5 / stage 1: justification of the research objectives

Policy studies reflect two kinds of objectives: those that require action and those that enable action through the presentation of information. The first type are called policy objectives, the second, research objectives. Determining what action will most effectively meet the policy objective constitutes the policy problem. Determining what kind of investigation will most effectively meet the research objective constitutes the research problem. In this chapter we deal with the policy problem as it impinges on the research problem. In policy research both kinds of objectives and problems must be dealt with. It is at the justification stage of the research design that these two problems, and the processes by which they are to be resolved, intersect. Justifying the research objectives is in effect demonstrating how their attainment will facilitate determining the proper course of action to achieve a given set of policy objectives. Developing a research design involves demonstrating how the research objectives can be met through a structured investigation.

A framework for making this connection between the policy-making process and the research process was provided in our discussion of the function of research in policy making in Part 1. There we noted that the objectives to be achieved by research depend in part on the stage of the policy-making process in which they are generated. Therefore, in order to formulate research objectives that will provide the policy maker with the needed information, the analyst must (1) develop a clear picture of the policy-making process under consideration and (2) identify the stage in that process which generates the need for information. For example, when the "entry stage" is the assessment of needs or specification of policy objectives, the research objectives will relate to the undesirable conditions the policy maker wishes to eliminate or the desirable conditions he or she wishes to promote. When, on the other hand, information is needed about alternative courses of action, the research objectives will relate to the means whereby the policy maker can attain his or her objectives. By contrast, if the analyst is required to estimate the consequences of alternative actions, the objectives will relate to the assumed effects of those alternatives and their distribution in a given population. Finally, if a policy action already taken is to be evaluated, the research will focus on the extent of its impact, both intended and unintended.

The need to justify research objectives is premised on the fact that not all policy problems require empirical research. Perhaps the problem arises from a lack of clarity about the goal or objectives to be attained. Such a problem may be solved by a deductive process in which the decision maker formulates alternative conditions or end-states and then ranks them in order of their priority. Or the problem may arise from a value conflict which inhibits a choice between alternative ends or means. Here the solution may lie in a social or political process in which all the parties involved in the policy-making process resolve their differences by means of a negotiated choice. Only when the analyst can identify within the policy problem a question of fact, the answer to which is a prerequisite for action, is there a researchable problem. Since the purpose of any problem-solving activity is to move from uncertainty to clarity, the analyst must identify at the very outset the basis and nature of that uncertainty. This is the function of the justification stage of the research design process.

The difference between an investigation that finds application and one that is ignored usually hinges on the writing of an adequate statement justifying the contemplated research. If the research is to have any relevance to the policy problem, its justification must be determined and so stated as the first step in the design process and not as an afterthought tacked on to the report of the research findings. If the analyst defaults at this important juncture, the design will probably result in findings of little use to either policy maker or analyst.

In this, the justification stage of the design process, the analyst assumes perhaps his or her most active role vis-à-vis the policy maker or client.* Frequently the policy maker may want to give the analyst a ready-made formulation of research objectives. Upon examination this agenda may turn out to be either an overly general statement of vaguely sensed tensions or, on the other hand, an overly specific prescription of the information to be obtained. If the analyst uncritically accepts the policy maker's formulation, he or she may be prone to conduct an investigation that results either in a plethora of information irrelevant to the specific decision upon which action is pending, or in a premature narrowing of the investigation so that it may address the wrong issue or ignore important alternatives. In both cases the findings will be only marginally

---

*This role is analogous to that of clinician as developed by Gouldner (1965).

applicable to solving the policy problem. This fact has been repeatedly corroborated by the experiences of social scientists who have been called upon to conduct studies for government agencies (Merton 1949). Accordingly, the analyst is strongly advised against automatically accepting someone else's formulation of the research objectives. Instead he must scrutinize them carefully, forcing them, so to speak, through the "justification screen" of the design process.

The advice we have just given may appear to sanction a manipulative role for the analyst vis-à-vis the policy maker, and ultimately toward the group or public he or she represents. It may seem to lead to the conclusion that the analyst should, where possible, impose a definition of the situation upon the decision maker. On the contrary, our view is that the analyst, by taking an active role in defining and evaluating the policy problem and the proposed research, and in challenging the decision maker or client to clarify the linkage between the two, in the long run actually helps the decision maker achieve his or her goals by formulating more relevant objectives and more effective courses of action. Our definition of the role of the analyst implies that one is more than a technician whose expertise is confined to data collection and data analysis applied to the attainment of research objectives given by the client. By virtue of training and experience, the analyst also has expertise in the reasoning process used in problem solving. Hence, an additional contribution is the application of this reasoning skill toward achieving that clear definition of the policy problem which is an indispensable element in its resolution.

It must be recognized, however, that even a strictly analytical process is not value free. Indeed, when the analyst challenges the policy maker's request for the research, the analyst's own values may well come into play. In evaluating the steps to be taken to alleviate certain conditions, for example, the analyst will of necessity proceed from his or her relatively imperfect knowledge of the policy situation, a knowledge which in turn reflects personal values. Furthermore, the analyst may selectively probe the logic of the several alternatives being considered for achieving the policy maker's objectives, and this selectivity will reflect the analyst's personal values and limited awareness of the client's situation. Hence, at all times the analyst must be on guard against bringing into the analyst-client relationship preconceptions that will affect an otherwise rational process.

CRITERIA FOR JUSTIFYING THE RESEARCH*

The request for research in the policy-making process most often stems from some felt difficulty experienced by the policy maker (Ripple 1960, Bross 1953). It may be a vague sense of dissatisfaction that the policy maker is not where he or she wants to be, that there are aspects of the present situation that

---

*Ackoff (1962) presents a more technical treatment of this subject.

can be eliminated or at least ameliorated. It is this sense of difficulty implying a motivation to act which justifies policy research.

Transforming this sense of dissatisfaction into research objectives that are relevant to action is often a tortuous and time-consuming process. The expression of felt difficulty on the part of the policy maker can refer to various aspects of policy making, not all of which are researchable. It is the job of the analyst to ferret out through probing interchanges with the policy maker the exact nature of that difficulty so that appropriate research objectives can be formulated. The felt difficulty may reflect an uncertainty about the ends of policy. For example, an administrator may express the difficulty as, "We need to make some changes because we are getting a lot of pressure to drop this program." Such a situation typically occurs when existing policies or programs are in a state of transition. The administrator's statement reflects a lack of clarity about program goals or objectives, which may be due to an incompatibility among the goals and objectives of the constituent groups in the policy-making system. Clarification and/or reconciliation of these conflicting goals is a prerequisite to fruitful research.

Sometimes the felt difficulty refers to a clearly defined policy problem; for example, "Should we close down neighborhood health centers and provide service through outpatient clinics of a central general hospital?" In this case, though the objective is not explicit, it can easily be explicated and, the alternative means evaluated. Now consider the statement, "We need to know how many unlicensed day care homes are in this community." Such an expression conveys no sense of policy objective, no sense of alternative actions being contemplated. The felt difficulty has been submerged by the statement of a research objective and must now be explicated before this specific objective can be justified.

There are four questions which both analyst and policy maker must address in order to determine the nature of a policy problem and the specific aspect of the problem that requires research. These are:

1. What is the policy objective, that is, the undesirable condition the policy maker wants to alleviate or the desirable condition he or she wants to bring about?
2. Is there a potential for two or more alternative courses of action for achieving that objective?
3. What is the relevant question(s) of fact; that is, what missing information is needed to adopt a course of action that will achieve the objective?
4. Is there a commitment to engage in action once the factual question is answered?

The answers to these questions, with their ramifications, constitute the substance of the justification statement of the research design.

Beginning with the client's policy problem, the analyst can use these questions to generate the objective(s) for research. Or, presented with a premature statement of the research objective(s) by the client, the analyst can filter that statement through these questions in order to identify the policy problem to which it is addressed, and, if necessary, to refine or to reformulate the preliminary statement as a justifiable research endeavor.

The Policy Objective

The first test for determining whether research into the policy problem is justifiable is to ascertain whether the policy maker can identify some end-state that he or she wishes to attain. The degree of specificity with which this end-state can be verbalized depends, as we have noted earlier, on the stage in policymaking at which the difficulty is felt. In articulating a felt difficulty, the policy maker may be able only to identify pressures exerted on his or her organization to change, or certain opportunities—for example, the availability of federal funds—to undertake new programs or policies. This would suggest that neither goals nor objectives have been established for policy making. Research cannot begin until the decision maker has identified some concrete condition to be attained. In such a situation the analyst's preparatory work will consist chiefly of helping the policy maker to think through a set of alternative goals and objectives, and of generating a dialogue among competing interests to bring out all of the potential policy problems.

If in the course of expressing a felt difficulty the policy maker is able to identify an observable condition he/she wishes to alleviate or a goal he wishes to attain, the first criterion for research has been met. Such a condition is reflected in the following examples: "The neonatal death rate is too high"; "The use of high-rise construction in public housing is damaging to social life"; "What can be done to improve the reading levels of children from low-income families?" In these statements the conditions to be acted on are (1) the high neonatal rate, (2) the social isolation in public housing, and (3) the low reading levels of low-income children.

The expression of an observable end-state represents a rudimentary statement of a policy objective. It is rudimentary because the statement does not specify the amount of change sought, and the population and time interval in which such change is to occur. The rudimentary character of the policy objective indicates that the difficulty has arisen in the stage of assessing needs, in which the condition to be dealt with has been identified, but its extent is not yet known. (See pp. 9-10.) A more precise statement of policy objectives would indicate that the felt difficulty has arisen later in the policy-making process and relates either to designing alternative courses of action, to selecting among alternative actions, or to evaluating actions that have been implemented.

Unless the analyst is able to express the policy objective in some rudimentary form, the design process cannot begin. Studies that focus on collecting data but lead to no action almost always lack an explicit policy objective that would give the research effort its raison d'être. For example, studies aiming to analyze the age and sex characteristics of first admissions to a given hospital or to develop indexes of living conditions by census tracts (sometimes referred to as social indicators) are common in the planning field. Such studies may be best characterized as data collection ventures. As such they are useful in generating information that may be applied to some future planning problem. But since they are not motivated by nor designed around a policy objective, they do not constitute policy research.

Alternative Courses of Action

Assuming that the decision maker is able to articulate a policy objective, the second test for justifying the research is to determine whether or not two or more courses of action are possible for attaining that objective. What is at issue here is not the validity of these alternatives—that issue will be taken up in the conceptual framework stage. Nor is their specificity at issue, because the need for clarity and elaboration of potential alternatives may itself become the focus of research. What *is* at issue in the justification stage is *the potential for taking more than one course of action.* As Ackoff (1953) has observed, unless there are alternatives open to the policy maker, the analyst cannot proceed with the investigation.

Two approaches exist in formulating alternative courses of action. One approach consists of stating the alternatives as whether or not to adopt (or continue) a given program or policy. This dichotomy is usually symbolized as A (to act) or $\overline{A}$ (not to act). Although policy makers frequently confront such choices, "all-or-nothing" alternatives are, more often than not, unacceptable politically. Public pressure usually calls for some form of action—the community rarely tolerates inaction. Also, organizational self-interest dictates against discontinuing a particular program without at the same time substituting for it another claim upon public support and/or resources. Much of the failure of evaluative research to influence the formation of public policy is undoubtedly due to evaluations that consider the merits of a single program or policy. For the analyst to formulate the research problem so narrowly is tantamount to guaranteeing the impotence of the research findings. However, such a formulation is perfectly appropriate in so-called "advocacy research." Here the research objective is to "demythologize," that is, to discredit the prevailing practice and thereby pressure decision makers to recognize the need to consider alternative courses of action, and, of course, preferably the one proffered by the advocate.

The political undesirability of the all-or-nothing formulation requires that a different approach be used in arriving at alternative courses of action, one in which genuine alternatives to an existing program are the focus of comparison (Fairweather 1968). Such a tactic is symbolized as A or B. Multiple alternatives may also be expressed as varying levels or variations of a given type of intervention. This tactic is usually symbolized as A_1 or A_2. If several alternative courses of action are uncovered, we have a series—A or B or C . . . N; or A_1 or A_2 or A_3 . . . A_n. The potential, or lack thereof, for taking more than one course of action derives from a number of factors. The technology or knowledge required for implementing different courses of action must be present if alternatives are to be available. Political commitment to the potential value of alternatives must be present if they are to be acceptable. And lastly, for the various courses of action to be feasible, adequate resources must be available for each.

The specificity with which alternative courses of action can be stated will depend on the stage in the policy-making process at which the felt difficulty arises. Therefore, by examining the specificity of alternatives the analyst will get some clue as to the research objective. For example, if the policy maker has articulated a policy objective but has not been able to specify alternative courses of action, then the difficulty arises in formulating those alternatives. However, the analyst must first determine that some form of action is possible. He must determine: Is the technology available? Is there enough political support (resources) within the policy-making system to act? If the option to act is available, then the second justification test is passed, and the research will probably focus on formulating alternative courses of action.

If, on the other hand, the policy maker explicitly specifies two alternative courses of action but has not implemented either, the felt difficulty probably arises in selecting one of them. In this case, the analyst must determine whether there is in fact a viable choice. If political support and resources within the policy-making system prescribe or are committed to one course of action, no real alternatives exist, and research cannot be justified.

Still a third possibility is for the difficulty to arise after a course of action has been selected and implemented. In this case the felt difficulty probably is in deciding whether the action was effective, that is, whether or not it should be continued. Even though the need for research occurs at the evaluation stage of the policy-making process, the analyst should still ascertain that two or more courses of action are possible. Unless the decision maker is free to discontinue or alter the program in question, the evaluation could be irrelevant.

In examining the policy maker's formulation of alternative courses of action, the analyst should be aware of the problem of "overspecification." This difficulty arises when the decision maker has confined his or her attention to a very narrow set of alternatives. For example, in considering ways to reduce the number of cases of child abuse and neglect, the decision maker may focus on increasing the availability of foster homes for abused or neglected children. But this is to ignore alternatives that allow children to stay in their own homes, including supplementing family income, creating self-help groups for abusive parents, and opening day care centers to relieve some of the pressure felt by parents of young children. We will have more to say about this flexibility in the decision maker's perception of the policy problem later in this chapter.

If the request for research passes the second justification test, the analyst will avoid three common pitfalls that plague the unwary. One consists of the situation in which the inquiry never proceeds beyond the needs assessment stage. When no course of action can be or has been formulated, any subsequent research may simply reiterate the need for action rather than shed light on possible action. Such is likely to be the case when the policy-making process is stalled due to a lack of commitment on the part of the decision maker. Additional studies of the nature and extent of undesirable conditions represent a way of avoiding a commitment to act.

A second pitfall takes the form of studies that elaborate the nature of the policy objective by relating it to a wide range of conditions that are not manipulable, that are not set in the *framework of a system of action*. The literature abounds with studies of the social class correlates of certain physical diseases and of educational failure, when in fact there is absolutely no capacity or even intent to manipulate the social class structure as a way of bringing about changes in physical health and/or educational achievement. From a policy viewpoint, to know that a person's low position in the social class structure "causes" (read "influences") his poor health or his poor reading skill does not further our knowledge about how to overcome class determinants of ill health and/or educational failure. Policy research must deal with actions that can either alter the nature or mitigate the effects of the factors that correlate strongly with the vexing problem under examination.

The third pitfall that can be avoided by ensuring an adequate set of alternative actions is undertaking a study that is essentially unnecessary. There are situations in which practical considerations and/or political pressures virtually constrain the policy maker to one course of action, thereby precluding alternatives. Here research is really superfluous. It may even be that the client's motivation, either conscious or unconscious, in requesting policy analysis is to legitimize the one and only course of action available to him or her. When the policy maker is locked into a single solution, the policy problem then becomes how best to implement that solution. This pitfall often occurs in planning research. A survey may be conducted to determine what programs are needed in a given setting when in fact the decision maker has already decided on the kind of program to finance. In this case there are really no alternative solutions to the particular problem selected. In the early days of the War on Poverty, surveys were conducted by community action agencies to determine what programs were needed in a given community for combating poverty, when in fact the federal government had already developed specific programs, each with its own financing. It is more appropriate to regard surveys of this kind as efforts to document a need which is already known to exist. Without gainsaying the value for community planning of such efforts, they do not constitute policy research in our meaning of the term. However, researchable problems may and do arise in the implementation process of such planning ventures, for example, deciding how to organize and operate the designated program.

The Question(s) of Fact

The third test of justification is to ascertain whether it is possible to specify one or more questions of fact about the policy problem identified in the first and second tests. To be more specific, having identified the policy maker's objective and ascertained what several courses of action are possible, the analyst now assists the decision maker in coming to a rational decision about how to bring about the desirable state of affairs. But if the decision is to be rational, it must be based on adequate factual information. When there is a gap in the requisite information, it is through research that the gap is filled. *Hence, research is indicated only when the analyst is confronted with one or more questions which must be answered by means of hitherto unavailable information.*

The form of such factual questions will vary depending upon the specific aspect of the policy problem or stage in the policy-making process that gives rise to the research. In the course of specifying objectives, policy making may be hampered by lack of information about the extensiveness or prevalence of the conditions to be altered. In order to specify the amount of change required to eliminate these conditions, the analyst must undertake descriptive research to identify their distribution in the population. Such research is often referred to as "needs assessment" in human resources planning.

In the stage of formulating alternative courses of action, a question of fact may arise regarding what courses are available. Here the analyst searches for the factors that have precipitated the unfavorable condition or that have prevented change from occurring, and tries to identify those among them that are amenable to manipulation. Such questions of fact call for exploratory research. In estimating the consequences of alternative courses of action, the analyst needs to know the relative contribution each alternative will make to the attainment of the policy objective. Hence, the analyst may need to specify how the various effects will be distributed throughout the population in question. This assignment would involve descriptive research.

Finally, by the evaluation stage, the decision maker seeks a judgment about the success or failure of his efforts. This judgment depends on information regarding the unintended consequences that may have resulted from a course of action (exploratory), the size and distribution of change in relation to a given objective (descriptive), and the causative nature of the intervention selected to achieve that objective (explanatory). The question of fact could relate to any one of these issues and would require the appropriate research method.

Although our presentation of factual questions has been general, in any given study they of course assume specificity, thereby suggesting the kinds of information required to answer them. Therefore, in the third justification test the analyst should (1) ascertain that a question of fact exists, (2) state specifically what that question is, and (3) indicate the research objective implied by that question.

It is important that the request for research pass the question-of-fact test if the analyst is to avoid getting involved in a situation where the choice between alternative actions rests on political rather than factual grounds. By the term *political grounds* we have in mind the relative power or degree of influence wielded in a policy-making situation by different decision makers who prefer different alternative courses of action. It is important to determine whether the inability to decide on a course of action is due to ignorance occasioned by the absence of requisite information or to failure on the part of the parties concerned to reconcile their differing preferences. In the public arena it is quite common to delay a decision about a given course of action because of an unresolved conflict among the various interest groups. The analyst may be called in to do a "study" that is motivated by a desire either to stall for time, during which the intergroup conflict might be resolved, or to shift the burden of having to choose among alternatives upon "an impartial outside agent." The study may be requested presumably to ascertain the probable consequences of each of the alternatives under consideration when, in fact, these consequences are already well known. Obviously such a "study" does not have as its true intent a desire for missing information. While such tactical stratagems are probably unavoidable in any social context, the analyst who becomes involved in them should be aware of their nature so that the expenditure of time, money, and resources on unnecessary research may be minimized.

Contrary to popular belief, political conflicts are not necessarily resolved by focusing the bright light of knowledge upon them. The solution to these conflicts does not lie in simply obtaining more information about the substantive issue(s) involved. When the choice between two alternative courses of action is entangled in a conflict of interests and/or of values, *partisan analysis* is more appropriate (Lindblom 1968, pp. 32ff.). In partisan analysis each participant seeks to exert a rational influence upon the policy maker in behalf of a personally preferred course of action. One proceeds by first identifying the goals of the policy maker and the values upon which they are premised. This accomplished, one then tries to marshal evidence that would demonstrate a connection between the proposed course of action and the goals that motivate the policy maker. Partisan analysis is really a form of persuasion and is more characteristic of the political rather than of the research process. An essential element in partisan analysis is a precise definition of the value preferences and of the goal commitments of those political actors to be persuaded. Around this matter questions of fact can and do arise. Such questions are, of course, researchable.

The Commitment to Act

The final criterion that allows the analyst to justify his or her research efforts is whether or not the policy maker is committed to act once the missing information is provided. The policy objective may be identified, the potential for alternative actions may be ascertained, questions of fact may exist about how to proceed toward that objective, yet the client may exhibit no intention to act even if all the relevant factors were known.

It is often difficult, in this sense, to distinguish the meaning of the second justification test from that of the fourth. When the analyst applies the second justification test, he or she uncovers constraints in the policy-making environment that limit the range of alternatives available to the policy maker. But when the fourth test is applied, the analyst becomes aware of constraints internal to the policy maker that inhibit taking such action. It is conceivable that situations exist in which the decision maker will not take action regardless of its feasibility.

This last criterion is perhaps the most difficult of all four to apply; such commitment is not easy to ascertain. However, if positive incentives exist that are likely to induce action—or negative sanctions to penalize inaction—the analyst can assume that some action will be taken. For example, public agencies have recently been confronted with a series of court orders requiring positive action to eliminate violations of constitutionally guaranteed rights—with respect to the location of subsidized housing, the school assignment of pupils, and the regulation of pollutants in the environment. A request for research in connection with any of these tasks can be assumed to be motivated by a high commitment to take action. On the other hand, technological advances may create the knowledge, and newly aroused public awareness may generate the financial support, for programs heretofore regarded as impossible. How to land a man on the moon never was a problem until space technology made the feat possible. As Lindblom has observed, "a problem is often a new opportunity, not an old sore" (1968, p. 14). Research requested under such conditions can be assumed to have a high probability of being utilized.

There is nothing completely fixed or unambiguous about a commitment to act in the field of policy making. Policy makers may have to and frequently do hedge their intent to act with the proviso "until all the facts are in." Circumstances surrounding the problem situation can and do change during the conduct of the requested research, thereby undoing the commitment made earlier. Therefore, in applying this last criterion, the analyst should not require ironclad assurances. Rather, he or she should ascertain whether the circumstances surrounding the policy-making decision favor eventual action or whether foreseeable blocks exist to prevent the implementation of the research findings.

USING THE FOUR JUSTIFICATION TESTS

By now it should be obvious that in order to apply the four criteria for justifying research, the analyst must communicate with the policy maker or client. Those who have had experience in providing policy research services uniformly suggest that the discussion between analyst and client be informal, unhurried, and free-wheeling in content. Ripple (1960) has characterized this approach as "relaxed probing." Using as his or her point of departure the client's opening statement of felt difficulty, the analyst moves from one test to the next, questioning, probing, and drawing out the client. This interchange compels the client to think about his or her problem in a new way. Perhaps the client's objective(s) has not been clearly expressed, so that it may be radically different from the analyst's first impression of it. Or perhaps there was ambiguity about the courses of action available to the client. Or, again, the alternatives may be readily visible, but the basis for choosing among them not at all so evident. This dialogue between analyst and client produces a progressive clarification of the issues. Such clarification is exceedingly valuable even if its outcome is the realization on the client's part that he basically does not want to, or realistically cannot, act to alter his situation.

The first step in this justification task is for the analyst to clarify the nature of the client who has the policy problem. The client may be a bureaucrat or head of an organization with access to certain resources; a politician or an official representing a constituency with interests to protect; or a governing body with certain statutory powers to exercise. The character of the client has a definite bearing on the courses of action that are possible; some clients have access to financial resources, some have manpower at their disposal, others can exercise legal sanctions. The relationship of the client to the total environment of the policy decision determines his or her commitment to act on the basis of the findings produced by the prospective research. The analyst must thus ask him or herself: Does the client have sole decision-making power? Must he or she consult others? Will it be necessary to persuade other relevant actors of the propriety of a given course of action? The less exclusive is the client's decision-making authority, the more likely is it that the prospective study may have to be refocused upon the decision-making environment itself, rather than on the condition that originally gave rise to the need for action.

Although we have described the four justification tests as though they constituted a sequential scheme, they should really be employed dynamically. As in formulating the research design itself, the analyst must constantly reassess the results derived from preceding tests in terms of more recent results. In this manner the original statement of the needed research becomes progressively reformulated, and correspondingly affects the statement of research objectives.

As an example, let us consider the policy problem stemming from an unacceptably high rate of neonatal mortality (see Figure 5-1). The client in this

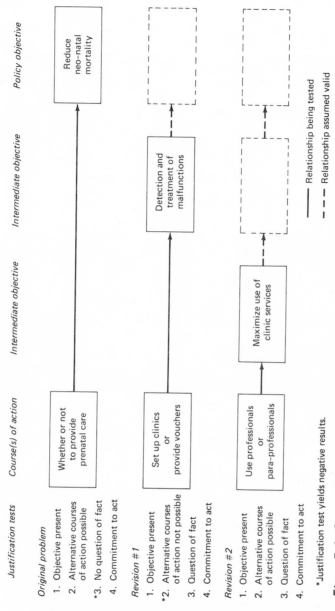

Justification test yields negative results.

Figure 5–1 Sequential revision of policy problem requiring research based on justification tests

example is a county health department in a large metropolitan area. The alternative courses are well known, namely, whether or not to provide prenatal care. However, there are no questions of fact around the alternative courses available; health experts uniformly agree that prenatal care is necessary in order to provide early detection and treatment of malfunctions that might cause complications in delivery, a major cause of neonatal mortality. Since there is no factual question about the course of action being proposed, research on that policy problem is not needed.

The policy problem, however, might be recast in terms of an intermediate objective: How can prenatal care be delivered so as to provide early detection and treatment of malfunctioning of the highest quality (see Figure 5-1, Revision No. 1)? Here two alternative courses of action are feasible, namely, to set up free public clinics at a number of locations or to provide financial assistance in the form of vouchers with which to purchase service from private physicians. Now there is a question of fact as to which of the two courses of action would maximize the intermediate objective. But let us suppose that the decision maker is committed to only one course, namely, the provision of public clinic services. If this is the case, again research is not justifiable.

However, a new intermediate objective might easily be envisioned in connection with the operation of such a public system of health care (see Figure 5-1, Revision No. 2): How to maximize the use of public clinic services? Again, courses of action present themselves in the form of alternative staffing procedures: to use either professionally trained doctors or neighborhood residents trained as paraprofessionals. There is a question of fact about the likely consequences of each alternative action. Furthermore, the commitment to act once the factual question has been answered is clear. Therefore, a justifiable research objective has been identified.

It should be noted that in reformulating the policy problem two things occurred. First, the problem moved from general to more specific factors. In terms of the policy-making model presented in Chapter 1, the decision process moved from the consideration of alternative policies or programs to the consideration of alternative means of implementing that policy. This substage of policy planning is often called program or operations planning. The second thing that occurred was that the end-state was recast from a policy objective to an intermediate objective involving a shorter linkage than that specified in the original formulation. Such an objective is often referred to as an output or bridging variable. We will have more to say about this in connection with our discussion of the conceptual framework in Chapter 3.

It should be noted that the process of analyzing the policy problem can force its reformulation in the opposite direction, from the specific to the more global. In terms of Figure 5-1 this would mean moving from the bottom of the diagram to the top. For example, if the decision maker originally stated the policy problem as "whether or not to use paraprofessionals in staffing public prenatal clinics," the analyst would probably question why the choices have been so narrowly conceived. In essence, the analyst would be challenging the policy maker's formulating the problem in terms of an intermediate objective. What is the policy maker's evidence that clinic services are the best means of providing such care? If the decision maker cannot produce such evidence, the analyst would refocus the policy problem to the second level, namely, that of choosing between alternative means of delivering prenatal care. Similarly, if the policy problem had been originally formulated at the second level, the analyst would ask the decision maker to justify his or her exclusion of alternative means of delivering prenatal care. That is, what evidence does the policy maker have that the provision of prenatal care will result in fewer neonatal deaths? And so the process continues.

The justification tests are used as a technique to zero in on what will turn out to be the research objectives. Like any technique, their use calls for flexibility and judgment. Applying the tests to the policy problem may not always yield clear answers. Ambiguous answers suggest the need for more thinking, probing, discussing. A negative answer to a test may well require the client to reexamine his or her conception of the policy problem and/or commitment to take action. This check will in the end circumvent the client's likely disappointment in what could turn out to be an abortive study; it will also prevent the waste of resources and effort. Applying the justification tests helps the analyst to shape and reshape his or her conception of the client's situation and contributes toward a clear formulation of the research objective(s).

ASSESSING VALUE ASSUMPTIONS

The use of the scientific method requires a clear distinction between fact and value. Statements of fact can be empirically verified, statements of value cannot. However, as was pointed out in Part 1, value assumptions inevitably intertwine with any policy research; they underlie not only policy objectives but also the actions proposed for attaining them. Such assumptions serve a useful function in formulating research objectives. They reveal the limits to policy objectives and to the action alternatives to be considered (Lindblom 1968, p. 23). In their absence policy analysis would become an enormous task. The explication of these assumptions, in the course of applying the justification tests, will clarify the boundaries imposed on research objectives by values.

But propositions which enunciate value assumptions are not always immutable; at times they can be reformulated so as to permit their empirical verification. When such is the case, they may become the preferred focus of research. The process of explicating and reformulating value assumptions involves reformulating the policy problem from specific to more general factors, as we did in moving from the bottom to the top of Figure 5-1. To understand this process requires an examination of the nature of value assumptions.

As was discussed in Part I, value assumptions are of two types: (1) those which reflect *inherent* worth valued for its own sake, and (2) those which reflect *instrumental* worth valued as a means to a desired end. Based on our earlier discussion of the policy-making process, we can say that a policy goal embodies an inherent value. Therefore, a policy objective, being an operational expression of a goal, cannot be validated empirically; it can only be validated with reference to its consistency with the value assumption underlying the goal it expresses. However, at times the objective under consideration is an instrument to the attainment of some other objective, as in the case of intermediate objectives. These objectives can be said to reflect an instrumental value and, therefore, can be validated empirically in terms of their functional relation to a policy objective.

The process of clarifying a policy problem by explicating and reformulating its value assumptions can be illustrated by our hypothetical example in Figure 5-2. Let us assume that the policy objective is the reduction of poverty, and that the task of the analyst is to identify alternative actions for attaining

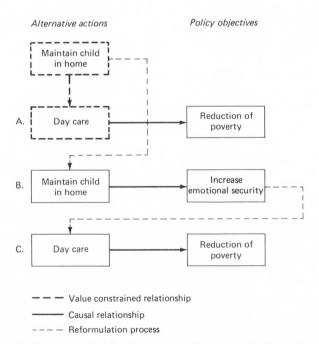

Figure 5-2 Clarifying a policy problem by explicating and reformulating a value assumption

that objective. Let us further assume that the analyst proposes to provide day care services to enable poor women who are also mothers to seek employment, and thereby reduce poverty. However, the policy maker precludes consideration of this alternative with the comment, "Children should be cared for by their mother in their own homes" (Figure 5-2, A). The expression of a "should" statement implies the presence of a value assumption. The analyst's approach, therefore, is to ask of the policy maker, "Why?" If the person responds, "Because I believe that a mother's place is in the home," the analyst concludes that the original preference is an inherent value which cannot be reformulated for empirical verification. If, on the other hand, the policy maker responds, "Because I believe that children raised by their mother in their own home will develop greater emotional security," the analyst concludes that the original preference is an instrumental value which can be verified empirically by being reformulated as a causal hypothesis (Figure 5-2, B). If verification results in the finding that maintaining a child in his or her home does lead to greater emotional security, the analyst concludes that the policy maker's original preference is valid. In such a case no further consideration of day care services is appropriate. If, on the other hand, the results of verification are that maintaining a child at home has no such benefit, the analyst concludes that the policy maker's original value assumption is invalid. In this case a return to consideration of the provision of day care services as a means of reducing poverty is warranted.

In a similar manner the value assumption underlying a policy objective can be explicated and its status as an inherent or an instrumental value can be determined. If it is found to be an instrumental value, the objective can be reformulated and its validity as an end of policy making can be tested in terms of its causal relationship with another value held by the decision maker. Returning to our previous example, if we find that the policy maker regards poverty essentially as an inequitable distribution of income, the analyst is forced to conclude that the objective of policy making (reduction of poverty) is an inherent value and no further justification of its pursuit is necessary. If, however, the policy maker replies that poverty should be reduced "because it leads to social unrest," the analyst concludes that the objective is merely an instrumental value and that its justification can be reformulated as a causal hypothesis and verified empirically.

The decision to refocus research on the validity of an instrumental value is guided by two criteria: (1) the credibility of the instrumental value assumption (that is, what is the probability of its being true?), and (2) the practical consequences of basing action on the value assumption if it is not true (that is, what are the risks if the assumption proves false?). Returning to our hypothetical example, the first criterion would impel the analyst to ask, "Would most informed observers accept the assumption that growing up in one's own home contributes to maximal emotional security, or the assumption that alleviating poverty reduces social unrest?" If most people do not regard these propositions as self-evident, they may need to be verified empirically. A refocus of the research toward that end is thereby justified.

The second criterion would impel the analyst to ask, "What consequence does the instrumental value assumption have for the attainment of the client's objective or goal?" "Are there alternatives to the inducement of mothers into the labor market, through the provision of day care services, that are equally feasible and effective in reducing poverty?" If not, then the client's instrumental value assumption acts as a constraint in achieving his or her objective and should become the focus of research. Similarly, by this criterion the analyst ascertains whether the client's instrumental value is the sole justification of pursuing his or her objective, or if other equally compelling bases exist. "Are there other reasons why reducing poverty is desirable even were it not to result in reducing social unrest? Will it stimulate economic growth, or will it reduce the cost of public services such as police and fire protection?" If reduction of social unrest is offered as the overriding justification for reducing poverty, and the relation between the two is of questionable validity, then the analyst should refocus the research toward verifying this instrumental value assumption. To proceed with efforts to reduce poverty without such verification may have no impact on social unrest.

Whether to focus research on the original statement of the policy problem or on the instrumental value assumption constraining it will be decided in part by experience and careful reasoning. Sufficient data are not always available to make such a decision on empirical grounds. The lack of sufficient empirical evidence does not, however, invalidate such a decision.

SUMMARY

The justification statement should present the results of applying each of the four justification criteria to the proposed research.

1. What is the objective to be achieved by policy making?
2. Is there a potential for two or more courses of action? (When specified by the policy maker, those alternatives should be reported in the justification statement.)
3. Is there a question(s) of fact which prevents the policy maker from taking action toward his policy objective? What is the specific question?
4. Is there a commitment to act on the part of the policy maker once the facts are known?

It should be noted that the question of fact foreshadows the formulation of the research objective(s). It should refer to the nature and prevalence of the condition that underlies the policy objective; to the discovery of alternative courses of action; to the distribution of the presumed benefits of each action alternative; or to the impact of a course of action already implemented. The question of fact should specify the information that is needed. When the research objective is formulated in stage 4 of the design process, the question of fact will become more precise. At the justification stage, this formulation is still tentative and must pass through two subsequent design stages. An examination of previous attempts to deal with the policy problem (stage 2) and the drafting of the conceptual framework for the policy problem (stage 3) may modify the analyst's conception of the research objective(s).

REFERENCES

ACKOFF, RUSSELL L. *Scientific Method, Optimizing Applied Research Decisions.* New York: John Wiley and Sons, 1962.

ACKOFF, RUSSELL L. *The Design of Social Research.* Chicago: University of Chicago Press, 1953.

BROSS, IRVIN, D. J. *Design for Decision.* New York: Free Press, 1953.

FAIRWEATHER, GEORGE W. *Methods for Experimental Innovation.* New York: John Wiley and Sons, 1968.

GOULDNER, ALVIN W. "Explorations in Applied Social Science," in *Applied Sociology,* ed. Alvin W. Gouldner and S. M. Miller. New York: Free Press, 1965, pp. 5–22.

LINDBLOM, CHARLES E. *The Policy-Making Process.* Englewood Cliffs, N.J.: Prentice-Hall, Inc., 1968.

MERTON, ROBERT K. "Notes on Problem-Finding in Sociology," in *Sociology Today, Problems and Prospects,* eds. R. K. Merton, L. Broom, and L. S. Cottrell, Jr. New York: Basic Books, 1959.

MERTON, ROBERT K. "The Role of Applied Social Science in the Formation of Policy: A Research Memorandum," *Philosophy of Science, 16* (July 1949), 161–81.

RIPPLE, LILIAN. "Problem Identification and Formulation," in *Social Work Research,* ed. Norman A. Polansky. Chicago: University of Chicago Press, 1960.

chapter 6/stage 2:
history of the
policy problem

At the justification stage of the research design the analyst focuses on identifying the policy problem that has motivated the request for research. The analyst views that problem from the perspective of feasible solutions. He or she uses the stated goals and the political forces operating in the decision-making environment as the principal framework for identifying the policy objective and for evaluating the means of its attainment. In the history statement, this formulation of the policy problem is reexamined from the viewpoint of prior attempts to resolve the problem.

The purpose of the history statement is twofold. First, it reduces the possibility that the prospective research will simply "reinvent the wheel." More positively, when research objectives are formulated on the basis of prior experience, the project can draw on cumulative efforts toward ameliorating the situation or bringing about the desired change. Thus, the history statement is important to both the analyst and the potential funding agent in making the best use of limited resources.

The history stage of the research design interacts directly with the justification and the conceptual framework stages. Often knowledge of prior efforts to attain an identical or a similar objective helps the policy analyst articulate alternative courses of action. In this sense it is impossible to separate the justification from the history stage of the design process. However, treating the history statement as a separate stage assures the analyst that a preoccupation with forces maintaining the policy problem and with those constraining potential actions will not go unchecked against prior experience. The history statement can also yield useful insights for the development of a conceptual framework. Knowledge of prior experience in dealing with the policy problem may help the analyst to identify constraints or consequences that have thus far remained unidentified by the policy maker. Therefore, the contents of the history statement are fed in two directions: backward to the identification of the policy problem and forward to the construction of a model for that problem.

In this chapter we will discuss the topics to be covered in a history statement; we will enumerate a variety of sources that the analyst can use in ferreting out the history relevant to the policy problem; and we will offer some guidance for selecting the evidence to be included in a history statement.

CONTENT OF HISTORY STATEMENT

The history statement should deal with the following topics: (1) trends in the nature and extent of the condition(s) which the policy maker is trying to alleviate or achieve (the policy objective), (2) existing models that portray alternative courses of action for achieving the policy objective, (3) evidence of the applicability and/or effectiveness of these models, and (4) implications of this history for the research design. A complete history statement will cover all four topics.

An understanding of the policy problem will be enhanced by historical data about the progress of the condition to be altered. These data may include simple time series that show either changes in the nature and magnitude of the condition or changes in the classes of people affected by it. Such data are often available in secondary sources such as the *Statistical Abstract of the United States,* the *U.S. Census* and other governmental reports, previous studies on the subject, and agency service statistics. Such historical data provide a developmental picture of the condition requiring action. This is helpful in appraising the importance of the current policy objective, evaluating the success of previous policies, and suggesting new types of intervention. These kinds of data may have been presented in connection with the identification of the policy objective in the justification stage. If so, they should be reexamined at this design stage to see what implications they hold for the research design.

A second important subject to be covered in a history statement is the sequence of models developed about the policy problem and about its possible solutions. Such models may be based on mathematically expressed relationships between the policy objective and the characteristics of the population affected, or its environment, that carry implications for intervention. For example, correlations between lung cancer and smoking do not necessarily comprise a model of the etiology of lung cancer, but they do provide clues about possible means of intervention. On a more sophisticated level, the literature may contain a record of prior attempts to conceptualize the problem condition in terms of its susceptibility to modification. For example, Cloward and Ohlin developed a model of the origins of juvenile delinquency that greatly affected the nature of programs designed to alleviate that condition throughout the 1960s (Cloward and Ohlin 1960). Such models may be formal, as in the case of theoretical treatises and research designs, or they may be subjective observations of practitioners who have worked with the condition in question. In any event, such models represent speculations about what factors might influence the presence, perpetuation, and alteration of that condition.

A third subject to be covered in a history statement, is information about the efficacy of models of intervention, when it is available. How well have such models worked when applied in the past? Ideally such information takes the form of empirical evaluations of the effects of each alternative course of action on the policy objective. With the extensive experimentation on social programs begun in the 1960s, there is beginning to cumulate a substantial body of literature about the outcomes associated with educational programs, various forms of publicly subsidized housing, manpower training, and patterns of health care. However, empirical evaluations of an explanatory nature are still rare, because often there is insufficient time in the policy-making process for the execution of such research. In addition, objective evaluations are often inhibited by pressure from powerful political interests wishing to perpetuate or to alter a course of action. In such circumstances subjective evaluations can be sought from practitioners who have dealt with the condition and the program or policy exemplified in the model. While such evaluations lack the rigor and clear generalizability of formal research findings, they often yield very useful insights because they are based on an intimate knowledge of the nature, variations, and impact of the policy or program.

And lastly, the history statement should contain a section drawing together the implications for the research design of prior experience in dealing with the policy problem. This section is most important, because the purpose of a review of prior experience is, after all, to determine whether the research is still needed, and to see how existing knowledge may be utilized to advantage in drafting its design. Awareness of this purpose will help the analyst avoid wasted time and energy in an aimless review of literature which does not contribute to policy-making.

As indicated earlier, prior experience has implications for both the justification statement and for the conceptual framework. With regard to the former, the analyst should ask him or herself, "Does this review of research and experience contain answers to the question(s) of fact raised in the justification statement?" Existing data on the extent of the condition to be changed may sufficiently define it and, thereby eliminate the call for "needs assessment" research. Or a review of prior experience and/or research may suggest potential courses of action and thus obviate the need for an exploratory study. Finally, prior research may document the effects of the various policy alternatives, and thus render an explanatory evaluation unnecessary. If the analyst can safely conclude that the question of fact has been answered, this does not ipso facto render research unnecessary. It just means that policy making should be applied to subsequent stages, during which new questions of fact will undoubtedly arise calling for the services of the analyst.

With regard to implications for the conceptual framework, the analyst should ask him or herself, "Have any new factors come to light that should be taken into account?" These factors may involve alternative courses of action for dealing with the policy objective beyond those already identified by the policy maker; auxiliary actions that may improve the effectiveness of any of the alternatives; constraints that limit (but do not void) the effectiveness of alternatives; operational measures usable in implementing an alternative; and unintended or latent consequences of the proposed alternatives. Each of these factors can be translated into policy variables within the conceptual framework of the policy problem. Hence, before undertaking a review of the literature or of prior experience, the analyst should read Chapter 3 on the conceptual framework, which discusses these variables in detail. Having this framework in mind will aid him or her in focusing the historical review.

SOURCES OF THE HISTORY STATEMENT

Traditionally, achieving an historical perspective in designing research has meant a review of the literature. While the literature is the primary source of background knowledge for academic research, it is much too limiting for policy research. Knowledge about previous attempts to deal with a policy problem arises from three sources: (1) the personal experience of persons affected by the condition requiring action, (2) the knowledge and experience of practitioners in the field, and (3) the relevant literature (Selltiz, Wrightsman, and Cook 1976).

Few persons are untouched by the consequences of public policy. Accordingly, the direct experience of the analyst with the problem at hand should not be overlooked as an information source (Abel 1948). Obviously, personal experience is the most important source of insight. One can do no more than speculate about the emotional impact of discrimination if one has not been the object of prejudice. It is hard to understand the demoralization resulting from unemployment unless one has repeatedly been "turned down" for a job. It is difficult to recognize the apathy resulting from having to stand in long waiting lines in a health clinic or other large service agency unless one has actually done it. Indeed, participant observation as a data collection technique is based on this very premise of generating understanding of the phenomenon under investigation through personal experience with it.

However, insights gained from personal experience must be translated into propositions that can be tested and verified for their generalizability. Knowledge derived form experience that remains private and personal provides no basis for public actions, because public actions apply to classes of persons and events, not to the unique. Therefore, in each personal experience the analyst must look for those characteristics and/or relationships which might apply to the class. He or she must also be clear about the boundaries of the class to which the experience applies.

The perspective from personal experience, however insightful, is obviously quite limited. A potentially wider source is the experience of professionals practicing in the problem area. Persons in service roles—teachers, health workers, employment counselors, social workers, and so on—having dealt with large numbers of individuals, have a wider base of experience from which to generalize. Direct service personnel also observe varied types of people and events. They are likely to deal with people from different income levels, occupations, subcultures, or life styles and to observe varying degrees or manifestations of the condition which is the object of policy making. This provides them with a comparative framework from which to view the policy problem and/or its solution. Because of their long-term association with the problem, practitioners are also able to think developmentally, in terms of both the etiology of the condition and the way that condition responds over time to attempts to modify it.

The clinical knowledge of persons in service roles is often a more valid and rich source of insight than is the literature. Research reports tend to deal with a subject in a more structured and rigorous fashion and thereby fail to convey a sense of its complexity or of its natural context. Furthermore, tapping the knowledge of practitioners is often the only way of obtaining the history of a problem at the local level. The literature on policy research tends to be dominated by studies of national scope because their funding has been largely federal.

To base one's understanding of a phenomenon solely on insights provided by third parties is risky. Service personnel clearly have a vested interest in the services they render, and in fact are often funded by dominant groups in society whose interests may be diametrically opposed to those of the recipients. One way of avoiding the influence of this bias is to consult personnel who are in a relatively impartial or "broker" role vis-à-vis direct service personnel and their clients. For example, if one is concerned about increasing the use of prenatal clinics, one might interview the staff of an independent visiting nurse agency whose responsibility is to make home visits to mothers of babies delivered in local hospitals. Such personnel are not the direct providers of care either before or during delivery, yet they have intimate knowledge of the recipients' health practices as well as of their history of medical service usage. When research analysts hold interviews only with service providers, they are likely to come away with a perspective that is blind to the failings of these agents. Another practice for overcoming the bias of direct service personnel is for the analyst to include in his experience survey the observations of both providers and consumers of the particular service in question.

The preferred method of ascertaining the experiential knowledge of practitioners is the open-ended, loosely structured interview. A particularly fruitful variation of this approach is to organize a round table discussion or a conference carefully planned to reflect varying disciplines and experiences. Such group interviews sharpen the analyst's understanding of the problem by pitting contrasting points of view against each other. They also stimulate additional insights as participants respond to others' observations in a sort of free association atmosphere. Thus, to learn about policies and practices that facilitate school desegregation one might convene a group of school administrators, civil rights leaders, teachers, parents, and students in a desegregated school system. In terms of the effort required to arrange them, group interviews are more expensive than a literature review, but they can be completed in less time and can be infinitely more rewarding.

When the interview technique is carried to an extreme, it assumes the form of an exploratory case study. Hence, there is a natural continuity between the history stage of the research design and an exploratory study. Occasionally the need to achieve an historical perspective may call for such a study, which will in turn require its own research design.

Reviewing the Literature

The traditional method used to develop a history statement is to review the literature. In adopting this approach the analyst may be confronted with what can best be described as a morass of written documents spanning periodicals, books, and reports of governmental research and service agencies. An effort to encompass such a literature without some shortcuts can bog down the research design process. One approach is to begin with a particular article or report that is known to deal with the problem at hand. It may be a report of a definitive investigation, such as the Coleman Report, *Equality of Educational Opportunity*, or the report of a governmental study commission, such as the Kerner Commission Report on Civil Disorder. One then examines all the footnotes and bibliographies in the volume for relevant references, and these may lead in turn to other references in a fanning out process. Another approach is to begin with a published bibliography on the subject, if one exists. Such bibliographies are available in most major libraries and can be located with the assistance of a reference librarian.

In the absence of well-documented articles or published bibliographies, the analyst will need to undertake a canvass of periodicals that deal with the subject at hand on a regular basis. Periodical literature is particularly useful in policy-oriented research because of its currency and accessibility; however, canvassing it can be an enormous task. A number of reference works are available to assist in this process. We have listed these works in a Guide to Resources for Reviewing the Periodical Literature (Figure 6-1). The Guide is not intended to be comprehensive. It is, rather, an introduction to the type of resources avail-

Figure 6-1 A guide to resources for reviewing the periodical literature by subject area and type of resource

SUBJECT AREA AND TYPE OF RESOURCE	TITLE OF RESOURCE
Social sciences	
Indexes	*International Encyclopedia of the Social Sciences*
	Social Sciences and Humanities Index
	Bonjean, Charles M., Richard J. Hill, and S. Dale McLemore, *Sociological Measurement, An Inventory of Scales and Indices*
Abstracts	(Each social science has its own abstract; the following are interdisciplinary abstracts.)
	Abstracts for Social Workers
	Poverty and Human Resources Abstracts
Major Periodicals	(Each discipline has several journals which cover theory and research in its field. The more general ones are listed here.)
	American Anthropologist
	American Journal of Sociology
	American Political Science Review
	American Sociological Review
	Psychological Bulletin
	Psychological Review
	(Several journals are focused on planning or policy making per se.)
	Administrative Science Quarterly
	Journal of American Institute of Planners
	Journal of Political Economy
	Public Administration Review
	Public Interest
Statistical Data Sources	*U.S. Census of Population*
	Current Population Reports
Health	
Indexes	*Cumulated Index Medicus*
	Medical Socioeconomic Research Sources
Abstracts	*Excerpta Medica* (public health and social medicine, health economics, occupational health and industrial medicine, environmental health and pollution control)

Figure 6-1 (Continued)

SUBJECT AREA AND TYPE OF RESOURCE	TITLE OF RESOURCE
Periodicals	*American Journal of Public Health*
	Health Services Reports
	International Journal of Health Services
	(Also see journals of medical and other health professional societies.)
Statistical Data Sources	*Morbidity and Mortality*
	Vital Statistics of the United States
	Vital and Health Statistics

Labor and economics

Indexes	*Business Periodicals Index*
	Index of Economic Articles
	Public Affairs Information Service
	Wall St. Journal Index
Abstracts	*Journal of Economic Literature*
	Employment Relations Abstracts
	Poverty and Human Resources Abstracts
Periodicals	*BLS Bulletins* and *BLS Reports*
	Employment and Training Reporter
	Industrial Relations Review
	Labor Relations Reporter
	Monthly Labor Review
Statistical Data Sources	*Consumer Price Index*
	County Business Patterns
	Editor and Publisher's Market Guide
	Employment and Earnings
	Handbook of Labor Statistics
	Occupational Outlook
	Sales Management, Survey of Buying Power
	U.S. Census of Business
	U.S. Census of Population

(continued)

Figure 6-1 (Continued)

SUBJECT AREA AND TYPE OF RESOURCE	TITLE OF RESOURCE
Education	
Indexes	*Current Index to Journals in Education* (ERIC)
	Education Index
	Research in Education (ERIC)
Abstracts	*Current Index to Journals in Education* (ERIC)
	Research in Education (ERIC)
Reports	*Research in Education* (microfiche) (ERIC)
Statistical Data Sources	*Digest of Educational Statistics*
Criminal justice	
Indexes	*The Criminal Justice Periodical Index*
	Index to Legal Periodicals
	Index to Periodical Articles Related to Law
Abstracts	*Crime and Justice Abstracts*
Periodicals	*Crime and Delinquency*
	Crime Control Digest
	Journal of Research in Crime and Delinquency (Also see individual law reviews.)
Statistical Data Sources	*FBI Report* (See also state crime reports.)
Housing	
Indexes	*Business Periodicals Index*
	Housing and Planning References
	New York Times Index
	Public Affairs Information Service
Abstracts	none
Periodicals	*Journal of Housing*
Statistical Data Sources	*HUD Annual Reports*
	U.S. Census of Housing
General	
Indexes	Bibliographies of the Council of Planning Librarians
	Government Reports Index
	Monthly Catalogue of Government Publications
	New York Times Index

Figure 6-1 (Continued)

SUBJECT AREA AND TYPE OF RESOURCE	TITLE OF RESOURCE
	Public Affairs Information Service
	Reader's Guide to Periodical Literature
Abstracts	*Dissertation Abstracts* (University of Michigan)
	Government Reports Announcements
Periodicals	*Journal of Human Resources*
	Urban Affairs Reporter
Statistical Data Sources	*Current Population Reports*
	National Atlas
	Statistical Abstract of the U.S.
	U.S. Census

able, and to their effective use, so that the literature relevant to a given subject may be quickly identified. A reference librarian can render invaluable assistance in locating additional resources and in using them.

The Guide to Resources for Reviewing the Periodical Literature is organized around subject areas and types of resources. The subject areas are comprehensive with respect to issues in social policy. They are the social sciences, health, labor and economics, education, criminal justice, and housing. Within each subject area four types of resources are identified: *indexes, abstracts, periodicals,* and *statistical data sources.* Understanding the differences among these resources will facilitate their use and reduce the time needed to review the literature.

In any review of periodical literature, the first resource to consult is an *index.* In every subject area there is at least one index which comprehensively lists, for that area, the articles appearing in major periodicals and, in some instances, the research reports issued by governmental agencies. These listings are by title, author, and subject. The introduction to each index lists the publications regularly reviewed therein. An index offers the quickest way to get a comprehensive picture of the literature on a particular subject.

However, indexes can be misleading and much time can be wasted in tracking down listings that at first glance appear promising but turn out to be irrelevant in content. *Abstracts,* the second type of resource, are extremely useful in overcoming this deficiency. In most of the areas listed in this guide, abstracts exist that summarize the contents of publications. A perusal of these abstracts reduces greatly the time required for a literature search, particularly when used in conjunction with an index.

The third type of resource consists of the major *periodicals* in the subject area. Where indexes and abstracts are not available, the periodicals themselves must be used as a resource. Each periodical has an annual index of the articles appearing in its issues listed by subject and author, which facilitates location of any given article.

The final resource listed in the Guide consists of major sources of statistical data for each subject area. An important element in the history statement is a description of the nature and size of the policy problem and the trends in its development. These collections of statistical data, although usually quite general and often gathered for other purposes, can in many instances be adapted to achieve a description of the problem at hand.

Turning to the Guide itself, the first subject area is the social sciences. Since the social science literature is generic to the various subject areas listed, one may consult it in addition to the sources listed for a specific field. The principal index in the social sciences is the *Social Sciences and Humanities Index,* a comprehensive and long-standing publication. The *International Encyclopedia of the Social Sciences* can also be used as an index. Each of its authoritative articles is accompanied by a list of references. In addition, the volume by Bonjean and his collaborators, while somewhat dated, is a very useful index of measurement techniques common to the social sciences. It provides descriptions of techniques and cites the literature in which their use is reported. As to abstracts, each social science has its own, for example, *Sociological Abstracts, Psychological Abstracts,* and so on. In the interest of brevity these are not listed in the Guide. However, two interdisciplinary abstracts may prove particularly helpful—the *Abstracts for Social Workers* and the *Poverty and Human Resources Abstracts.*

There is a myriad of periodicals in the social sciences, making it difficult to list them exhaustively. We have listed the more general ones that provide points of entry to the various subject areas. We have also included a number of journals related to planning and policy analysis. They deal not so much with the theoretical analyses of problems as with governmental efforts to manage them.

The principal source of statistical data relevant to social behavior is the *U.S. Census of Population.* Both the reports on general characteristics of the population—age, sex, family composition, and so forth—and those on social and economic characteristics, containing data on education, ethnicity, income, and labor force participation, are useful. Through skillful cross-tabulations it is possible to evolve data for individual census tracts on many complex variables, for example, the number of women with children under six years of age in the labor force.

Since the population census is decennial, a source of current population data is the *Current Population Reports,* issued by the Bureau of the Census in several series. Among them are *P-20, Population Characteristics,* covering not only the usual variables that appear in the decennial report, but also mobility, fertility, voter participation, and others; *P-23, Special Studies,* dealing with specific subject areas; *P-25 Population Estimates,* providing estimates of the U.S. population by major subdivisions; *P-28, Special Censuses,* commissioned for states or "standard metropolitan statistical areas" between decennial censuses; and *P-60, Consumer Income,* providing data on poverty, household income, consumption patterns, and employment.

In the subject area of health, there are two excellent indexes. The *Cumulated Index Medicus* is a comprehensive listing of the biomedical periodical literature. Although primarily oriented toward clinical issues, it does have a limited section on health facilities, manpower, and services. The *Medical Socioeconomic Research Sources* covers books, newspapers, and journals, and is oriented more to the sociological and economic aspects of health and health care organizations. An excellent abstract is *Excerpta Medica,* which consists of separately bound sections by subjects, the more relevant ones being *Public Health and Social Medicine, Health Economics, Occupational Health and Industrial Medicine,* and *Environmental Health and Pollution Control.*

There are many periodicals in health and medical care, most of them too specialized for us to include here. One periodical with a rather broad outlook that makes it suitable for planning and policy analysis is the *American Journal of Public Health.* Two periodicals with an international perspective and particularly related to health planning, administration, and the social aspects of medicine are *International Journal of Health Services* and *Social Science and Medicine.* Of the medical journals, the *Journal of the American Medical Association* and the *New England Journal of Medicine* occasionally have articles useful for planning. Another important periodical is the *Health Services Reports* (formerly known as the *Public Health Reports*), issued by the Health Services and Mental Health Administration. The continuity of this last publication is a serious problem because of the frequent reorganization of health agencies in the federal government.

There are three principal statistical data sources in the health area. *Vital Statistics of the United States* provides continuity of statistics on births, deaths, marriages, and divorces by state. A source of data on periodic health examinations and household interviews of population samples, as well as on surveys of health care institutions, is the publication by the National Health Survey, *Vital and Health Statistics.* It is the principal source of data on the morbidity, health status, and medical care practices of the U.S. population. The Center for Disease Control of the U.S. Public Health Service publishes current data on the state-by-state incidence of contagious diseases by age of the afflicted.

Resources in the subject area of labor and economics are more diffuse. The principal indexes are the *Business Periodicals Index,* which lists both books and periodicals, and the *Index of Economic Articles* published by the American Economic Association, a very good resource for reviewing the scholarly literature. More general indexes of use are the *Public Affairs Information Service* and the *Wall St. Journal Index*. Abstracts in this subject area are also diverse. Of these, the *Journal of Economic Literature* is the most comprehensive, while the *Poverty and Human Resources Abstracts* are particularly good on labor matters.

There are several periodicals published by the U.S. Bureau of Labor Statistics (BLS). *The Monthly Labor Review* contains monthly statistics on labor force characteristics as well as articles on developments and programs in the labor field. The *BLS Bulletins* carry the findings of surveys and wages by occupations and localities. The *BLS Reports* carry reports of studies of productivity, working conditions, minimum wages, work stoppages, and cost of living. There are two periodicals dealing with relevant federal and state policy published biweekly by the Bureau of National Affairs. *Employment and Training Reporter* summarizes legislation and administrative regulations having to do with manpower programs, and *Labor Law Reporter* does the same for labor relations and fair employment practices.

There are many excellent statistical data sources on labor and business conditions. The *Editor and Publisher's Market Guide* and *Sales Management, Survey of Buying Power* are two annual commercial publications on population, income, and consumption patterns by states and local market areas. These publications, because they contain annual statistics, are an important supplement both to the *U.S. Census of Business* and to the *U.S. Census of Population*, which carry quinquennial and decennial census data, respectively. The *Consumer Price Index, Occupational Outlook,* and *Employment and Earnings* are published by the BLS on a monthly or quarterly basis. The *County Business Pattern*, an annual publication of the U.S. Census Bureau, carries employment and payroll statistics by county and industry. The *Handbook of Labor Statistics,* an annual BLS publication, is also a rich source of data on employment, unemployment, compensation, productivity, prices, living conditions, unions, industrial relations, and occupational injuries.

The subject area of education has a centralized resource network. *Research in Education,* the principal organ of the Education Resources Information Center (ERIC), provides an integrated set of indexes, abstracts, and microfiche reproductions of the research literature. Through this system of publications one can quickly run down any article, governmental report, or book dealing with research in education. ERIC also publishes *The Current Index to Journals in Education,* which is both an abstract and an index, covering some 350 journals. Contents of the *Education Index* refer to books and journals as well as to publications of the U.S. Office of Education. The major statistical data source in the education area is the *Digest of Educational Statistics* prepared by the U.S. Office of Education, which carries references to other more specialized data sources. The *U.S. Census of Population* also has important data on education related to census tracts.

The subject area of criminal justice has less developed information resources. Since criminology is a recognized discipline within the social sciences, the social science literature should also be checked. *The Criminal Justice Periodical Index,* published by University Microfilms International, provides a relatively comprehensive listing of the emerging literature dealing with various parts of the criminal justice system. *The Index to Legal Periodicals* is a comprehensive overview of the rich sources that are usually found in law libraries. Legal periodicals carry research reports on the administration of the judicial system as well as useful analyses of the implications for public policy of court rulings. The National Council on Crime and Delinquency publishes *Crime and Justice Abstracts,* a bimonthly comprehensive source of abstracts of reports on research and programs. It also publishes two periodicals, *Crime and Delinquency* and *Journal of Research in Crime and Delinquency.* The various law reviews published by the major law schools constitute an important resource in this subject area. The *Crime Control Digest* is a periodical serving law enforcement agencies and personnel. As for principal statistical data sources, there are the FBI and the state crime reports.

The subject area of housing has the sparsest literature. *Housing and Planning References,* prepared by the U.S. Department of Housing and Urban Development, is the only index dealing specifically with housing. Hence, one should consult more general indexes such as the *Business Periodicals Index,* the *Public Affairs Information Service,* and the *New York Times Index.* The principal periodical is the *Journal of Housing,* which primarily covers developments in public housing programs. The analyst doing research on housing should also consult periodicals in the social sciences and economics. For statistical data, the researcher will find the *U.S. Census of Housing* comprehensive and useful.

And, lastly, resources of a general character are worth noting. *The Reader's Guide to Periodical Literature* is familiar to most readers. Less familiar but equally important is the *Monthly Catalog of Government Publications,* which lists the publications of all agencies of the U.S. government. Since the federal government is a profuse publisher, this catalogue is a reference to an important and abundant literature. In addition, the *Public Affairs Information Service,* mentioned earlier, covers governmental and nongovernmental publications of current public interest. Another useful source for the policy researcher are the bibliographies of the Council of Planning Librarians, which appear regularly and deal with a wide range of public issues. *Governmental Reports Index* and *Government Reports Announcements* index and abstract researches performed by publicly funded nongovernmental organizations. A good review of education, manpower, and welfare policies is contained in the *Journal of Human Resources* published by the University of Wisconsin Press. A general reference to legislation and administrative regulations in all areas of federal domestic policy is *Urban Affairs Reporter,* published biweekly by Clearing House, Inc. An important source of general statistical data is the *Statistical Abstract of the United States,* which summarizes selected statistics published by governmental agencies. More references can be obtained by following up the sources cited in that abstract. The *Current Population Reports* and *U.S. Censuses* have already been described. Finally, there is the *National Atlas,* consisting of maps that portray the geographical distribution of various social and economic characteristics of the country's population.

In using Figure 6-1, certain precautions should be taken. First, both the publications and the methods of reporting data are constantly changing. New periodicals are published and old ones cease. Government agencies responsible for data collection change their priorities, or are themselves dissolved or merged with other agencies. In order to minimize obsolescence, we have confined ourselves to resources characterized by relatively greater permanence. For this reason we have omitted from the Guide many new and promising periodicals. In any event, the reader should use this Guide with imagination, keeping in mind that new and alternate resources may be available. Second, the Guide is not comprehensive, hence it should not be regarded as a detailed inventory but as an outline of the available literature. Lastly, the Guide lists resources that are available in libraries of major cities and universities, so that the investigator doing research on rural or small town phenomena will have to make use of the better known facilities for a survey of the literature.

The Guide we have presented has been confined primarily to a description of resources for reviewing the periodic literature, for that is the analyst's primary source of information about the policy problem at hand. It is the journals that carry news of current developments in any discipline: the latest research reports, novel theoretical formulations, and up-to-date statistics. However, there is a secondary source which should not be neglected, namely, the book literature. Some books contain the results of major research projects on issues of current public interest; others propound new theoretical formulations that may have relevance to the policy problem at hand. Still other books are educational texts, which, though not as current in content as recent journals, are the depository of theories, concepts, and models that have graduated from journal status because they have withstood the test of time. Within the covers of a meaty book often may be found quantities of information that would otherwise be scattered in countless journal articles. For this reason, the analyst would do well to include relevant books in his or her literature search.

The search for information in the book literature may have to assume a somewhat different form than the review of periodical literature. The leading journals in each discipline are invariably well known and constitute standard sources in the policy field; but individual books usually do not gain such renown. To help compile a bibliography of books, we suggest a combination of the following four approaches. The first is to be alert for titles of promising books cited in the footnotes and bibliographies of various articles in the periodical literature. A second approach is to make a list of those authors the analyst feels are the leading authorities on the topic under study. If authors' names do not readily come to mind, the analyst might tap the knowledge of the practitioners whom he interviews in his experience survey. Who, in their opinion, are the authorities on the topic? Equipped with these names, the analyst can then locate their books in the author file of the card catalogue of the library.

A third approach is to make use of standard reference works on books in print. The *Library of Congress Subject Catalogue* lists all books in print by subject, and is issued monthly and annually. The *Cumulative Book Index,* published monthly, and *Books in Print,* published annually, list all books in print by subject as well as author and title. In addition, there are many published bibliographies on subjects of major interest. The reference librarian at any metropolitan library should be consulted about such resources. The fourth approach is simply to use the card catalogue of a given library to look up the subject of the problem policy.

Whether the analyst is using a reference work on books in print or a card catalogue, it is advisable that he or she draw up a list of subjects with which to search for the titles of relevant books. To illustrate, let us return to a policy problem presented in the previous chapter, namely, an unacceptably high rate of neonatal mortality and what might be done to solve it. Lengthy dialogue with the policy makers about the problem would probably have yielded the analyst the following subjects:

1. health	9. nutrition
2. health professionals	10. paraprofessionals
3. hereditary diseases	11. pregnancy
4. infant care	12. prenatal care
5. infant mortality	13. prenatal clinics
6. maternal health	14. public clinics
7. maternity	15. voucher system
8. neonatal mortality	

Equipped with such a list, the analyst can proceed to the reference or card catalogue, recording under each subject the titles of those books that appear relevant. By combining the four approaches here described, the researcher should obtain a comprehensive bibliography of books.

One caution is advised about selecting books to be included in a review of the literature. We remarked earlier that articles listed by title in an index may at first glance appear relevant, but later prove not at all germane to the subject under investigation. This same remark is even more true of books, inasmuch as book titles are usually more cryptic than article titles. This calls for some technique for screening the content of books for their potential relevance. In contrast to a journal article, a book is a bit more difficult to screen, because it has so much more content that must be appraised. When examining a book, the analyst should first peruse its preface or foreword, which conveys the central subject of the book, and its table of contents to derive clues from the chapter titles about how that subject is treated. Then, to gain an overall impression of the book's content, he or she should leaf through its pages and read the section headings within chapters. Next the analyst should scrutinize carefully the subject index at the back of the book. A subject index, especially if it is detailed, will convey a great deal about the text. This is where the previously drafted list of subjects comes in handy. Comparison of the analyst's subject list with the book's subject index is a reliable way of estimating the relevance of the book's content. Also, since the subject index will contain page references to the text, the analyst may want to sample some of the relevant passages. Captions to statistical tables, figures, charts, and diagrams also convey a good deal of information about the book's content. Lastly, the analyst can perform a spot-check of the book by reading every *n*th page. The employment of these devices inevitably yields a reliable appraisal of a book's content. It will also reduce the bibliography to manageable proportions.

A GUIDE TO EVALUATING PAST RESEARCH AND EXPERIENCE

Thus far we have described some of the possible sources of information available to the analyst in preparing a history statement of the policy problem. In this, the final section of the chapter, we offer some guidelines to help the analyst evaluate the information derived from these sources. A common pitfall which the analyst must guard against is the temptation to use every bit and piece of information that he or she reads in the literature or that is reported by informants. One of the most frequent defects to be found in written reviews of the literature is the aimless recitation of all prior research on the topic under study. Such reiteration is of limited value in defining the analyst's objective(s) in a particular study. In collecting material for and in writing the history statement, *selectivity* should be the watchword. Two criteria for distinguishing between information to be retained and that which is better discarded are *relevance* and *accuracy*.

Relevance of Evidence

How is the analyst to evaluate the relevance of the various sources of information about the condition to the actual policy problem at hand? The fact is that the analyst does not approach the quest for historical information and the writing of the history statement with a completely blank mind. He has by now traversed the justification stage of the research design in the course of which he has learned much about the policy maker's difficulty. Depending on the stage of the policy-making process at which the request for research emerges, the interchange between the analyst and policy maker may yield some conceptualization of the policy problem, albeit tentative. And their mutual search for alternative courses of action will undoubtedly yield at least one intervention model. Should the policy maker not be very clear about the implicit theory that guides his or her thinking, it is the analyst's task to explicate it. Having already completed this part of the task, the analyst now searches the literature and interviews informants.

As each bit of evidence is considered, the analyst must determine whether it is derived from experiences with a policy problem similar, or at least analogous, to the problem presently facing the policy maker. In other words, do both problems fall within the same class of phenomena? In considering evidence derived from a reported investigation, the analyst must ascertain the relevance of the variables described therein to those that comprise the condition presently under investigation. That is, does the model implicit in the reported research resemble the model that the analyst has in mind for the policy problem at hand? Similarly, the decision to include any given material in the history statement should be governed by whether or not it can be applied toward (1) defining the condition to be addressed by policy; (2) formulating alternative courses of action, as these have been identified in the justification state; or (3) assessing the relative effectiveness of those courses. The analyst should detail only those historical developments that yield these implications and not be misled into retracing every pursuit reported in the researches reviewed.

It is conceivable that the analyst's search may yield little or no background information relevant to the problem being analyzed. This is a rare situation, indeed, given the richness of human experience and the breadth of interest of social scientists and of social service practitioners. But it is possible. The total lack of research and firsthand experience with the phenomenon might prevent the analyst from going on to the next stage of the design process and from developing a conceptual framework that includes all the relevant variables. It might leave him or her with the impression that past experience contains no guides for the present situation. Lacking a specific and precise model directly relevant to the problem at hand and to its solution, the analyst has two roads open.

One approach is to start with the class of problems within which the policy maker's difficulty falls and to widen that class to include related phenomena previously not considered, in the hope of finding some suggestive parallels to the present case. In this way the analyst exploits every possible clue that the literature and the experience of practitioners can provide. For example, the issue of racial balance in the public schools was entirely novel to the field of education in the late 1960s. But there was a fairly abundant literature on the process and effects of racial desegregation in public housing during the 1950s. Similarly, violent parental reaction to forced school desegregation in the 1970s had its precursor in the community conflict around fluoridation of water supplies which raged in the late 1940s. The analyst must use ingenuity in locating some analogous phenomenon that can serve as a prototype for the current problem. The second road open to the analyst in the absence of relevant evidence is to undertake an exploratory study designed to identify the variables in the policy maker's problem and to define them precisely. However, the researcher should opt for this alternative only after the first possibility has been exhausted. It is always less expensive to utilize the studies of others than to undertake a study of one's own.

Accuracy of Evidence

Evidence obtained either from reading the research literature or from talking with knowledgeable people must, of course, be scrutinized to determine its accuracy before utilizing it to write the history statement or to draft the research design. Accuracy refers to the absence of bias and error and is a criterion distinct from relevance. Information may be very accurate indeed and yet be quite irrelevant to the policy problem under consideration. Conversely, evidence which is directly relevant may turn out upon careful scrutiny to be of questionable accuracy to be usable.

In appraising the accuracy of evidence obtained by talking with presumably knowledgeable persons, the analyst should remember that information is only as reliable as its source. However, survey methodologists have devised techniques for evaluating the accuracy of interview responses by means of checks built into the interview questions (Hyman 1955, pp. 149ff.). This method of internal consistency has also been used to evaluate the responses of several interviewees reporting about the same event from the same perspective. Marked inconsistencies between respondents indicate the likelihood of errors.

In the case of an empirical study, error may stem either from its design or from its execution. The analyst must scrutinize the design to see if it provides a logical basis for the reported findings. The principal design features that he or she should examine are: (1) the conceptualization of the research problem, (2) the definition of the independent and dependent variables, and (3) the method and techniques employed in collecting and analyzing data. Having done so, the analyst must now ask, "Given the concepts, variables, and procedures of the study, could they have yielded the inferences reported?" Points of doubtful consistency between findings and design are indications of error.

However, even consistency between the study design and its findings is no foolproof guarantee against error committed during the execution phase of the study. Hence, the analyst should also ask a number of questions about the specific techniques involved in conducting any given piece of research, "Was the study sample properly drawn from its population? Were qualified observers and/or interviewers employed to collect the data? Do the data appear to be reliable and valid? Were the statistical techniques carried out properly?" If we apply these criteria to the Coleman Report on equality of educational opportunity, for example, we find sufficient weaknesses in both its execution and its design to cast serious doubts on its findings (Weinberg 1970, pp. 284-92).

Evaluating the Evidence

Inevitably difficulties will arise in the analyst's quest for and use of evidence derived from prior research and experience. Of these the most vexing is that posed by obviously conflicting evidence. Not infrequently a review of the research literature and/or interviews with practitioners will present a picture of ambiguity, some evidence confirming and other evidence negating the conceptualization of the problem arrived at during the justification stage.* Confronted with such a situation the analyst is tempted to invoke a "curse on both your houses," or else settle for indecision, concluding that "it all depends on the given circumstances." To refuse to seek further clarifying evidence is not very helpful to the policy-making process. Conflicting reports from different studies must be confronted if the problem-solving process is to be facilitated. In this connection the following suggestions are offered.

A basic tenet of the scientific method is that two independent investigators observing the same phenomenon with the same research design executed under the same conditions will emerge with the same findings. Any difference between studies in any one of their essentials will of necessity result in a difference in their findings. Therefore, when comparing two items of apparently conflicting evidence, one must ask whether they are indeed comparable. The findings of two studies are comparable only if the studies resemble each other in terms of their concepts, variables, observational and analytical procedures, *and* the conditions under which they were carried out. Two studies may well purport to treat the same subject, but if their design and execution have been different, they cannot be equated. Therefore, inconsistencies in the evidence derived from such studies are to be expected.

To illustrate, suppose there are two separate studies of the effect of manpower training on employment, one of them dealing with training accompanied by a guarantee of employment, the other lacking such a guarantee. The studies may yield differing sets of findings, both perfectly valid, precisely because different variables have been incorporated into their designs. Hence, in ascertaining the comparability of findings from two or more investigations, the analyst should ask, "Do the conceptualizations of the respective problems involve the same variables?"

Further, two studies may be noncomparable because, although they both focus on the same critical variables, the variables themselves are differently defined. Hence, in comparing research findings, the analyst should ask:

---

*A classic case is the conflicting evidence of the effect of school busing on academic performance (Wilson 1973).

Are they based on the same definition of key variables? A classic example in this regard may be cited from the field of labor and economics. For years the federal government defined as unemployed any person who was out of work but was still looking for work. By this definition persons who were discouraged from looking for work because of repeated failures to find jobs were excluded from the unemployed category. Changing the definition to include the hard-core unemployed made a considerable difference in the size of the resultant estimates of the unemployed population.

Differences in the technical procedures employed in two studies may also render them incomparable. Technical features include delimiting the population exhibiting the observed phenomenon; sampling from the population; collecting the data by means of techniques and instruments; and manipulating the collected data to generate measurements. Hence, in comparing research findings, the analyst should also ask, "Were the same population, units, techniques, measures, and so on employed in the two studies?" For example, data on family income derived from household interviews may differ markedly from data derived from personal income tax returns. Hence, the measures derived from these two studies are not comparable. Also, it is impossible to compare the average family incomes of two populations when one is given in terms of the mean and the other in terms of the median income. The properties of these two averages are different.

Utilizing the Evidence

If two studies that are comparable in all respects do indeed offer discrepant findings, the analyst may consider undertaking an investigation to resolve or explain the discrepancy. Such a study could yield information of much value. On the other hand, the analyst may conclude that in essence the discrepancy is of minor importance. Small discrepancies are tolerable provided the accumulated findings are mutually corroborative to a degree sufficient to indicate a marked tendency. Hence, the analyst must ask, Does the accumulation of evidence from prior research and experience *tend* to confirm or to negate the conceptualization of the policy problem and its solution that emerged during the justification stage of the design process?

Confirmatory evidence indicates that the intervention model the analyst intends to propose has already been tried elsewhere and been found successful. This would imply that any research designed to ascertain the feasibility of *this* course of action would be superfluous. Why spend valuable time, money, and energy investigating the feasibility of a mode of action when past experience has already demonstrated its utility? The analyst can advise the policy maker to proceed with the implementation of the planned course of action.

Negative evidence indicates that the intervention model contemplated has already been tried and found wanting; it did not produce the effect which, in the analyst's opinion, should have followed from it. However, this need not necessarily dictate that the intervention model be abandoned. Should the model be a reflection of the inherent values of the policy-making system, it cannot be so easily abandoned. The analyst might retain it. But then the questions of fact which should become the object of the analyst's research become, "Why didn't the model work?" and "How can it be made to work?" For example, research has uncovered little beneficial effect resulting from existing strategies of school desegregation on the relative academic achievement of different ethnic groups. In view of the considerable social value placed upon heterogeneity among the groups comprising American society, research might be undertaken to determine how school desegregation can be carried out so that it will indeed have the beneficial effects on academic achievement hoped for.

SUMMARY

The history statement should cover four topics:

1. Trends in the nature and extent of the condition which the policy maker is trying to alleviate.
2. Existing models of alternative courses of action for achieving the policy objective.
3. Evidence of the applicability and/or effectiveness of these models.
4. Implications of the history statement for the research design.

In ascertaining the history of the policy problem, the analyst should draw not only upon the literature, but also upon the observations of persons who have experienced the condition to be alleviated. Unbiased third parties— independent practitioners and service agents—are also an invaluable source of information. Before writing the history statement, the information thus obtained must be evaluated for its relevance and accuracy. Norms exist for assessing both, although there are no absolute standards by which to evaluate social science propositions.

REFERENCES

ABEL, THEODORE. "The Operation called Verstehen," *American Journal of Sociology, 54* (November 1948), 211–18.
CLOWARD, RICHARD A., and LLOYD E. OHLIN. *Delinquency and Opportunity.* New York: Free Press, 1960.
HYMAN, HERBERT. *Survey Design and Analysis.* New York: Free Press, 1955.

SELLTIZ, CLAIRE, L. S. WRIGHTSMAN, and STUART W. COOK. *Research Methods in Social Relations* (3rd ed.). New York: Holt, Rinehart and Winston, 1976.

WEINBERG, MEYER. *Desegregation Research: An Appraisal.* Bloomington, Ind.: Phi Delta Kappa, 1970.

WILSON, JAMES Q. "On Pettigrew and Armor: An Afterword," *The Public Interest*, No. 30 (Winter 1973), 132–34.

chapter 7 / stage 3:
conceptual
framework

In this chapter we turn to the drafting of a conceptual framework for the proposed investigation, the third stage in the design process and the one prior to the actual formulation of the research objective(s). What is the conceptual framework? What is its function?

A conceptual framework is a causal orientation toward the contemplated study. As such, it formulates a detailed model of the given policy problem and of its proposed solution. It also furnishes a supportive framework for the model, based on the empirical evidence garnered from prior research and/or experience plus the value assumptions underlying the proposed solutions. The conceptual framework presents all this in relatively abstract terms. It identifies, defines, and elaborates the concepts reflected in the policy problem, its proposed solutions, and the various social forces impinging upon them. The conceptual framework may be thought of as a mental diagram, or map, which interrelates these concepts, showing where, when, and how they fit together. The written statement of the conceptual framework is, therefore, the analyst's description and explanation of this conceptual map.

The very exercise of thinking through and writing the conceptual framework compels the analyst to become aware of additional factors besides those identified during the justification and history stages. He or she may thus identify auxiliary actions and situational constraints which the policy maker would be advised to consider, as well as probable negative consequences that should be avoided if the benefits of intervention are to be maximized. In this manner the conceptual framework provides the analyst with a more promising orientation toward the contemplated study than would otherwise have been available.

Specifically, the conceptual framework fulfills four functions of the research design. First, as has already been intimated, the conceptual framework spells out the variables that the analyst must take into account if the proposed study is to bear fruit for the policy maker. It is when the component concepts of the framework are defined that they point to the variables which will be the focus of observation. The conceptual framework also indicates the relationships that probably exist among these variables. The search for these relationships then becomes a principal aim of the investigation. Without prior specification of the important variables and of their interrelations, the analyst would be unable to define, in stage 6, precisely which ones among an infinite variety of possible data he or she is supposed to collect.

The second function of the conceptual framework is a corollary of the first. It is to delimit the boundaries of the prospective investigation by suggesting which variables are to be considered as irrelevant and hence to be ignored. Ideally the conceptual framework should detail those aspects of the policy problem that the analyst will disregard as being of minor importance. But even when this step is omitted, specifying the relevant variables will by implication suggest the irrelevant ones. It is absolutely essential that a research undertaking be circumscribed by defined limits. It is, of course, a truism that no phenomenon can be fully understood without examining all the other phenomena that in some way impinge upon it. This does not mean, however, that innumerable variables should be included in a single investigation, for then the specific relationships under study would no longer stand out, but would merge with the larger reality. It is the function of the conceptual framework to provide, in Ripple's phrase, an iron ring around the planned research (Ripple 1960).

Third, the analyst must keep in mind that the conceptual framework is the structure that imparts meaning to the research findings. After the data have been analyzed, the research results must then be interpreted. The analyst is faced with the question: What do these results mean? It is by reference to the conceptual framework that the analyst can answer this question. In explicating how the concepts—about the policy problem, its solution, and their accompanying social forces—are interrelated, the conceptual framework provides a basis for accounting for these relationships should they be corroborated by the research. The research findings are thus raised above the level of blind empiricism.

In the same manner the conceptual framework enables the analyst to interpret the generalizability of the findings. Inasmuch as the conceptual framework specifies the important variables that must be considered, should an attempt be made to apply the research findings to policy problems in which certain variables are lacking, the analyst is in a position to assess the risks involved in such applications. For it is axiomatic that the applicability of a set of research findings is limited to situations composed of variables comparable to the ones in the research design.

A fourth function served by the conceptual framework is to provide the premises from which the analyst can deduce the objective(s) of the research. It is difficult to imagine by what logic the analyst could formulate his or her research objective(s) without the deductive basis furnished by the conceptual framework. Thus the conceptual framework serves as a bridge to stage 4 of the research design process.

At this juncture we should like to differentiate the term *conceptual framework* from two other terms also employed to refer to this phase of the research design. The term *theoretical framework* is used frequently to describe the content of scientific investigations. It implies a causal explanation of the relationship among concepts or variables that have been verified through formal research or deduced from formal theory. Such a framework is relatively abstract. By contrast, in policy research the propositions dealt with are often based on practical experience supplemented by conventional wisdom. The causal reasoning involved is often simply the analyst's best guess about what is going on in the problem situation, rather than the application of theoretical laws. In addition, such propositions tend to be less abstract.

Rationale is a term that is frequently used to designate the framework of policy studies. It refers to an exposition of the reasons (in the form of available empirical evidence and underlying value assumptions) why a proposed solution to a policy problem is to be regarded as plausible and hence as meriting advocacy. However, a rationale does not provide a conceptual structure to serve as a context for that solution. Hence, it does not offer a set of concepts that the analyst can use to identify those variables which must be observed in the contemplated research. Thus, a conceptual framework includes rationale plus a conceptual structure, and is the more inclusive term of the two.

In view of these distinctions, we prefer the term *conceptual framework* as the most appropriate one for designating stage 3 in the design of policy research. However, since all three terms are often used interchangeably, therefore, in describing this stage of the research design, the analyst should clarify for his or her audience the connection between self-chosen terminology and that customarily employed by the audience.

The development of a conceptual framework for a policy study may seem a somewhat esoteric exercise. Traditionally, conceptualizing and theorizing have been identified with basic research in the sciences rather than with applied or policy research. Past studies in program planning have usually been guided by research questions derived unsystematically from conventional wisdom or from the experience of practitioners. Thus previous attempts to conceptualize the policy problem usually met with resistance as impractical and as belonging to the "ivory tower" of the university. However, the 1960s witnessed a rising clamor for innovation and experimentation in dealing with social problems, accompanied by an increasingly sophisticated approach toward problem solving. These developments in turn resulted in a growing demand for analysts who possessed the ability to conceptualize policy problems and thereby to generate new solutions for them. Now it may be said that, to the extent that planning and policy making involve the generation of alternative courses of action, conceptualizing, and even theorizing, has become inseparable from social problem solving, thereby confirming the adage that "there is nothing as practical as a good theory."

By now it should be clear to the reader that the sequence of the three design stages leading up to the specification of the research objective(s) depends to a considerable extent upon the analyst. An analyst who is committed to a particular ethical or theoretical position would naturally approach the research design process with an a priori conceptual framework. For example, an analyst who is already committed to the concept of community medicine, or who is convinced of the validity of the dual market theory of unemployment, has a conceptual framework regarding these social issues before he or she reaches stage 3 of the research design process. However, in the case of policy studies the problems presented for research arise in the world of practical affairs, and for them ready-made solutions are rarely appropriate. Thus, the conceptual framework employed is much more likely to emerge a posteriori during the design process. In any event, the analyst must first articulate a conceptual framework that provides a suitable context for the policy problem before he or she can define the objective(s) of the prospective study.

STRUCTURE OF THE CONCEPTUAL FRAMEWORK

Our model of a conceptual framework will necessarily be of a general nature. It incorporates the types of concepts that are relevant to the analysis of most policy problems. Consequently, not every concept or relationship that we posit will apply to a particular problem under consideration. In building a conceptual framework, the analyst must select from the model those elements that are essential to understanding the given policy problem. In this sense the model is comprehensive—it is intended to encourage the analyst to consider all the forces relevant to the selection of the course of action most likely to achieve the given policy objective.

In referring to the elements of a conceptual framework, we will use the terms *concept* and *variable* interchangeably. Concepts can vary in their level of abstractness and their complexity. Those that are most abstract and complex we will call "global concepts." Those that are more concrete, referents of which are readily apparent, we will call "variables." A variable, therefore, is a low-level concept the referents of which are relatively easy to identify and observe, and which thereby is easily classified, ordered, or measured. We will discuss this distinction at greater length later in this chapter. Suffice it to say that when we speak of the elements of a conceptual framework we refer to concepts that constitute variables.

In developing this model we have made use of "causal modeling," a technique that has emerged in the behavioral sciences.* The literature on research methodology has gone beyond the simpler models of independent, dependent, control, and intervening variables to much more complex models of causal relationships. We have adapted these to depict the action orientation of the policy-making process. For the benefit of the reader trained in the behavioral sciences, we will indicate the similarities between our terminology and that employed in these disciplines. Our model of a conceptual framework centers around a policy problem, that is, it depicts some action to be adopted in order to attain some policy objective. The research objective(s) will be derived from this conceptual framework. It will consist of one or more questions of fact about the concepts, operationalized as variables, and their relationships as depicted in the framework.

The heart of the conceptual framework is the relationship between the *alternative courses of action* and a *policy objective*. In causal analysis terms, it is a relationship in which changes in an *independent variable* account for changes in the *dependent variable*. Since this relationship is rarely so simple, however, the conceptual framework must be expanded to portray multivariate, not just bivariate analysis. (See Figure 7-1.)

Several types of concepts can be added to the bivariate model to depict a policy problem more accurately. One is what is known in the behavioral sciences as an *intervening variable*. An intervening variable is assumed to come between the independent and the dependent variables in a cause-effect sequence. The intervening variable influences the dependent variable, but is in turn an effect of the independent variable. It must be taken into account in explaining the relation between the independent and the dependent variables because the former acts on the latter through it. Weiss distinguishes between two types of intervening variables (1972, pp. 47-51). The first type are *implementation variables,* specific administrative strategies adopted to carry out the policy or program; as such they are distinct from the substance of the program. For example, the analyst may wish to provide prenatal care to reduce neonatal mortality. However, the way in which prenatal care is provided (here, the implementation variable) may prevent the intended effect from occurring. If the doctors providing the prenatal care are incompetent, or if their attitudes toward patients are punitive or hostile, or if the service operates at inconvenient hours, then the desired effects of prenatal care are not likely to be achieved. The implementation process can be broken down into a sequence of events from staff hiring and training, application for service, intake, and treatment to termination of service, which itself constitutes a causal chain.

---

*This discussion is inspired by the work of Blalock (1969). It departs from his theory of causal analysis in that we differentiate causal variables in terms of their function in policy making, whereas Blalock treats them in an undifferentiated manner, being interested only in the size and direction of their relationships.

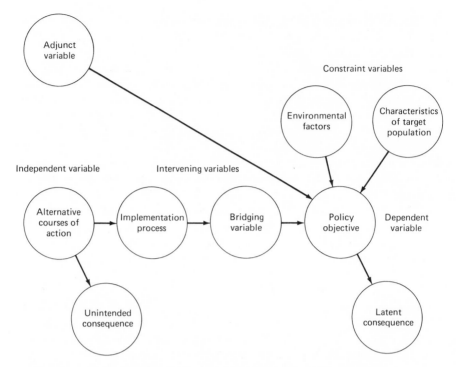

Figure 7-1 Structure of a conceptual framework of a policy problem

The second type of intervening variable is what Weiss calls a *bridging variable*. These are intermediate outcomes that must occur as prerequisites to the attainment of the policy objective. Let us assume, for example, that the objective of a manpower training program (here, the independent variable) is to enable the trainee to secure a job (here, the dependent variable). However, before he or she can secure the job, the trainee must acquire some marketable skill (here, the bridging variable). If the trainee is unable to maintain attendance in the program—or if, for whatever reason, he or she fails to learn while in attendance—the program will not result in the trainee's securing a job. The difference between an implementation variable and a bridging variable lies in the fact that the policy maker can presumably manipulate the first but not the second. Thus an implementation variable may be thought of as an action to which the policy maker can resort to achieve the policy objective, whereas a bridging variable is an attitude or behavior necessary to attaining the policy objective but beyond the policy maker's direct control. Understanding the success or failure of policy may often hinge on the decision maker's awareness of a bridging variable.

The question of which intervening variables to include in a conceptual framework is answered by determining how directly or strongly these processes impinge upon the policy problem. In some cases the relationships of implementation and bridging variables to the policy objective are so simple or so deterministic that they need not be considered. For example, should the proposed policy call for an automatic income transfer strategy, such as that employed by the Internal Revenue Service or the Social Security system, the framework need not feature the mode of implementation as a separate variable. However, the typical policy problem is by nature so complex that intervening variables can be expected to feature importantly in any conceptual framework constructed for it.

Another type of variable that figures importantly in the conceptual framework is termed in behavioral science research a *control variable*. Because such a variable offers an alternative explanation for variations in the dependent variable, it is also known as a "rival hypothesis." Its influence must, therefore, be controlled in the evaluation stage, to verify that the policy does in fact account for the attainment of the objective. Control variables in policy-oriented research are of two types: *adjunct* variables and *constraint* variables.

An adjunct variable refers to any auxiliary action the policymaker might take to enhance the effectiveness of the adopted policy or program. It may be thought of as a supplementary policy or program. Because an adjunct variable can be instituted independently of the alternative courses of action, it should not be considered just another alternative. Because it can occur simultaneously with the independent variable rather than sequentially to it, the adjunct variable also should not be confused with the intervening variable. Let us consider a manpower training program (the alternative course of action) proposal to enable unemployed persons to obtain jobs (the policy objective). The added provision of family counseling (the adjunct variable) should enable participants in the program to handle personal problems better and thus devote more attention to the training, thereby improving their employability. One caution, however: In evaluating policy, any adjunct variables must be held constant in order to verify the effect of the policy itself.

A constraint variable represents any factor influencing the policy process over which the decision maker has no control.* Constraint variables may be of two types; *environmental factors* or *characteristics of the target population.* An environmental factor is any factor in the social or physical environment of the target population that is beyond the power of the decision maker to change within the context of the policy problem. A characteristic of the target population is a property of members of the population to be affected by the policy which is relatively unchangeable within the duration of the policy under consideration. (More will be said about the target population in Chapter 9.) To return to our previous example, the rate of economic growth or the rate of unemploy-

*These constraints differ from constraints deliberately introduced into the design of the policy by the decision maker. The two types of constraints mentioned here are imposed upon the policy maker by the situation. The research design must therefore take account of them.

ment would be an environmental constraint on manpower training. Similarly, characteristics of the trainees, for example, their ages or prior education, would also act as constraints on the effectiveness of such training.

A constraint variable can be distinguished from an adjunct variable in that, unlike the latter, it is not manipulable by the policy maker. Awareness of constraint variables in a policy situation permits the decision maker to focus his or her efforts most effectively, that is, to apply the policy in that context and to that segment of the population where it will have maximum benefit. In evaluating a policy, any constraint variable must likewise be held constant in order to determine the true effect of a course of action on the policy objective.

The distinction between a manipulable and a nonmanipulable variable is not always inherent; it may be relative to a particular context. The age or racial distribution of the prospective beneficiaries of policy may not be manipulable in one context yet manipulable in another. For example, a school administrator has a fixed racial composition within his or her district. In an effort to achieve desegregation, the adminstrator must treat the racial composition of the system as a constraint variable. However, from the standpoint of the city council, the racial composition of the school-age population can be altered by housing and land development policies. Hence, in its effort to achieve desegregation of the schools, the city council may treat racial composition—or, more accurately, urban development policies acting on racial composition—as an adjunct variable.

The final type of variable that should be added to the conceptual framework is the so-called side effect, or secondary effect, of policy. Such a variable represents any effect that occurs outside the policy action-policy objective (independent-dependent variable) causal nexus. It can be either an *unintended* or a *latent consequence* of policy. When the side effect flows directly from the fact that a course of action has been taken (the independent variable), it will be considered as an *unintended consequence* of the policy. For example, reducing personal income taxes, thereby creating an increased demand for goods and services, is one way to reduce unemployment. Under certain conditions, however, this increased demand also creates inflation. Thus, the policy produces two simultaneous effects: reduction in unemployment, the policy objective, and inflation, the unintended consequence. When the side effect flows directly from the fact that the policy objective has been achieved (the dependent variable), it will be considered a *latent consequence* of policy. For example, the institution of the Federal Housing Administration's home mortgage program was designed to increase the availability of single-family housing. However, the impetus it gave to new housing construction was felt disproportionately more in suburban areas (where it was more feasible) and thus produced the latent consequence of increased economic and racial segregation of urban populations. This segregation has aggravated inequality in educational opportunity, a policy problem of considerable current importance. Thus, the original policy did indeed bring about the intended consequence, but this in turn set off a sequence of events resulting in still another consequence which we call "latent."

We recognize that the distinction we are making between unintended and latent consequences is not found elsewhere in the literature. In fact, the terms are usually used interchangeably. However, the difference between the timing of the two types of consequences has considerable practical significance for the policy-making process. In the case of an unintended consequence, corrective measures must be introduced simultaneously with the policy, otherwise the policy objective may never be realized. With a latent consequence, the policy objective itself is not threatened, but the policy maker must be ready to tackle the new problem that arises once that objective is reached. Therefore, in the absence of a better set of terms, we will use "unintended" and "latent" to refer to the differential consequences we have identified here.

The anticipation of unintended and latent consequences is critical in policy analysis, since the decision maker has only limited control over the course of events in a given environment. In the two examples we cited, the secondary effects were negative from the viewpoint of the policy maker. Such effects can prevent or cancel the benefits that follow from the attainment of the policy objective. However, this need not always be the case. Of course, positive effects create no particular problem in policy making—they simply enhance the desirability of the action to be taken. In any case, the introduction of side effects into the conceptual framework forces the analyst to come to terms with the multiple effects of any public policy, both those intended and those unintended.

Our generalized model of a conceptual framework takes on flesh and blood in the research design developed for a study of school desegregation (see Figure 7-2). Here the policy objective is to equalize educational attainment, which stems from the goal of equality of educational opportunity as provided for in the Constitution. It can be measured by student performance on standardized academic achievement tests. Thus, our dependent variable is *relative academic achievement* among racial and ethnic groups, that is, the ratio of black students' scores on an achievement test to those of white students. The alternative course of action is the degree of racial-balance in the attendance plan, a policy urged on school systems by the courts to achieve this objective. Thus, our independent variable is *school attendance plan,* of which racial balance is but one form. Two intervening variables are also involved. One is the *amount of bussing* used in implementing the plan. The second, a bridging variable, is the *social interaction* among racial and ethnic groups considered necessary in order to equalize academic performance among the respective groups. Thus, the cause-effect chain runs from school attendance plan to amount of bussing, to degree of social interaction, to relative academic achievement.

The mixing of racial and ethnic groups in a school will not lead to educational equality without the occurrence of other changes within the school, for example, the adoption of a curriculum which reflects a multiracial or multi-ethnic

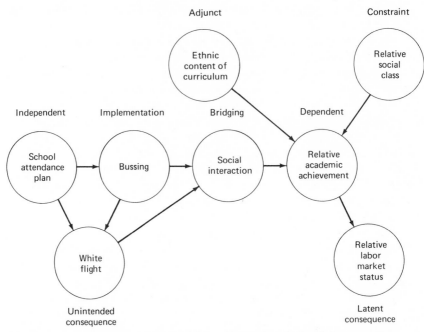

Figure 7-2 A conceptual framework for the study of school desegregation

point of view. Hence, the *ethnic content of the curriculum* is included in the conceptual framework as an adjunct variable. Furthermore, the framework recognizes that the effect of a school attendance plan on relative academic achievement depends in large measure on the degree of equality in social class between black and white students. Since social class is not manipulable in this situation, it represents a limitation on the effectiveness of policy. Therefore, *relative social class* becomes a constraint variable.

An unintended consequence of the policy may well be *white flight* from the schools, the tendency of white parents to transfer their children to private segregated schools or to move their residences out of the central city school district (which is multiracial) into suburban or county districts (which are predominantly white). The degree of white flight is an unintended consequence because it is affected directly by the independent, rather than the dependent variable. This means that it appears before the independent variable has influenced the dependent variable and thus operates on the other variables simultaneously with the independent variable. Accordingly, white flight can affect social interaction by reducing the number of whites with whom blacks can interact in the public schools. White flight is an example of a mixed variable: It is an effect with respect to the school attendance plan, but a cause with respect to social interaction. In this example the latent consequence that flows directly from the dependent variable is *relative labor market status,* that is, the relative ability of blacks and whites to get comparable jobs after finishing school.

It should be noted that the variables in a conceptual framework are stated in neutral terms, as is appropriate to a causal model. For example, the policy maker's objective is to equalize academic achievement among racial and ethnic groups. However, when this is converted to a dependent variable it appears as "relative academic achievement." Similarly the intervention to be tested, the adoption of a racial-balance attendance plan, is restated as "(type of) school attendance plan." The purpose of this restatement is to enable a causal model to be tested empirically. All the variables are "set," so to speak, at a value of zero at the outset of the test. Then the model is set into motion by changing the value of the independent variable in a specified direction to see whether the dependent variable will change in the desired direction. Thus, unless otherwise expressed in a neutral value, it is assumed that the term for each variable is preceded by some neutral label such as "degree of," "amount of," or "type of."

A conceptual framework is relevant to all research whether it be exploratory, descriptive, or explanatory. The specificity and completeness of the conceptual framework and the way it is used will differ with its purpose. We shall return to a discussion of these differences later in this chapter.

CONCEPTUAL CLARIFICATION

Essential to the construction of a conceptual framework are concepts which are unambiguous and which have a direct connection to phenomena. Deriving concepts to meet these criteria involves a process called conceptual clarification. Since this process is essential to all phases of constructing a conceptual framework, we will discuss it in some detail.

The Importance of Conceptual Clarification

One reason why the analyst must clarify concepts before putting them to use is to dispel whatever confusion may surround them. As the analyst confers with the policy maker, as he or she taps the experiences of knowledgeable practitioners and reviews the relevant research literature, vagueness and ambiguity may arise, imprecision and disagreement about the meanings of the terms that keep recurring in talk and in print. More specifically, the analyst may come across such anomalies as these: The same term is used as a label for different concepts and thus stands for two or more different phenomena; or a given concept is symbolized by a variety of terms, thereby creating the impression that the terms are labels for different ideas. The appearance of such semantic confusion is an indication that the relation of the concept to its referents calls for clarification.

Another reason why the analyst must clarify concepts is that even the most simple concept is difficult to use in empirical research and this difficulty is magnified as more abstract concepts are brought forward. Hence, the analyst is advised to be very clear about the concepts to be utilized in the prospective study. All concepts, by definition, are abstract, in contrast to their referents which are concrete. But concepts are not all equally abstract; obviously, the concept of "chair" is less abstract than that of "furniture," and the concept of "society" is more abstract than that of "neighborhood." The nature of the phenomenon from which the concept is abstracted, and to which it refers, contributes to the degree of abstractness. For one thing, the broader the range of objects, subjects, or events to which the concept refers, the more abstract the concept. Thus, the following concepts are in an ascending level of abstractness: street, neighborhood, district, city, region. Second, the more varied, subtle, and complex the phenomenon being conceptualized, the more abstract the concept. Thus, concepts such as "educational equality" and "personal adjustment" are more abstract than are those of "student" or "patient." For these reasons, concepts that are highly abstract are referred to as global.

Relatively abstract concepts are convenient tools in the policy-making process because they provide a simple means of conveying complex phenomena. However, the more abstract or global a concept, the more difficult to employ as an observational tool. For example, an interview schedule item intended to ascertain the number of unemployed in a community is easier to use and yields more accurate data than an item intended to ascertain the number of persons who are well adjusted and content. The concept of "unemployment" is less abstract than the concept of "personal adjustment." For this reason, investigators are forever engaged in the laborious process of converting the very abstract and global concepts that they want to employ into ones that are less abstract and hence more usable in their researches.

The Nature of Conceptual Clarification*

Conceptual clarification is the careful scrutiny of the interrelation among a term, the idea symbolized by the term, and the reality to which the term refers. Its aim, roughly stated, is to tighten the mental links holding together the three points of the triangle of reference which were discussed (See Figure 2-1 in Chapter 2, and the related discussion). This process is particularly important when dealing with highly abstract concepts, in which the linkages tend to be loose, thereby contributing to their ambiguity. With global concepts, conceptual clarification involves an additional process, that of breaking a concept down into sub-

---

*The mental process that we have referred to as conceptual clarification appears under a number of labels in the methodological literature. Merton has called it "conceptual analysis" (1957, p. 86); while Lazarsfeld (1958) has termed it "concept specification."

concepts of which it is composed and by which it is more easily understood. Thus the mental process of conceptual clarification has a multidimensional quality. It moves from a more abstract to a more concrete level at the same time as it moves back and forth between the term and the referent of the idea.

As we already suggested, the sure sign that conceptual clarification is indicated is when discourse reveals ambiguities in the idea-term relation. A given idea may, of course, be symbolized by two synonymous terms, which are thus interchangeable—for example, "client" and "consumer," "doctor" and "physician." But just as often terms that pass for synonyms are really not interchangeable, because they differ enough in shades of meaning to be not quite equivalent, as, for example, "crime" and "delinquency," or "education" and "schooling." When the analyst encounters such pseudo-synonyms, he/she must turn to the phenomenon for which these stand for clarification. Clarification involves two steps: (1) breaking a global concept down into its subconcepts, which results in a connotative definition; and (2) specifying the referents of the subconcepts, which constitutes an operational definition. To understand this process we must examine the nature of highly abstract or global concepts.

A global concept necessarily refers to a complex phenomenon, which is to say a phenomenon that possesses many facets or properties, and hence can be viewed with respect to more than one facet. In the technical literature these facets are called dimensions. Such a phenomenon is referred to as multidimensional, and is to be distinguished from its opposite, a simple or unidimensional phenomenon. Each of these dimensions, when identified and abstracted from its phenomenon, constitutes a subconcept of the global concept (see Figure 7-3). It is these subconcepts which become the variables that later are operationalized by specifying their indicators.* Some global concepts are not so easily analyzed, however, and may require an additional differentiation to the level of sub-

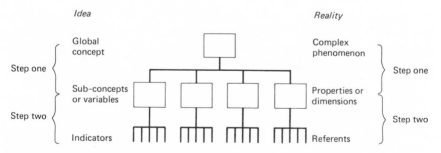

Figure 7-3 Steps in conceptual clarification

---

*Lazarsfeld (1959) uses the term *variate* instead of "variable," claiming that this is a more neutral term that includes also attributes (for example, dichotomies) which are nonquantitative, as well as variables which are quantitative and yield measures.

concepts, which then become the variables. In this way the ultimate referents of the concept can be specified.

Formulating the Connotative Definition

As we indicated in Chapter 2, the connotative definition of a given concept is always expressed in terms of subconcepts which are more easily understood. To identify these concepts the analyst begins with any ambiguity in the terms used to express an idea.

When two or more terms are used in discussion of a given phenomenon, it could be that they refer to the dimension of a unidimensional property, to different dimensions of a multidimensional phenomenon, or to entirely different phenomena. In order to determine which is the case, the analyst turns to the reality for which these terms stand and tries to determine whether the terms pertain to identical, to similar, or to distinct phenomena. He or she does this by asking those using the respective terms to describe and, if possible, to point to the reality they have in mind, or by reviewing the literature to determine the meanings imputed to the terms by their authors.

Let us illustrate this process with an example. Although global concepts often involve many dimensions or properties, we will choose a concept with only two in order to simplify our illustration. In debates over the status of minority groups in primary and secondary public education two terms are often used interchangeably: *educational equality* and *equality of educational opportunity*. Are these terms synonyms for the same idea, do they symbolize different aspects of the same idea, or do they symbolize distinctly different ideas? To answer this question we must ascertain what are the properties with which each term is associated. The user of the term *educational equality* might tell us that it stands for a situation in which members of various ethnic or minority groups on the average show the same level of academic achievement as members of the majority. The user of the term *equality of educational opportunity* might tell us that it stands for a situation in which members of various ethnic or minority groups attend schools with educational resources equal to those attended by majority students. Thus we have two terms, each of which is associated with a different property:

> Educational equality is associated with equality in academic achievement.
>
> Equality of educational opportunity is associated with equality of educational resources.

We can conclude that the two terms are not synonyms, because they do not refer to the same property. However, we must still ascertain whether they refer to different properties of the same phenomenon, or to different phenomena. We can make this determination by examining the interrelatedness of the associated properties. This is done by displaying all their possible combinations, as in Figure 7-4A. The four possible combinations resulting from the two properties are:

1. schools with equal resources and equal achievement
2. schools with equal resources and unequal achievement
3. schools with unequal resources and equal achievement
4. schools with unequal resources and unequal achievement.

The next step is to engage in conversation with those using the original terms and find which combination best reflects the meaning they intended. In doing so we would undoubtedly discover that combination 1 is eliminated because it is unreal. Given the accumulated economic and educational deprivations of certain minority groups in our society, it is virtually impossible for such groups to achieve parity in performance with the same educational resources given to others. This finding, therefore, allows us to rule out the possibility that the two original terms refer to different properties of the same phenomenon.

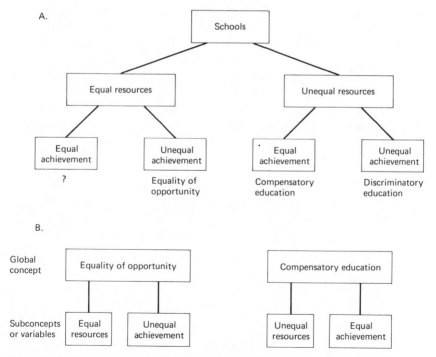

Figure 7-4 Conceptual clarification of the terms *educational equality* and *equality of educational opportunity*

Combination 2 conforms well to the idea held by those using the term *equality of educational opportunity.* The constitutional obligation, they would argue, lies simply in assuring that members of all groups have access to the same level of public resources, not that they perform equally with those resources. Combination 3 corresponds to the idea held by those using the term *educational equality.* They would argue that due to accumulated deprivations, more resources must be allocated to the education of certain groups in order to bring their performance up to that of the rest of society. In order to differentiate more clearly this combination from the idea reflected in combination 2, we have chosen to relabel it *compensatory education.* Finally, combination 4 corresponds to the traditional understanding of discriminatory education.

We conclude from this analysis that the original terms symbolize distinct ideas that refer to different phenomena. *Equality of educational opportunity* refers to education in which all groups receive equal resources, but do not necessarily achieve equally. *Compensatory education* refers to education in which disadvantaged groups receive additional resources, and are expected to achieve at a level comparable to that of advantaged groups. Thus we have arrived at a connotative definition of the two concepts (see Figure 7-4B).

Where a single term symbolizes several different ideas, conceptual clarification is somewhat easier. The analyst need only elicit from the user of the term, or from the literature, the properties referred to by each of the ideas symbolized by that term. By examining these properties the analyst can ascertain whether they are interrelated to constitute a multidimensional phenomenon, or they are single properties of several distinct phenomena, each with its own label. For example, the term *mental retardation* often stands for several ideas about behavioral incapacity. Sometimes it stands for physiological impairment of the brain or central nervous system, sometimes for learning disabilities exhibited in the classroom, and at still other times for a certain emotional quality of behavior. It is obvious that each of these concepts implies a distinct etiology, treatment, and prognosis, which would seem to indicate that they refer to three distinct phenomena. These three phenomena should be recast as *mental retardation,* referring to the phenomenon of physiological impairment; *learning disability,* which stands for cognitive difficulties not accompanied by physiological impairment; and *emotional disturbance,* which stands for behavior problems not involving cognitive or physical impairment.

Formulating the Operational Definition

In formulating the operational definition of a concept we convert an abstraction into a device that tells us both what to observe and how to observe it. We accomplish this by means of the reduction of a highly abstract concept into a number of subsidiary concepts, or variables, the referents of which are more easily identifiable and observable. Thus, the global concept becomes linked indirectly to its ultimate referents. We may now legitimately ask whether, by means of this process, the analyst has operationalized that concept. Insofar as the identification of the variables brings the analyst closer to what will turn out to be the ultimate referents of the concept, yes. But insofar as the variables themselves still remain to be operationalized, no. Having identified the variables, the analyst has, so to speak, acquired orientation; he or she knows the direction in which the observations are to be made, but is still unaware of the specific manifestations to be observed. It is clearly useful to know that the variables of compensatory education are "inequality of resources" and "equality of achievement," but what are the referents of "resources" and "achievement"?

We must now concretize each variable by specifying a series of observables—be they things, behaviors, objects, events, sensate entities—for which these variables stand and to which they refer. For example, the referent for educational resources might be a school's budget, the level of training or experience of teachers, or the amount of books or facilities. The referent for achievement might be a score on a standardized achievement test. These are the measurable referents that comprise what methodologists call the "indicators" of the global concept. These indicators will enable the analyst to recognize each occurrence of the phenomenon to which the global concept ultimately refers. Without its indicators the concept cannot become a research instrument. In fact, the sum of a concept's indicators comprises the operational definition of that concept—a set of instructions telling the analyst what data to gather (Lazarsfeld and Barton 1951). (This step in the research process will be discussed in Chapter 10.)

One concluding remark before turning to the actual construction of the conceptual framework: Because properties of a phenomenon vary from one occurrence to another, they have been conceptualized and labeled as variables. Qualitative variables vary in their form, and quantitative variables vary as to degree.* Qualitative variables are usually treated as dichotomies; for example, the variable, "ethnicity" can be dichotomized as "foreign born" and "native born." But what of quantitative variables such as "per pupil expenditure"? For ease of treatment, such a variable may also be dichotomized into "high expenditure" and "low expenditure" by cutting the continuum arbitrarily into halves. To facilitate further discussion in the construction of the conceptual framework we will treat all variables as dichotomies.

CONSTRUCTING A CONCEPTUAL FRAMEWORK

It may happen, as we noted in the introductory section of this chapter, that the analyst approaches this third stage of the design process from a specific perspective to which attaches a ready-made conceptual framework. It may like-

---

*Unfortunately current terminology is not particularly consistent. Qualitative variables are also called "attributes," and quantitative variables, "variables."

wise happen that the analyst comes across a seemingly appropriate conceptual framework in the course of reviewing the research literature or of interviewing knowledgeable practitioners. Whether such an a priori framework is partially or fully developed, it gives the analyst the advantage of being able to move into this design stage with something tangible. As a rule, however, the situations just described are rare. It is the raison d'etre of policy making to tackle new problems arising in novel and specific circumstances. Accordingly, the analyst must in most cases construct de novo a conceptual framework befitting the given problem.

The purpose of this section is to describe, within the limitations of space, the mental process of constructing a conceptual framework. For ease of description, the process will be broken down into five sequential steps (although the reader is reminded of the dynamic, interlocking nature of the process): (1) reviewing prior design stages for policy variables, (2) clarifying concepts, (3) deducing missing variables, (4) locating variables in the framework, and (5) checking the framework deductively. We will illustrate these steps in constructing the conceptual framework for the study of school desegregation presented earlier. In this manner we will demonstrate how that framework was actually constructed.

Reviewing Prior Design Stages

The analyst begins constructing the conceptual framework by reviewing those variables that appear in the justification and history statements, with a view to identifying which ones will fit the model presented in Figure 3-1. What the analyst finds will vary greatly in levels of abstractness. Many will appear only as global concepts, frequently undefined and rarely operationalized. A few will be quite specific, expressed in observable, manipulable, and measurable form.

Even though a formal policy objective may not have emerged during the justification stage, the justification statement should have enunciated the condition that forms the basis of the policy maker's objective. This statement also lists the various courses of action that came up for discussion between the policy maker and the analyst. If no specific alternative courses were or could be identified, as may occur when the analyst is called into the policy-making process at its earliest stage, this fact would indicate the need for an exploratory study. It should be noted that only those alternatives actually under consideration in the present policy-making context are entered in the framework.

Having identified the two principal variables (independent and dependent) in the justification statement, the analyst next searches for other policy variables needed to complete the framework. These are more likely to be found in the history statement. To begin with, a review of the research literature and of practical experience may suggest that the policy be implemented with certain administrative procedures to ensure the attainment of its objective (implementation variable). Or it may suggest that, if the policy were to be supplemented with an auxiliary program, its effectiveness would be enhanced (adjunct variable). Similarly, the history statement may point up certain features of the relevant environment that would inhibit or enhance the attainment of the policy objective; or certain subgroups of the target population for whom the policy or program is likely to be ineffective (constraint variables). Then, too, the analyst may have learned from previous studies or from interviews that the desired objective does not automatically follow the proposed policy, but that certain mediating events must link policy and objective together (bridging variables). Finally, the history statement may alert the analyst to possible undesirable results that might follow either from the implementation of the policy or from the attainment of its objective, results that are too important to ignore (side effects).

Let us illustrate this step by means of the conceptual framework constructed for the study of school desegregation (see Figure 7-2). This study grew out of a desire of the U.S. Office of Education (USOE) to evaluate the effect of school desegregation on the academic achievement of various racial and ethnic groups. In the justification stage it was learned that interest focused on different types of desegregation plans (at this stage, unspecified) currently in use by school systems around the country. USOE hoped that research would determine which type(s) of plan would have the greatest impact on equalizing academic achievement, so that the more successful plans could be encouraged by federal grants and technical assistance. Thus from the justification statement we identify "relative academic achievement" as the objective and "type of desegregation plan," a global concept, as the policy.

In reviewing the history of the policy problem, very little research was available on systemwide school desegregation because of the recency of the U.S. Supreme Court's mandate for the immediate elimination of racial duality in primary and secondary schools. However, a well-known study by Deutsch and Collins of a related phenomenon, the planned desegregation of public housing, was found to be relevant (Deutsch and Collins 1965). That study verified what has come to be known as "the equal status contact theory" of prejudice reduction. The authors argued that members of one racial group would become less prejudiced toward members of another racial group if members of the two groups interacted on the basis of equal status. Status was a multidimensional variable comprised of age, income, education, and occupation. Although the reduction of prejudice was not the objective in the USOE study, it does seem a highly relevant constraint variable. Any positive effect which a desegregated school environment might have on learning would be hampered by the existence of prejudice or hostile interactions among members of the various races. Therefore, since social class is the most relevant dimension of status in this situation, we have identified "relative social class" as a variable to be included in our conceptual framework.

Clarifying Concepts

At this point the analyst will undoubtedly have only a partial listing of those variables to be included in the conceptual framework. Before proceeding to generate additional concepts, however, the analyst should clarify those already identified. While conceptual clarifity is necessary for each of the variables in the framework, it is particularly crucial with respect to the independent and dependent variables. These variables must be totally clear, so that the analyst can go on to relate other variables to them, knowing that the "nucleus" of the framework is secure. If the independent and dependent variables are global and imprecise, the analyst will have difficulty in distinguishing them from implementation, bridging, and adjunct variables. Furthermore, clarifying a global concept in terms of its more precise meaning will help identify related phenomena that may later appear as additional variables within the framework. The analyst is advised to begin the clarification process by defining the objective of policy (the dependent variable), for the concrete form it eventually assumes will undoubtedly affect the design of policy (the independent variable).

We noted earlier in this chapter that when a global concept is broken down into its component variables, the concept has still been only partially operationalized, because these variables must be restated as indicators. But this task can be postponed to stage 6 of the design process. Since the function of the conceptual framework is only to specify those variables that comprise the policy problem and to depict their interrelations, partially operationalized concepts will do.

Let us return to our study of school desegregation to illustrate this step in the construction of a conceptual framework. It will be recalled that "relative academic achievement" was identified as the policy objective. This concept is easily operationalized as a variable measured either by some form of standardized testing or by a grade-point average. Therefore it needs no further clarification. However, the independent variable, "desegregation plan," is a global concept. It is not readily apparent what constitutes a desegregated school. The concept requires clarification in order for the appropriate variable to be specified.

In the course of the justification and history stages, the analyst discovered that different terms were used by different staff members of USOE in discussing school desegregation. White staff members used the term *desegregation* interchangeably with the term *integration* when referring to the process of reassigning pupils to different schools on the basis of race or ethnicity, as mandated by the courts. On the other hand, black staff members used only the term *desegregation* and objected to the use of *integration* in this context. This ambiguity in terminology led the analyst to question what was the true meaning of desegregation, whether *desegregation* and *integration* were synonymous, or whether they stood for different phenomena. This ambiguity indicated the need to submit the policy alternatives, and thus the independent variable, to conceptual clarification.

Staff members were asked to identify the properties associated with each term. White staff members identified a single property for both desegregation and integration: some mixture of racial and ethnic groups in the student composition of a school. Black staff members associated the same property with desegregation; however, with integration they associated two properties: a racial and ethnic mixture in the student composition of a school, and equal social status of the respective groups in the school system. In order to determine whether these properties belonged to a common phenomenon or to separate phenomena, their interrelatedness was diagrammed as follows:

Statuses

		Equal	Unequal
Enrollment	Mixed	(1) Integration	(2) Desegregation
	Homogeneous	(3) Separatism	(4) Segregation

It was agreed by all concerned that these four combinations represent four distinct phenomena. Combination 1 represents a state of affairs which had not yet been articulated in public policy and for which the term *integration* seemed appropriate. Combination 2, desegregation, represented the current connotation of the federal government's policy. Combination 3 was recognized as the concept advocated by some black militants and was labeled "separatism." Combination 4 was recognized as the actual situation under segregation. Therefore, "school attendance plan," a generic term covering all combinations that resulted from talking about *integration* and *desegregation,* was entered in the conceptual framework as the independent variable.

At the same time, it was recognized that equalizing status within the school would greatly affect the outcome of the policy. It was decided, therefore, to enter "relative status in the school" in the conceptual framework. But this subconcept itself remains global and requires further clarification. When questioned, users of this term were able to identify a number of variables that are components of this concept: the treatment of ethnic and racial groups in the curriculum; the composition of the faculty and administration; relative participation of racial and ethnic groups in extra curricular activities; mutual respect for the dress, language, and other behavioral manifestations of the unique cultures of the respective groups. For simplicity, "ethnic content of the curriculum" was selected as the variable to represent equal status within the school in the conceptual framework.

Deducing Missing Variables

Even after thoroughly reviewing the justification and history statements for policy variables, the analyst may still emerge with an incomplete conceptual framework. The missing variables would then be regarded as unknowns, and may become the focus of an exploratory study should they be critical to solving the policy problem. The analyst would use the conceptual framework as already formulated to guide the study. However, before committing him or herself to such an investigation, the analyst should attempt to arrive at the missing variables deductively, by using as premises the propositions of the extant framework. In other words, by a combination of logic and speculation, the analyst attempts to generate the additional concepts needed to complete the framework. Whether they are indeed the proper ones, only application of the framework to a specific situation will demonstrate.

As a point of departure, the deductive process should begin with the independent variable (assuming one exists), which in this case is operationalized as "school attendance plan." The analyst first seeks to identify certain consequences that both flow from the adoption of a course of action and are necessary antecedents to the attainment of the policy maker's objectives. The adoption of an attendance plan calling for major shifts in the enrollment of constituent schools would require some mechanism for its accomplishment. Two mechanisms are most frequently debated: one is the drawing of school attendance boundaries in such a way as to achieve a desired racial and ethnic mixture; the other is the provision of bussing. Of the two, bussing will more likely result in major shifts in enrollments and, therefore, will be added to the conceptual framework.

The analyst then turns to other consequences which may flow from the adopted policy, but which are unintended and are not necessary to the attainment of the policy objective. Relying on what he or she has thus far learned of the policy problem, the analyst might reason that the course of action planned could initiate an exodus of white families with school-age children from the school district. Since such an event would have considerable impact on the policy problem, "white flight" will be added to the conceptual framework. Ultimately, if the policy runs its full course and is successful, it can be expected to equalize the opportunities for black and other minority group students in the labor market. Thus "relative labor market status" of racial and ethnic groups will be added to the framework.

The analyst can also reverse the deductive process by moving from the dependent variable backward in time. That is, instead of searching for the consequents of the independent variable (cause-to-effect inference), he or she searches for the antecedents of the dependent variable (effect-to-cause inference). Now he or she looks for factors that will either facilitate or inhibit the achievement of the objective. The analyst poses the question, "Assuming the end product of relative equality of academic performance among racial and ethnic groups, what precipitating factors (in addition to the independent variable) must be present for this to be achieved?" The analyst will recognize that an equalization of academic achievement will not result solely from the presence of different racial and ethnic groups in the same school, or in the same classroom. One of the assumptions underlying school desegregation as a public policy is that it would make possible positive social interaction between students of different racial and ethnic groups, which would in turn lead to an equalization in their self-esteem and, ultimately, their motivation to learn. Thus, we will add "social interaction" among racial and ethnic groups as a variable in the conceptual framework.

The analyst can push the deductive process, no matter with which variable he or she begins, as far as it is deemed fruitful. As the inferential chain lengthens, it also fans out, multiplying the number of logically likely consequents. And if the process is pushed sufficiently far from both the independent and dependent variables, then the consequents of the former and the antecedents of the latter eventually overlap. In such an elaborate process, the analyst will discover that all consequents and all antecedents, although equally logical, are not equally probable. Having mapped out all the possible consequents of the policy and all the possible antecedents of the policy objective, the analyst selects for incorporation into the conceptual framework as variables those chains which seem to be most relevant to the policy problem and most probable in reality terms.

Locating The Variables in The Framework

Having executed the previous steps, the analyst is now in possession of a list of variables deemed relevant to the conceptual framework. It should be noted that each concept entered into the framework must be expressed as a variable, the measurable indicators of which are readily apparent. If the analyst is unable to so define a concept, then he or she must further clarify it. Only the framework of an exploratory study may contain global concepts; here the objective of the study is to identify the properties of the phenomenon to which such concepts refer. When the phenomenon to which a global concept refers has more than one property, the various terms which stand for the respective properties may be incorporated in the diagram. If this practice is cumbersome, the term symbolizing the global concept may be used, as long as the text accompanying the diagram specifies the properties of the phenomenon to which the concept refers.

Now the analyst must locate each variable appropriately in the framework. For some variables the location will be obvious, either because the relationship of the variable to the others is clear, or because the framework so dictates its position. However, the placement of other variables will cause the analyst considerable difficulty. For that reason, we will elaborate in some detail four criteria of placement: (1) causal sequence, (2) manipulability, (3) priority of the decision maker, and (4) intent of the decision maker.

The alternative courses of action and the policy maker's objective can be located easily. By definition they are the independent and dependent variables, respectively. The treatment of alternative actions in constructing the framework requires comment. When the alternatives are whether or not to enact or to retain a single policy or program, the independent variable is a dichotomy. When the alternative courses of action represent different degrees of a given intervention, they constitute differing ordinal- or interval-values of a single variable. Hence the alternatives can be entered in the framework as a single variable. However, when a variety of programs is being considered, each associated with different implementation and bridging variables, each alternative should be treated as a separate independent, dichotomous variable. In this way, the effect of each intervention on its respective intervening variables and ultimately on the dependent variable can be made clear. When, by contrast, only their overall impact on the dependent variable is at issue, the set of interventions can be treated as a single variable, taking the form of a dichotomous attribute when they are only two, of a manifold attribute when they are more than two.

Locating an intervening variable is a more complicated matter. It must be distinguished from the independent variable, on the one hand, and from the dependent variable, on the other hand. The key here is to establish a plausible *casual sequence* among a set of variables and to note their respective positions in that sequence. For example, let us suppose a set of three variables, namely, A, B, and C, in which A is the independent and C the dependent variable. B can be considered the intervening variable if the following conditions are met: B must occur before C can occur, and A must occur before B can occur; *and* B must occur in order to sustain the relationship between A and C; that is, if B were eliminated from the sequence, the relation between A and C would significantly decline or disappear. It should also be noted that an intervening variable may occur within the causal sequence of any two variables, even though our model depicts it only between the independent and dependent variables.

Once an intervening variable has been identified, it must be further classified as either an implementation or a bridging variable. This differentiation is made on the criterion of *manipulability*. If the intervening variable is manipulable by the decision maker within the existing policy-making context it is considered an implementation variable. If, however, the variable refers to attitudes or behaviors of other people, which by definition the decision maker cannot control, it is to be considered bridging. For example, the administrator of a health clinic cannot change the attitudes of the staff toward clients, but he or she can hire staff with certain attitudes. The attitudes of staff would constitute a bridging variable; hiring practices, an implementation variable.

Manipulability is also the criterion by which an adjunct variable can be distinguished from a constraint variable. If a variable has been found to be an antecedent of the dependent variable but *not* a consequence of the independent variable, it may be either an adjunct or a constraint variable. Both act on the dependent variable independently of the independent variable. However, the adjunct variable presumably can be manipulated by the policy maker in the context of the policy problem, while the constraint variable cannot. For example, an employer cannot change the age of a worker but he or she may be able to change the age requirement of a job specification.

Since both the adjunct and independent variables are manipulable, a criterion is needed to distinguish the two. The independent variable represents the intervention to which the decision maker is committed, as determined in the justification stage. The adjunct variable is usually identified subsequently, and represents an intervention which the decision maker could elect to take above and beyond that represented by the independent variable. Thus the *priority attached by the decision maker* to respective manipulable variables represents the distinguishing criterion.

Finally, unintended and latent consequences are distinguished from the other variables by the criterion of *intent*. They both represent unintended effects that flow from the policy. An unintended consequence is further distinguished from a latent consequence by the causal sequence of their occurrence. Thus, any variable which follows the independent (or an intervening) variable in a causal sequence *and* is not intended by the policy maker is considered an unintended consequence. Any variable which follows the dependent variable in causal sequence *and* is unintended by the policy maker is considered a latent consequence.

Returning to our example of the study of school desegregation, at this step in the development of our conceptual framework we have identified a number of variables:

> school attendance plan
> relative academic achievement
> relative social class
> ethnic content of curriculum
> bussing
> white flight
> relative labor market status
> social interaction between racial and ethnic groups

By means of the four criteria just discussed, we can now logically reconstruct the conceptual framework diagrammed in Figure 7-2. From the justification statement we have already determined that

> relative academic achievement = dependent variable
>
> school attendance plan = independent variable

"Relative social class" occurs in a causal sequence prior to "relative academic achievement," but it does not occur in a causal sequence following "school attendance plan." Since the origins of social class lie outside the policy problem, "social class" cannot be an intervening variable. In addition, social class cannot be manipulated by the decision maker in the content of this policy problem. Therefore we conclude that

relative social class = constraint variable

By the same process we determine that "ethnic content of the curriculum" is not an intervening variable. It occurs in a causal sequence prior to "relative academic achievement," but in this policy context it does not follow from a "school attendance plan." However, the ethnic content of the curriculum is manipulable by the decision maker, and so we conclude that

ethnic content of curriculum = adjunct variable

"Bussing" is a variable that occurs in a causal sequence following from "school attendance plan" and prior to the occurrence of "relative academic achievement." Since it is manipulable in this policy context we conclude that

bussing = implementation variable

Likewise, "social interaction" is a variable that occurs in a causal sequence between the independent and the dependent variable. It occurs prior to "relative academic achievement" but subsequent to "bussing." Since social interaction is a function of what students choose to do and is thus not manipulable within this policy context. Therefore we conclude that

social interaction = bridging variable

Finally, the amount of "white flight" from the school system and the "relative labor market status" of racial and ethnic groups are unintended by the decision maker. Since the first follows in causal sequence the independent variable, and the second, the dependent variable, we conclude that

white flight = unintended consequence

relative labor market status = latent consequence

Having located these variables in a conceptual framework, we may now wish to make some adjustments (see Figure 7-2). For example, it is reasonable to assume that the amount of bussing will also have an effect on the amount of white flight. We symbolize this relation by adding an arrow pointing from "bussing" toward "white flight." Similarly, we can now see that "white flight," by removing white students from the system, will have an impact on the bridging variable, "social interaction" among racial and ethnic groups. We symbolize this relation by adding an arrow between the two variables directed toward the latter.

Checking the Framework

Before using the framework as a launching pad for the proposed research, the analyst is advised to check it for accuracy, consistency, and validity. To be sure, only the actual application of the framework to the research design will verify it in practice. But it is always preferable to embark on an investigation with a conceptual framework that appears sound on an a priori basis. Checking consists essentially of recapitulating the process whereby the framework was constructed, making sure that the variables have been labeled and entered into the framework correctly. This time, however, the relationship between each pair of variables is seen against the background of a completed framework.

The variables of the conceptual framework comprise a network in which every variable is in some way related to every other variable. For some pairs of variables the relation is direct, whereas for others it is indirect. Most obvious is the relation of independent to dependent variable through the intervening variables. Less obvious is the relation of, let's say, an adjunct or a constraint variable to the latent consequence.

Testing the validity of the framework consists in rechecking the deductive process whereby these relations were reached. The eight variables that make up the model of a conceptual framework comprise 28 possible pairs of relations. Although desirable, it is practically impossible to check every one of them for deductive validity. However, there are seven basic pairs of relations that do merit the analyst's attention. These are

1. independent variable → implementation variable
2. independent variable → unintended consequence
3. implementation variable → bridging variable
4. bridging variable → dependent variable
5. adjunct variable → dependent variable
6. constraint variable → dependent variable
7. dependent variable → latent consequence

The proposition asserting a relationship between a pair of variables is derived from one or a combination of the following kinds of premises. For one, it may be a segment of scientific or practical theory the analyst has adopted from the literature. Second, it may be a piece of relevant information furnished to the analyst by seasoned practitioners. Third, it may consist of the analyst's personal observations. Lastly, it may be a proposition deduced logically from other demonstrated relations. Deductive testing of any given relation between two variables consists in reexamining the premises from which the analyst inferred that these variables do indeed influence each other.

Returning to our example of the study of school desegregation, we can look at the links between "school attendance plan," "bussing," and "social interaction" and consider them reasonable enough. On the basis of logic and personal observation, it seems obvious that the adoption of a school attendance plan involving a high mixture of racial and ethnic groups in enrollment would require increased levels of bussing, and that bringing such students together in one building would result in greater social interaction among the respective groups. However, it is not so obvious why increased social interaction would lead toward an equalization in academic achievement. This link requires some scrutiny. On the basis of personal experience as well as existing theory (Deutsch and Collins 1965), we can reason that social interaction among members of different racial and ethnic groups leads to the recognition of common interests. A recognition of common interests leads to an exchange of aspirations, norms, and information, which in turn leads to more equal levels of academic performance. Since these sublinks seem reasonable, we have accounted for the original link between social interaction and relative academic achievement.

An asserted relation between two variables may fail to meet the deductive test, because the deductive chain by which it was inferred is found to be invalid. Much more likely, however, is that the premises from which it was deduced are seen on reexamination to have been erroneous. Perhaps the theory that was brought to bear does not apply directly to the policy at issue; or the factual evidence that was invoked comes from research conducted under totally different conditions; or the information used as a base was obtained from practitioners who had acquired it without rigorous controls. And so on and on. A relation that fails the deductive test can itself become the focus of an investigation. However, even if a relation does appear to have deductive validity, it should be regarded as only more or less probable, precisely because the premises on which it is based are rarely, if ever, foolproof. The supporting theory, while somewhat relevant, rarely covers directly the relation in question. The supporting research, while applicable, rarely conforms precisely to the problem at issue. The supporting information obtained from expert practitioners is rarely free of a heavy mixture of intuition. Finally, we remind the reader that because a relation appears valid on logical grounds does not ipso facto make it factually true. For that, the asserted relation must pass the inductive or empirical test.

In concluding this discussion we should note some general characteristics of the model that may create problems in this last stage of constructing the conceptual framework. First, the boundaries of the framework are largely arbitrary. In reality there are always additional variables which precede the independent variables and influence them. In systems terms, all variables left out of the framework are *exogenous*, that is, external to the operation of the system.

In constructing the framework their influence is assumed either as a given or as being inconsequential. If such an assumption is found to be unwarranted, the framework must be expanded to include them. The "new" variables would become the independent, adjunct, or control variables, thereby relegating the "older" ones to intervening variables. In our example of the study of school desegregation, the existence of court orders to eliminate racial duality in a public school system leads to a change in the school attendance plans of that system. If the existence of such orders cannot be assumed, then "court orders" should be entered into the framework as the independent variable, and "school attendance plan" should be relegated to the status of an implementation variable. Similarly, a latent effect which takes on the significance of a policy objective may be elevated to the dependent variable, necessitating the quest for a "new" latent effect to replace it.

Second, the designation of each variable within the framework depends on which pair of variables is the focus of the research. If the focus changes from one relationship to another, the designations change. For example, a change in priorities for action may result in the conversion of an adjunct variable to the independent variable, in which case the original independent variable would become the adjunct variable. In the study of school desegregation, the policy maker may decide to focus on changing the respective statuses of racial and ethnic groups within the school rather than on changing the composition of the enrollment. Thus, "ethnic content of the curriculum" would become the independent variable, and "school attendance plan" would become the adjunct variable.

Third, the model presented here is an ideal model. Each variable is assumed to influence only one other variable and thus, presumably, to serve only one function. In a real situation, any one variable may affect several other variables and thus serve more than one function. For example, an independent variable may act on an adjunct variable as well as on the dependent variable. In such a case, the relative strengths of the respective relationships must be considered in designating the variable. When one relationship is relatively weak, it may be ignored in the framework. If this is not justifiable, the variable must be considered as having multiple functions each of which can be analyzed statistically.

USING THE CONCEPTUAL FRAMEWORK

The conceptual framework is comprised of the variables (concepts) and the relationships that form the causal context of the investigation and is therefore indispensable in any research design. However, the specificity and validity of the framework will vary with the extent of knowledge about the policy problem, and this will in turn affect the design of the study. Consequently, the way in which the conceptual framework is used in the design process will vary from one type of study to another. We will now examine the nature and use of the conceptual framework in an exploratory, a descriptive, and an explanatory study.

Exploratory

If the analyst is unable to identify policy variables that are missing from the conceptual framework, or succeeds in identifying only global concepts, the objective of the research may be to discover those variables or to clarify those concepts. Such an investigation is exploratory in its method. The conceptual framework assists the analyst in determining the type of variables for which he or she must search.

In the early stages of the policy-making process, when the conceptual framework is rudimentary, only the dependent variable (the policy objective) may be known. In that instance the purpose is to discover the independent variable(s) (alternative courses of action). The reverse also occurs; the policy maker may be forced to take a course of action and wants to know its likely consequences. In both instances the conceptual framework is used to provide structure for an exploratory study. Cases must be found which have opposite values of the known variable. The contrasting cases are then examined to determine what other characteristics differentiate them. These other characteristics, if they are manipulable by the policy maker, represent potential courses of action. For example, the policy maker may want to improve the quality of intergroup relations in a desegregated school, but is unclear about what programs or policies might lead to that objective. To answer that question, he or she might observe schools with very good intergroup relations, to see what programs or policies they have in common, and then compare them with schools that have poor intergroup relations to see what programs or policies distinguish the former from the latter. In this manner, as we have shown in Chapter 2, the analyst invokes the two inductive canons.

This approach is more fruitful when additional policy variables can be included in the conceptual framework. Figure 7-5 depicts a conceptual framework containing three constraint variables along with the dependent variable. It is reasonable to assume that "size of the school," "intergroup relations in the community," and "level of education of the adult population," would all have an impact on the quality of intergroup relations in the school. These constraint variables can be used to match the contrasting cases and thereby narrow the range of properties that must be searched in order to identify the missing policy variables. For example, schools with harmonious and schools with conflicting intergroup relations can be selected so as to be equal in their sizes, in the character of intergroup relations in their communities, and in the level of education among their adult populations. When, in addition, the contrasting schools are also strati-

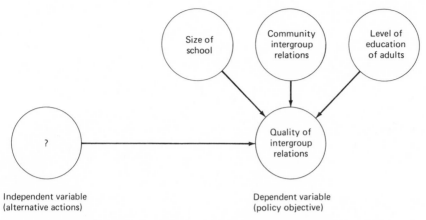

Independent variable   Dependent variable
(alternative actions)   (policy objective)

Figure 7-5 A conceptual framework for an exploratory study of policies to improve intergroup relations in desegregated schools

fied with respect to each constraint variable, for example, when there is one large, one medium, and one small sized school in each of the contrasting groups, a range of policy alternatives appropriate for all circumstances can be more easily identified.

Descriptive

When the analyst wishes to ascertain the distribution of the condition calling for intervention in order to be able to define the policy objective, a form of description referred to as needs assessment, he or she does not require a conceptual framework. The definition of the condition, i.e., the dependent variable, suffices. However, in policy research we are interested in information to guide actions to change undesirable conditions. Therefore, it is not sufficient to determine the extent of a given condition reflected in the policy objective—we need to ascertain the distribution of all known factors which precipitate that condition. Only then can we estimate the number of units of the target population that can be helped by each of the available interventions. We do this by ascertaining the number of units likely to be affected by factors that are amenable to change (bridging variables) through the respective interventions (independent variables), and the number of units that might be affected by factors that are not amenable to change (constraint variables) within the given policy context. The conceptual framework aids the analyst in differentiating these various factors.

For example, the experience of employment agencies indicates that a number of factors determine the ability of an unemployed person to get a job. Among them are his or her skill level, prior work history, education level, and employer discrimination based on race, sex, and age. Thus the conceptual

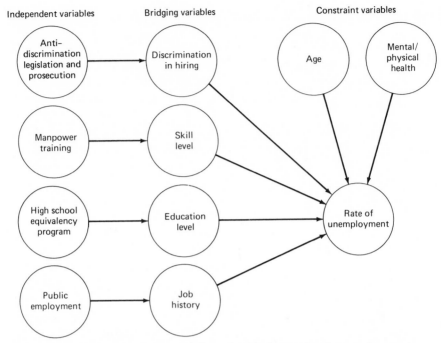

Figure 7-6 Conceptual framework for a descriptive study of unemployment

framework for a descriptive study of unemployment should protray all of these factors and their relationship to unemployment (see Figure 7-6). Next, the framework should include the interventions (independent variables) appropriate to each factor amenable to change (bridging variables). For example, enforcement of recently enacted legislation prohibiting race, sex, or age discrimination in employment would reduce discriminatory hiring practices; the provision of manpower training would raise the skill level of unemployed workers; a high-school equivalency program would raise educational levels; and a public works program would provide employment for those with unstable work records.

Of course, the framework should also identify precipitating factors that are not amenable to change through actions that can be taken by the decision maker (constraint variables). Thus persons under 14 or over 65 years of age are not likely to find jobs given present labor market concepts. Persons with chronic illness or serious handicapping conditions, as well as the severely retarded and the mentally ill, will be limited in competing for jobs.

Sometimes, for the sake of efficiency, a description of the distribution of bridging and constraint variables used in estimating the consequences of alternative actions (stage 5 in policy making) is combined with a description of the distribution of the condition calling for intervention (stage 2 in policy making). The result is a description of the "population at risk," differentiating those units which have from those which do not have the condition in question. Then, the former, called the "target population" are further divided into groups of units exhibiting each of the bridging and constraint variables. This form of needs assessment constitutes *bivariate description.*

Thus, the conceptual framework plays an important part in descriptive studies. Rather than challenging the validity of the causal relations among variables, however, the analyst uses the framework to identify the alternative courses of action that are appropriate for dealing with the policy maker's objective.

Explanatory

In an explanatory study the level of knowledge about the variables involved in the policy problem is maximal. Therefore, the conceptual framework for such studies follows the general model for policy research introduced at the beginning of this chapter. The study of school desegregation presented earlier provides an illustration of such a framework.

Some general comments should be made about the way the conceptual framework is used in an explanatory study. The purpose of an explanatory study is to verify one or more causal relationships stated in the conceptual framework. But only one such relationship can be tested at a time. Most importantly, it is the conceptual framework which distinguishes for the analyst the principal relationship, that between the independent and dependent variable, from other relationships that should be controlled, namely, those between the adjunct, the constraint, the intervening variables, and the dependent variable. Now, in terms of a simple experiment, the explanatory study requires two situations, one in which the independent variable is present, and one in which it is absent. Both situations must be alike in terms of the other variables. As the analyst moves to test one relationship after another, each in turn must be varied while the rest are held constant. The development of statistical techniques such as path analysis and causal modeling has made it possible to test many relationships within the same study design (Blalock 1969). Such techniques permit the testing of very complex conceptual frameworks.

SUMMARY

The process of developing a conceptual framework of the policy problem assumes five stages: (1) reviewing prior design stages for policy variables, (2) clarifying concepts, (3) deducing missing variables, (4) locating variables in the framework, and (5) checking the framework deductively.

The conceptual framework which the analyst includes in his research design should incorporate three elements:

1. a diagram of the relevant policy variables and their interrelationship, that is a graphic representation of the conceptual framework
2. a connotative definition of each policy variable, that renders it understandable in terms of other, more familiar concepts (Operational definitions come in stage 6 of the design process.)
3. a brief explanation of each relationship depicted in the diagram as that has revealed itself in the deductive testing of the framework

With the completion of the conceptual framework, the analyst is in a position to specify the precise question(s) of fact about the conceptual framework which constitute his or her research objective(s). To the specification of that objective(s) we turn in the next chapter.

REFERENCES

BLALOCK, HUBERT M. JR. *Theory Construction.* Englewood Cliffs, N.J.: Prentice-Hall, 1969.

DEUTSCH, MORTON, and MARY EVANS COLLINS. "Interracial Housing," in *American Social Patterns,* ed. William Petersen. Garden City, N.Y.: Doubleday and Company, Inc., 1965, pp. 7–62.

LAZARSFELD, PAUL F. "Evidence and Inference in Social Research," *Daedalus,* 7, (Fall 1958), 99–130.

LAZARSFELD, PAUL F. "Problems in Methodology," in *Sociology Today, Problems and Prospects,* eds. Robert K. Merton, Leonard Broom, and Leonard S. Cottrell. New York: Basic Books, Inc., 1959.

LAZARSFELD, PAUL F., and ALLEN H. BARTON. "Qualitative Measurement in the Social Sciences," in *The Policy Sciences,* eds. Harold D. Lasswell and Daniel Lerner, Stanford, California: Stanford Univ. Press, 1951, pp. 155–192.

MERTON, ROBERT K. *Social Theory and Social Structure* (rev. ed.). New York: Free Press, 1957.

RIPPLE, LILIAN. "Problem Identification and Formulation," in *Social Work Research,* ed. Norman A. Polansky. Chicago: University of Chicago Press, 1960, pp. 24–47.

STINCHCOMBE, ARTHUR L. *Constructing Social Theories.* New York: Harcourt, Brace and World, Inc., 1968.

WEISS, CAROL H. *Evaluation Research.* Englewood Cliffs, N.J.: Prentice-Hall Inc., 1972.

chapter 8 / stage 4: statement of the research objective(s)

The research design process began with the analyst assisting the decision maker to identify the policy problem and to define the information needed to move toward effective action. Next, the analyst examined prior efforts to deal with the policy problem on a theoretical, on a research, and on a practical level, thereby illuminating the action choices available and desirable. On the basis of the knowledge that he or she thus accumulated, the analyst constructed a model of the many variables that comprise the policy problem and its solution, depicting the interrelations of these variables. With this as a background, the analyst should now be able to state clearly the objective(s) of the contemplated research.

The statement of research objective(s) designates the specific variables and the question(s) of fact about their nature, distribution, or interrelations which must be answered to resolve the policy problem. In this sense there may be more than one objective, as there may be more than one question of fact. By specifying which variables will, indeed, be observed, the statement defines the parameters of the investigation. Hence, in formulating a statement of the research objective(s), the analyst is committed to the study of a given set of variables. This stage of the research design completes the conceptual phase of the design process and serves as a transition to the technical phase that follows.

The statement enunciating the objective(s) of the prospective research is derived from the conceptual framework. When the conceptual framework is extremely complex, attempts to compress all of it into the research objective(s) rarely succeed. Under such circumstances the research objective(s) must focus on a manageable portion of that framework. The analyst can, of course, return to the framework and revise it to conform to the more modest objective(s). However, we advise against this. Better to leave the framework in its expanded form and to justify the exclusion of certain variables and relations from the research objective(s). By the time the analyst is ready for the research statement, he or she sees clearly the priority among the relations depicted in the framework and the sequence in which various aspects of the policy problem should be investigated in order to facilitate policy making. Leaving the framework in its expanded form is preferable, because it provides a context in which the research findings take on a greater meaning. In addition, an expanded framework provides the basis for a series of research efforts based on a number of questions and hypotheses. Such serial investigations would be discrete and disconnected were they not interrelated by an overarching conceptual framework.

Once the objective(s) of the contemplated study has been clearly formulated, the analyst can attend to the technical aspects of the design. The statement setting forth the research objective(s) implies the method of research to be employed in obtaining that objective(s); and this method in turn determines to a large degree the techniques that must be implemented in stages 5 through 8. Thus, only because the research objective(s) is known, can the analyst work out the details attached to specific data-gathering techniques. For example, the research statement will invariably specify who will be observed and what variables will be observed about them. Such information enables the analyst to visualize the study population, the data to be collected about it, and the analysis to which the data will be put. The technical details of population sampling, data collection, and data analysis are then worked out in design stages 5, 6, 7, and 8. *Hence, a clear statement of the research objective(s) imparts direction and focus to the design stages that are to follow.*

We have already referred to the dynamic character of the design process, namely, that the design stages influence each other. While the statement of the research objective(s) sets the parameters of the investigation, these may have to be modified here and there as a result of technical and/or practical constraints encountered during subsequent design stages. Perhaps the precise population required by the research statement is inaccessible, or the data called for are either unavailable or necessitate infeasible techniques for their collection. Or, again, the way in which the variables can actually be measured differs from what was implied in the research statement. Hence, it is not uncommon for the statement of research objective(s) to undergo some modification to accord with one or more of these contingencies, although the set of variables specified for observation remains basically unchanged. To this extent the initial formulation of the research statement has a certain tentativeness. It is something for the analyst to work with as he or she moves into the technical stages of the design and may thus be thought of as a "working statement."

The experienced reader will recognize that what we have called the "statement of the research objective(s)," some textbooks in social research refer to as the "statement of the research problem." We believe there is an important distinction between the two terms. A research objective connotes an end to be attained, a specific piece of information that will answer the question of fact that motivates the research. The term *problem* implies a puzzle to be solved. It is often used to connote both the end, or solution, and the means or method by which that solution is to be derived. It is therefore a less precise term. In our view, the technical stages of the research design that follow the statement of research objectives operationalize the method by which the policy objective is to be attained. We recognize, however, that in every statement of a research objective is implied a method of research—either exploratory, descriptive, or explanatory—that is appropriate for its attainment. It is this method which governs the selection of techniques in the design stages that follow. Therefore, in stating the research objective(s) the analyst should explicate the method implied.

THE RESEARCH OBJECTIVE(S)

The statement of the research objective(s) concentrates on the specific variables and their relations to be investigated. It is unusual for an investigation to focus on an entire conceptual framework. To do so may result in a study of inordinate complexity, or may involve resources in time and money that exceed those available to the analyst. It is important to recognize, however, that the variables and relations to be investigated depend largely on the stage of the policy-making process at which research is required.

If the need for research occurs at the stage of specifying the policy objective, it is likely to focus on the dependent variable of the conceptual framework. If research is done to facilitate formulation of alternative courses of action, it will focus on the independent variable. If research deals with the estimation of the consequences of these courses of action, it will focus on the relation between the independent and dependent variables, as mediated by the bridging variables. To increase the accuracy of such estimates, the analyst must incorporate into the analysis the relation of adjunct and constraint variables to the dependent variable. Clearly, the analyst can achieve greater precision in estimating how fully the policy objective can be reached by each alternative course of action when he or she considers the varying effectiveness of these alternatives upon different segments of the target population, within different environments, and in the presence of auxiliary actions which influence such effectiveness. Similarly, a more complete picture of the consequences of policy would include consideration of the unintended and the latent as well as the intended effects.

If the research occurs during the implementation stage of the policy-making process, it will focus on the intervening variables, either in establishing their presence or in verifying their relation to the independent and dependent variables. If the decision maker is interested in evaluating the outcome of a policy that has already been implemented, the research may have one of several foci. For example, if the policy maker wants simply to know whether the objective was achieved, research will focus on the dependent variable. If instead he/she wishes to verify a "theory of intervention" (that is, that a given policy brought about the attainment of its objective), then the research will focus on the relation between the independent and dependent variables. If the interest is in the side effects of policy, then the research will focus on the unintended or latent consequences. Again, the more variables and relations that are included in the research, the more valid the evaluation. For example, if constraint and adjunct variables are included with the independent variable, the verification of an intervention theory will have greater validity by virtue of the elimination of rival hypotheses.

In determining the research objective(s), the analyst is actually delimiting in a precise manner the variables and their relations to be studied. How many variables and relations to include rests, in part, on the benefits for decision making to be gained from each additional variable versus the cost of studying it. Each variable raises the cost of research by increasing the populations to be observed, the data to be collected, and the analyses to be undertaken, a fact to become apparent later. Because the analyst wants to resolve the policy problem with the least cost, he or she tries to formulate a research objective that will be simple and yet result in an acceptable solution.

THE FORM OF THE STATEMENT

The objective of policy research is to obtain some specific piece(s) of information needed to carry out the policy-making process. In the previous section we noted that the objective(s) derives in large part from the stage in policy making at which the need for research arises. But what method of research should be adopted in pursuit of that objective(s)? Elsewhere in this book (see pp. 50-57) we noted that the method of an investigation—that is, whether it be exploratory, descriptive, or explanatory—depends on the level of knowledge about the variables or their relations needed to solve the policy problem. We further pointed out that this level is often determined by the stage in the policy-making process at which research is initiated. For example, research required during the specification of objectives is most likely to require the descriptive method; that required in designing alternative courses of action, the exploratory method; that required to estimate the consequences of those alternatives, the descriptive method; and that required to evaluate the effects of policies once implemented, the explanatory method. But we also noted that there are frequent exceptions to this pattern (see pp. 57-60). The actual method required depends on the level of knowledge needed to solve the policy problem at whatever stage of policy making that problem arises. If the need is to identify a property of the phenomenon which is the subject of policy making, i.e., to discover a policy variable missing in the conceptual framework, the method required is exploratory. If the need is to determine the size or distribution of a policy variable, the method required is descriptive. If the need is to verify the causal nature of a relation between policy variables, the method required is explanatory.

If properly drawn, the form in which the research objective(s) is stated reflects the level of knowledge needed. Therefore it behooves the analyst to examine carefully the form in which that objective(s) is worded because it has implications for the particular method to be incorporated in the remaining stages of the research design. The wording of the objective(s) of the proposed research will inevitably vary, depending on the subject matter investigated. And yet research statements do tend to assume certain modes, so that it is possible to speak of the form of the statement. In general, research statements assume three forms: the open-ended question, the closed-ended question, and the causal hypothesis.

The Open-Ended Question

When policy maker and analyst initially confront the policy problem, their knowledge about it and its context may be quite minimal. They are, of course, able to recognize the phenomenon to be studied, because they are dealing with it. But they may not understand it well enough to specify its distinguishing properties—the variables that constitute it and set it apart from similar phenomena. Thus the objective of research is to identify those properties. The form in which such objectives are stated is an open-ended question, so called because the properties of the phenomenon in question cannot be specified. In terms of the triangle of reference, we can say that an open-ended question refers to a concept of which the idea and term are known but the referents are unclear. The intent of such a question is to complete the triangle.

To illustrate, consider the possibilities of the following open-ended question for research, "What are the factors that characterize a maximally successfully desegregated school?" Here the analyst's thinking runs somewhat as follows, "I can recognize an exemplary school which has desegregated itself so successfully that it can serve as a model for emulation. I can also recognize its opposite, a school in which desegregation has failed. But I cannot name the properties that distinguish the two, and this task will therefore be the objective of my investigation." At times the open-ended question focuses upon the policy —that is, the independent variable in the conceptual framework, as in this example, "What kinds of attendance plans have districts adopted in an effort to achieve school desegregation?" At other times the open-ended question might focus on the dependent variable in the conceptual framework. For example, "What types of jobs do graduates of job training programs obtain?"

An open-ended question is not always confined to the identification of the component variables of a concept; it may also be used to identify the antecedents or consequents of a key variable in the conceptual framework. For example, the question for research might be, "What are the factors that impede unemployed persons from obtaining a job?" Here the analyst reasons, "The objective of the policy maker is to reduce unemployment, the properties of which can be specified. However, there are factors that must be overcome (bridging variables) to achieve that objective, factors that cannot be specified on the basis of available information." Another research question might be, "What are the consequences of adopting a racial balance attendance plan?" Here the analyst is reasoning, "The policy maker has identified a policy to be adopted (and, by implication, the objective that policy is intended to achieve), but we do not know what unintended consequences might occur were the policy to be adopted."

The Closed-Ended Question

Next, there is the situation in which the analyst is well aware of important properties or variables that comprise the policy problem but has little or no knowledge about their size or frequency. Perhaps the analyst cannot say how these properties are distributed in a given population in terms of the classes, categories, or values that they assume; or perhaps it is not known whether such properties are interrelated.

To produce information about either type of objective, the research statement would take the form of a closed-ended question. Such a statement is considered closed-ended because it specifies properties of the phenomenon under study, the alternative forms and limits of which are known beforehand. For example, age, sex, education, and neonatal fatality are properties expressible in terms of a priori classes, or quantitative values. At times the closed-ended question might focus upon a single variable within the conceptual framework. For example, "How many people are unemployed?" or "How many births resulted in neonatal fatality?" Sometimes the closed-ended question might focus upon the simultaneous distribution of two or more variables in the conceptual framework. For example, "What is the distribution of unemployed persons by age, sex, and level of education?" At other times the closed-ended question may focus on the relation or covariation between two or more variables in the framework. For example, "What is the degree of association between the amount of prenatal care received by women and neonatal fatality among their offspring?"

The Causal Hypothesis

Lastly, there is the situation in which the analyst knows both the properties of a phenomenon and their size or distribution but lacks information that would allow him or her to account for this phenomenon in terms of the size or distribution of one or more other phenomena. Knowledge is needed about whether the variation exhibited by one variable is accountable in terms of the variation exhibited by another. The descriptive information that may be available does not fully satisfy this need. The form assumed by the research statement in such a study is what we call a causal hypothesis. In order to specify the form of a causal hypothesis, we must recall briefly the requirements for testing causality.

As we pointed out in Part I (p. 33) three conditions must prevail in order to validate a causal hypothesis: (1) variation in one variable must be associated with variation in the other(s); (2) the variable which is the presumed cause (independent variable) must precede in time the variable which is the presumed effect (dependent variable); and (3) the effect of the presumed cause was not produced by some third variable. Therefore, covariation of two variables does not in itself permit the analyst to conclude a causal connection between them. The analyst must posit or hypothesize that variation in one (or more) variable(s), A, precedes variation in a second variable, B, in the absence of variation in a third (or more) variable(s), C.

In order to demonstrate that some other variable C, also an antecedent, did not produce the consequent B, we must control the suspected factor by holding it constant. If the suspected factor C is indeed exerting some effect, we must then demonstrate that the presence of the antecedent A in the relation under examination results in an overall effect B in excess of what would otherwise be. This condition is known as the falsification principle in hypothesis testing and was discussed in Part I (p. 28). It recognizes the impossibility of proving a causal hypothesis true. All one can do is to falsify alternative hypotheses and thereby increase the plausibility of the research hypothesis. For this reason, the validity of a causal hypothesis lies in the number of alternative causal hypotheses that can be refuted (Blalock 1960, pp. 92f). Similarly, a given hypothesis can be said to be true only in relation to the specific factors that have been refuted as alternative causes through the research.

It is important at this point to comment on the difference between a research hypothesis, as we conceive it, and a null hypothesis. Much confusion has been bred because of the changing interpretation of this difference since the introduction of the null hypothesis. The reader is urged to consult the more recent literature (Morrison and Henkel 1970). The null hypothesis is sometimes treated, erroneously, as an alternative to the research hypothesis. In actuality the two hypotheses are distinctly different, and serve different purposes. The research hypothesis posits or predicts an observable covariation between two or more variables. The null hypothesis refers to the probablistic nature of that observed covariation. It posits that the observed covariation is the result of factors not controlled in the research design, namely unknown factors that are presumed to operate on the dependent variable in a random manner. Testing the null hypothesis, therefore, is a way of adding to the validity of the research hypothesis by ruling out the influence of factors uncontrolled in the research design. Such a test is applicable, however, only when randomization has been used in the design of the study (Selvin 1957). We will say more about the null hypothesis, or the statistical significance of the findings regarding a research hypothesis, in the data analysis section of research design (Chapter 12) where that discussion properly belongs.

Let us turn now to some examples of causal hypotheses that serve as statements of research objectives. (1) "The provision of a manpower training program will be associated with an increase in the entry of unemployed persons into full-time employment, assuming employment opportunities remain constant." (2) "The utilization of prenatal care services by pregnant women will be associated with a decrease in the neonatal death rate of their offspring, given no change in the mothers' living standard." (3) "The adoption of a racial balance attendance plan in a given school district will be associated with an eventual reduction in the gap in academic performance of white and black students, controlling for the ethnic content of the curriculum and the relative social class of the two racial groups." Each of the foregoing hypotheses posits a covariation between at least two variables, one of which is the antecedent and, by implication, the cause of the other. In addition, each hypothesis rules out the influence of at least one other relevant antecedent variable by the inclusion of such clauses as "assuming employment opportunities to remain constant" and "given no change in their living standard." If the analyst is able to utilize in the research design a "pure experiment," in which randomization governs exposure to the independent variable, then the phrase "all other factors being equal" may be used in the hypothesis. In such a design both known and unknown factors are controlled (see Chapter 9).

Upon careful examination the analyst may find that his or her statement of a research objective does not fit one of these three forms. This may be the result of lack of precision in the statement or of lack of clarity in the analyst's mind about the level of knowledge being sought. In such cases the analyst should reexamine the policy problem and the first three stages of the design process until the research objective can be more precisely stated in one of these forms. Failure to state the objective(s) with the proper degree of clarity will prevent the analyst from specifying with certainty the method to be employed in the research.

METHODOLOGICAL IMPLICATIONS

Thus far we have spoken of the substance and the form of the research statement. In substance it sets forth the information needed; in form it is either a question or an hypothesis. The research statement thus specifies the *what* of the research, the objective, but it does not specify the *how,* the means for achieving the objective. It does not tell the analyst in so many words what method to employ to obtain the needed information. At the same time, however, both the form and the substance of the research statement carry methodological implications. And these the analyst must now explicate. The justification statement, which defines the policy problem, and the conceptual framework, which identifies its variables, already contain preliminary suggestions for method, without actually making the choice explicit.

In order to facilitate the design decisions that are to follow, the analyst must now explicate the research method the study will employ. The type of method determines a number of technical details. It determines how the study population is to be defined, how the population units are to be sampled for observation, and how they are to be exposed to the independent variable(s). It determines what kind of data will have to be collected, how they are to be collected, and, once collected, how they are to be analyzed. Hence, explication of the type of method has the effect of narrowing the range of the technical decisions yet to come.

For example, once the analyst has chosen a research method, he or she can already visualize the requisite data collection and data analysis techniques. As already noted in Part 1 (pp. 52-57), each research method entails its own requirements for research techniques. Of course, specifying a method will not alone determine the techniques to be employed; these decisions will also depend on certain field conditions and cost constraints that will be examined in greater detail in the chapter to follow. For example, the nature of the phenomenon, or its sensitivity to observation, may preclude making a large number of observations or may limit the manner in which they can be made. Thus, although the analyst at this stage can specify with certainty the method of inquiry, this decision will only indicate the range of techniques to be employed in executing that method.

To specify the method we return to the form of the statement of research objective(s). (See Figure 8-1.) A study guided by an open-ended question, whether directed at the identification of the properties of a given phenomenon or at the identification of its antecedents or consequences, calls for the exploratory method. As we shall see in the design stages that follow, the exploratory method has the least rigorous specifications. Such a method allows flexibility in procedure to pursue whatever promising opportunity arises for the identification of missing properties or variables. In order to maximize efficiency, a relatively small study population is observed intensively, and cases are selected on a purposive, nonrandom basis. Observational techniques are open-ended or intentionally unrefined. The data yielded by an exploratory study are qualitative in character, being the classes or types of the property or variable identified, and the inferences to be derived are about the range of these classes or types. Such a study, of course, provides no way of knowing the size or distribution of property or variable throughout a given population.

A study guided by a closed-ended question calls for the descriptive method. Its design requirements are much more exact. When the population

Figure 8-1 Methodological implications of the statement of research objective(s)

LEVEL OF KNOWLEDGE REQUIRED	FORM OF RESEARCH OBJECTIVE	RESEARCH METHOD IMPLIED	TYPE OF INFORMATION PRODUCED
Discovery of missing property or variable	open-ended question	exploratory	qualitative data
Estimation of size or distribution of known variable or relation	closed-ended question	descriptive	quantitative data
Causality of relation	causal hypothesis	explanatory	verification of conditions of causality

being studied is large, samples are drawn for observation by some random procedure. Observations are made by standardized and rigorous procedures. The data generated are quantitative in character. They may come in the form of enumerations, of a frequency or percentage distribution, or of averages, rates, ratios, or proportions based on previously established types, classes, or categories. They may also come in the form of measures or coefficients of association. It is possible to infer from such a study the size or distribution of a known property or variable in the population under study within a specified range of error.

A study guided by a causal hypothesis calls for the explanatory method. Its objective is the testing of causality, which is accomplished by verifying the conditions specified in the causal hypothesis. The explanatory method requires the observation of at least two cases which differ with respect to the presumed cause and which have at least one other potential causal variable in common. Observation requires precise and systematic procedures. Such a study yields a conclusion regarding the relative acceptability of the presumption of causality. One can infer causality only with respect to the cases observed and the variables controlled. It is not possible to generalize beyond those cases unless they also meet the requirements of a descriptive study. Therefore, the larger the study population and the greater the number of variables controlled, the greater the generalizability of the causal findings.

At the outset of this chapter we recognized the possibility that a given study may have more than one research objective. Such a situation arises when more than one question of fact must be answered at a given stage of policy making. Assuming that they share the same conceptual framework, multiple research objectives can be accommodated in the same design with relative ease when they involve the same method of research. For example, an exploratory study may be guided by two or more open-ended questions; a descriptive study, by two or more closed-ended questions; and an explanatory study, by two or more causal hypotheses. The principal constraint is in finding a study population large enough to accommodate all objectives.

However, if the research objectives involve different research methods, the ensuing study design can become quite complicated. The overall study design must meet the requirements of all methods involved. Such a feat involves more than a matter of the size of the study population. It also involves accommodating in one study two or more requirements for the composition of a population, as well as the corresponding techniques of data collection and analysis. Given these complications, it may be wiser to design separate studies for each objective. Nonetheless, there are times when, owing to the cost of data collection procedures, it is advantageous to combine several objectives in one study. A general rule of thumb in such circumstances is that the design for a less rigorous method may be incorporated into the design for a more rigorous method, but not vice versa. For example, it is possible to incorporate an exploratory research objective in the design of a descriptive study, but it is not possible to incorporate a descriptive research objective in an exploratory study. If multiple research objectives involving different methods are to be accommodated in the same study, the method for each objective should be clearly stated, both at this stage of the design and at each subsequent stage.

EXAMPLES OF RESEARCH OBJECTIVES
AND THEIR METHODOLOGICAL IMPLICATIONS

Let us return to our study of school desegregation in order to illustrate how research objectives are formulated in exploratory, descriptive, and explanatory studies. Let us assume that we are in the early stages of decision making, and have defined our policy objective as "equalizing academic performance between racial and ethnic groups" (dependent variable). Let us also assume that prior research indicates that social interaction between the groups (bridging variable), providing they are status equals (constraint variable), assists in achieving such equality by raising the performance of low achievers. However, we are unable to formulate a course of action (independent variable) for promoting greater social interaction among racial and ethnic groups and, therefore, that policy variable is missing from our conceptual framework. This calls for the exploratory method. We shall state our research objective as follows:

> What policy actions are available for generating social interaction among racial and ethnic groups when they are status equals?

Note that we stated the variable to be identified in terms of its relation to a known variable in the conceptual framework (social interaction), a relation critical to identifying it. The variable of social interaction is used here on the assumption that such interaction promotes the policy objective. If that assumption were untenable, we would look for actions that lead directly to the objective without benefit of a bridging variable. Note the inclusion in the research statement of the constraint variable (status equals), which will help define our study population and thus focus our exploration. The more complete the conceptual framework—that is, the more variables relevant to the policy objective it includes—the more fruitful an exploratory study.

Now let us assume that our conceptual framework is entirely complete and that we are at the stage of estimating the consequences of alternative courses of action. Let us further assume that our exploratory study resulted in identifying several alternatives, each one based on a different assumption about barriers to academic performance. One alternative is a racially and ethnically balanced attendance plan, which we have already discussed. A second alternative might be a supplemental appropriation to schools with a predominantly black or minority group enrollment to bring up the quality of their education programs. A third alternative might be special education services designed to help underachieving students develop perceptual and cognitive learning skills. Thus, three alternative courses of action reasoned from separate assumptions are proposed for equalizing academic achievement between racial and ethnic groups:

1. a racial and ethnic balance attendance plan to promote social interaction among racial and ethnic groups
2. a supplemental appropriation to predominantly black or minority group schools to increase the quality of education
3. provision of special education services to increase perceptual and cognitive skills of underachieving students

In estimating the consequences of these alternatives, the analyst must know how much of the policy objective might be achieved by each. In other words, how many persons in the target population might be changed in the direction of the policy objective by each alternative? To answer this question, we must ascertain the number of students in the target population whose academic retardation is attributable to each of the several conditions to be remedied by the alternatives. Such an objective calls for the descriptive method, and can be stated as follows:

How many black and ethnic students with below average achievement scores exhibit (1) social isolation from white students; (2) attendance at inferior schools; or (3) perceptual and cognitive disabilities?

Undoubtedly these conditions are not independent of each other, a fact that would have to be kept in mind in estimating the effects of each course of action.

Underlying the study is the assumption that each course of action has a probability of success equal to that of the others.

Note that this statement of the research objective assumes a causal relation between each of the alternative courses and the policy objective sufficient to warrant its consideration as a solution to the policy problem. As an inquiry about the frequency and distribution of the members of the target population who would be benefited by each course of action, the study would use the descriptive method.

Finally, let us illustrate how a research objective might be chosen for an explanatory study. Assume that a course of action, namely, the adoption of a racial and ethnic balance attendance plan, has been selected and implemented; our job is to evaluate its outcome. Further, let us assume that the policy maker is concerned with determining the effectiveness of the policy in bringing about the objective (explanatory), not simply with ascertaining the extent to which the desired outcome occurred (descriptive). In our conceptual framework we may have determined that certain intervening factors (for example, social intercation), certain adjunct factors (for example, a multiracial and multi-ethnic curriculum), and certain constraint factors (such as status equality among students) are necessary to the success of the policy. Since we are interested in verifying the causal relation between the independent (attendance plan) and dependent (relative academic achievement) variables, we control (hold constant in value) all other variables. The research objective is stated as follows:

> The adoption of a racial and ethnic balance attendance plan will be associated with an equalization of academic performance when undertaken with a multiracial and multi-ethnic curriculum and with social interaction among status equals.

Note that the assumed causal relation between policy and outcome that is to be verified is stated as a correlation, while the relations to be controlled are stated as constants.

SUMMARY

The statement of the research objective(s) should specify: (1) the variable(s) and/or relations to be observed, and (2) the method of research required for its attainment. For an exploratory study the statement will specify the type of policy variable(s) to be identified or the global concepts, which must be clarified. For a descriptive study the statement will specify the already identified variable(s) and/or relations to be observed. For an explanatory study the statement will specify the conditions of causality to be verified, i.e., the presumed causal relation to be observed and the alternative causal relations to be controlled. The method identified to attain that objective must be consistent with the form in which the research objective is stated.

The research objective(s) may be modified by decisions made at subsequent design stages. Thus the choice of study population will result in a refinement of the variables and relations to be investigated. The selection of procedures for the collection and analysis of data will result in their further refinement. At the conclusion of the design process these refinements are then fed back into the statement of the research objective(s), resulting in a very precise specification of what is to be investigated.

REFERENCES

BLALOCK, HUBERT M. JR. *Social Statistics.* New York: McGraw-Hill Book Co., 1960.

MORRISON, DENTON, E., and RAMON E. HENKEL. *The Significance Test Controversy.* Chicago: Aldine Publishing Co., 1970.

SELVIN, HANAN C. "A Critique of Tests of Significance in Survey Research," *American Sociological Review, 27* (October 1957), 519–527.

chapter 9 / stage 5:
study population

With the statement of the research objective(s) in hand, the analyst turns to the first technical stage of the research design process, the determination of the population to be studied. The study population consists of those individuals, objects, or events which are subject to observation by the analyst. Its design involves specifying four things: (1) the unit of observation; (2) the particular population of units to be observed; (3) the procedures for selecting units for observation, and (4) the number of units to be observed.

The primary objective in the design of the study population is to operationalize the method of the research, be it exploratory, descriptive, or explanatory. Indeed, traditionally, research design has been equated with the design of the study population. When the method is exploratory, the study population will be designed in such a way as to discover variables or their properties. When the method is descriptive, the population will be designed to permit generalizations about properties of that population on the basis of the fewest possible observations. When the purpose is explanatory, the population will be designed to verify the conditions of causality. We will describe these differences in more detail later in this chapter.

In addition to operationalizing the method of research, the study population serves another important function. It identifies the limits within which the analyst can generalize his or her findings. In policy research, interest lies in some population defined by the policy-making system as in need of public action. This we call the target population. It may be defined in legislation by the eligibility requirements to qualify for service from a public agency, or in the expression of public sentiments in the media or other public forums. However, all studies take place within a finite population of their own, that is bounded in time and space and is limited to a particular experience with the variables being observed. We call this the study population. Ideally, the analyst tries to select a study population that is identical to the target population. However, because of limited time, resources, and technical feasibility, he or she often falls short of this objective. In the next section we deal with the problem of maximizing the fit between these two populations. Since accessing the target population is common to all types of studies, we will discuss this process in a generic sense before discussing how to design a study population for each method of research.

ACCESSING THE TARGET POPULATION

Gaining access to a target population requires the analyst to distinguish among three interrelated phenomena: a target population, a sampling frame, and a study population. The *target population* is that aggregation of persons, objects, or events, called units of observation, to which the study findings are to apply; in other words, that segment of the resident population which the policy maker desires to reach with a program or, alternatively that group specified in the policy objective which has the condition to which policy making is addressed. The target population may be all unemployed persons in a given geographical locale, all elderly persons below a certain income, or all organizations operating in some sphere of public interest. However, a problem often arises in that the target population may be inaccessible as an entity for observation by the analyst. That is, one may find individual persons who are unemployed, or poor and elderly, but unless one has access to the group of unemployed or elderly persons as a whole, one has no way of knowing how many they are, or how typical are the individuals who were encountered.

This situation has given rise to the invention of the *sampling frame.* A sampling frame can be defined as a natural aggregation of units to which the analyst has access. It is represented by an enumerated or listed population of events, objects, or individuals which is bounded and remains constant over time. The elements of a sampling frame are called sampling units. In the case of the unemployed, such a frame might be applicants to all locally advertised job openings, recipients of unemployed benefits, or registrants at employment agencies. In the case of the elderly it may be recipients of social security. In the case of organizations it may be all those receiving public funds or being regulated by some public agency. The principal characteristic of such an aggregation is that some reference list or process exists whereby the aggregation as a whole can be identified. Sampling frames are used to gain access to target populations. However, it should be obvious that the two aggregations may not be identical. A

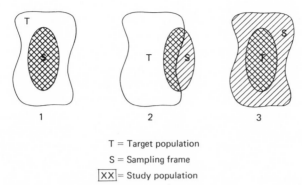

T = Target population
S = Sampling frame
XX = Study population

Figure 9-1 Alternative relationships between the target population and the sampling frame.

sampling frame of applicants to advertised job openings is substantially different from a target population of unemployed persons.

The relationship between the sampling frame and the target population is important for defining the *study population,* which can be defined as *those units which are part of the target population* and *the sampling frame.* This relationship can take any of three forms (see Figure 9-1): (1) the sampling frame can be contained within the target population, (2) the sampling frame can overlap the target population, and (3) the sampling frame can be larger than and contain the target population.

When the sampling frame is contained in the target population the study population equals the sampling frame, and may be smaller than the target population. Since no enumeration of the target population exists, one can only estimate the relationship between the study population and the target population. A special study can be undertaken in which a sampling frame is constructed of a representative portion of the target population to estimate the gap between the two populations. When the sampling frame overlaps the target population the study population is smaller than either. Again, the only way to estimate the difference between the study population and the target population is through special pilot studies. When the sampling frame is larger than the target population and thus contains it, the study population equals the target population. Such a situation provides the greatest accuracy because the target population can be completely enumerated. However, this situation creates the greatest expense in data collection, since extra units must be observed which are not part of the target population. When the excess is not large, data can be collected on the sampling frame with the addition of items, called screens, by which nonmembers of the target population can be identified and eliminated from the study findings. When the sampling frame is significantly larger, the study population must be derived in a two-step process. First a survey is conducted of the sampling frame to enumerate the target population. This enumeration then becomes a new sampling frame which is coterminous with the target population and thus the study population.*

It is crucial that the analyst maintain a clear distinction between study population, target population, and sampling frame when making inferences from the study findings. A sampling frame allows us to draw a probability sample, and from it to make precise estimates about characteristics of the study population. However, we have no such device for inferring these same characteristics about the target population. That is to say, with sampling techniques we can generalize from a sample to the study population, but not from the study population to the target population. In order to take this step, we must rely on logic or the face validity of the similarity in definition of the two populations, and on the importance which any dissimilarities may have for the conclusions to be drawn.

Up to this point we have been discussing the study population as a function of the relationship between the sampling frame and the target population. However, in some studies the unit of observation is not the same as the reporting unit. A reporting unit may be a public record or a person. Minutes of meetings may be used as a report of actions taken by an organization, and teachers or health workers may be asked to report data on their clients. When a reporting unit differs from the unit of observation, the analyst must clearly specify the unit of observation as distinct from the reporting unit, so that data collected may be analyzed in terms of the proper units. For example, if the analyst wishes to estimate the number of children with learning disabilities in a given school, and uses as the basis of observations teachers' reports, his or her estimate should be expressed in terms of the number of children in the school so observed, and not the number of teachers making such reports.**

Variations in the relationship between the study population and the target population can be illustrated by four examples (see Figure 9-2). The most typical is probably the *U.S. Census of Population.* The target population is all

---

*We have been discussing the relationship between the sampling frame and the target population under the assumption that the sampling units are the same as the units of observation. When the units are different, an additional step is needed to define the study population. For example, in the case of a study in which the sampling frame consists of dwelling units and the target population consists of elderly persons, some sampling units will contain more units of observation than others; some households may have one elderly person and some may have two or more. A decision must be made about which units to observe in each sampling unit: all may be observed, some set proportion of each household may be observed, or some random procedure for picking a respondent in each household may be adopted.

**In studies involving secondary data from such sources as the U.S. Census, public records, or surveys of business activities, the set of respondents may not be apparent. However, all such data were derived from some reporting unit, be it a household member, public official, or firm representative. Such respondents should be explicated as a check on the reliability and validity of the resulting study population.

Figure 9-2 Four examples relating study population to target population, sampling frame, and reporting unit

STUDY	TARGET POPULATION	SAMPLING FRAME	REPORTING UNIT	STUDY POPULATION
U.S. Census	citizens of the U.S.	dwelling units in U.S. and registries of U.S. embassies	head of household in dwelling unit	residents in U.S. dwelling units or registered with U.S. embassies, as reported by head of household
School dropouts	students who drop out of high school before graduating	former high-school students who are not enrolled and have not graduated	former high-school students who are not enrolled	former high-school students who are not enrolled, did not transfer to another school, or did not graduate
Skid row	skid rowers	beds in transient facilities located in geographical area encompassing skid row services	occupants of beds in same	occupants of beds in same who participate in skid row way of life
Client study	clients of service agency	clients of service agency	clients of service agency	clients of service agency

U.S. citizens. However, there is no ready access to such a population—there is no up-to-date list of citizens. Since everyone has to reside somewhere, the most systematic and feasible sampling frame is dwelling units. It should be noted that even for purposes of a complete enumeration (when samples are not drawn), a sampling frame is necessary in order to determine the extent to which the entire target population has been observed. The census is a reasonably good example of diagram 1, Figure 9-1, in which the target population exceeds the sampling frame. A few persons will be on the road or in transient facilities at the time of the enumeration. An attempt is made to reduce this gap by interviewing occupants of all hotels on a given night. Some citizens will be out of the country, and an attempt is made to enumerate them through U.S. embassies abroad. Heads of households are used to gather information about all units of observation in each dwelling unit. Therefore, the study population can be defined most precisely as *residents in dwelling units in the United States and citizens registered at U.S. embassies abroad, as reported by heads of households.*

A different pattern is illustrated by a hypothetical study of school dropouts. Here the target population is all students who drop out of high school before graduating. However, there is no sampling frame of school dropouts. The only systematic records are of former students who have not graduated and are not enrolled in a given semester. Former students who transfer to another school can be identified only if a transfer record has been requested. Therefore, the sampling frame will be a list of former students who have not graduated and are not enrolled in high school. Such a situation is an example of diagram 3 in Figure 9-1, in which the sampling frame exceeds the target population. Some units of observation in the sampling frame will have transferred to other schools, a few might even have graduated ahead of their age group. In such cases, data collection procedures must identify members of the sampling frame who are not members of the target population. In this example the reporting unit is the same as the unit of observation. Therefore, the study population can be defined as *former high-school students who are not enrolled, have not graduated, and did not transfer to another school.*

Studies of skid row provide an example of a study population that represents a significant overlap between a sampling frame and a target population and thus illustrates diagram 2 in Figure 9-1 (Bogue 1963, pp. 511–514). The target population of persons who live on skid row or participate in the skid row way of life is not listed. To draw up such a list would be inordinately expensive, since the target population is a relatively small proportion of the total number of households in any community. However, the residents of skid row inhabit distinctive types of dwellings, namely missions and cheap rooming houses, that are usually clustered in identifiable sections of a city. Such facilities can provide the basis for a sampling frame.

Since there are no explicit physical boundaries to skid row, the criteria to be used to determine which buildings to include becomes a problem. The criterion usually relied on is the location of services commonly utilized by skid rowers. A geographical boundary can be established within a certain distance from all consumer facilities frequented by skid rowers. Any residential facility catering to transients (rooming house, mission, hotel) falling within that boundary would locate the sampling frame, the beds in those facilities constituting the actual frame.

The residential instability of the skid row population creates a unique problem in identifying the study population. Since the sampling frame is defined by place of rest, and the beds in the rooming houses are the sampling units, the sampling frame is stable over time. The study population will consist, therefore, of all occupants of beds on a given night. When a stable sampling unit is used to observe an unstable target population, the assumption must be made that the target population is relatively homogeneous, that any individual who falls into the sampling frame on any given occasion is similar to any other individual he or she may replace.

The problem of overlap in such a case is considerable. Not all occupants of beds in transient facilities will be participants in the skid row way of life. They can be screened out by data on labor force characteristics and/or drinking habits. However, a substantial portion of the target population will fall outside this sampling frame. They are the skid rowers who sleep on the street or in the parks, who stay in facilities outside the geographical area of the sampling frame, or who may be "on the road." The resulting study population underrepresents the target population by an unknown and probably significant amount. Thus the study population for a skid row study can be defined as *occupants of beds in transient residences located within a geographical district that incorporates services used by skid rowers, and who participate in the skid row way of life.* The target population is skid rowers, the sampling frame is beds in transient facilities located in a skid row district, and the study population is occupants of such beds who have skid row characteristics.

The final example is the case in which the sampling frame is coterminous with the target population. Such situations occur when the target population *is* a sampling frame, as in the case of the membership or client roster of formal organizations such as service agencies, places of employment, and membership organizations.

The process of deriving a study population is guided by a simple principle. The analyst should endeavor to select a sampling frame that comes closest to incorporating the target population or has a known relationship to it.

STEPS IN DESIGNING A STUDY POPULATION

Up to this point we have been discussing how to define a study population that accurately reflects the target population of concern to the policy maker. We turn now to a discussion of the steps involved in designing that population so as to attain the research objective. Four steps are involved: (1) specifying the unit of observation, (2) specifying the population to be observed, (3) specifying procedures for selecting units for observation, and (4) specifying the number of units to be observed.

Specifying the unit of observation. The analyst must first specify the unit of observation to which the findings are to apply. The units are those proto-typal persons, objects, or events that comprise the target population specified in the policy objective.* As we already noted, this specification indicates the unit in terms of which the data will be analyzed and the findings reported, even though data collection is accomplished through some other unit. The analyst may have a complex unit of observation, which is then observed by collecting data from its subunits. For example, the analyst may be measuring "organizational effectiveness," in which case the unit of observation is an organization; or "neighborhood stability," in which case the unit of observation is a neighborhood. In both cases, however, the sources of information may be expressed as characteristics of lower-level units of observation, for example, employees or households. The analyst must somehow combine the observations from the subunits into some composite reflection of the complex unit of observation.

Specifying the population to be observed. Once the unit of observation has been identified, the analyst must specify that particular population or aggregation of units which is the subject of observation—that is, the study population. The boundaries of the study population are determined, according to our definition, by the fit between the respective boundaries of the target population and the sampling frame. The boundaries of the target population are expressed in the statement of the policy objective that appears in the conceptual framework. When the policy objective has been adequately specified, it refers to a finite population with explicit boundaries. When the objective has not been explicitly identified, such boundaries may have to be ferretted out through probing discussions with the policy maker. The boundaries of the sampling frame are defined by those characteristics according to which persons, events, or objects are listed in the frame. Thus, in executing step 2, the analyst must do three things; he or she must (1) identify the boundaries of the target population, (2) identify the boundaries of the sampling frame, and (3) when the first set cannot be completely superimposed on the second, identify the convergence of the two sets of boundaries.

The boundaries of any one of these aggregations—the target population, the sampling frame, or the study population—are expressed in three dimensions: temporal, spatial, and experiential (Hyman 1955, pp. 109f.). The *temporal*

---

*When the focus of the research is some variable in the conceptual framework other than the policy objective, such as an intervening variable or the policy action itself, then the person, object, or event to which that variable pertains is the unit of observation.

dimension refers to the specific period of time during which the population is observed or listed. The temporal dimension of the sampling frame may differ from the time of observation, and the time of observation may differ from the time of implementing a policy. Thus, the temporal dimension of the study population has an important bearing on the generalizability of the study findings and should, therefore, be identified. The nature of unemployment in 1980 is quite different from that in 1960, as changes in the supply of jobs, the level of education of job seekers, the role of women, and the prevalence of the work ethic converge to create a qualitatively different phenomenon. The *spatial dimension* refers to the specific geographical area in which the population is located, be it a neighborhood, city, county, state, or other geographical subdivision. The spatial dimension should be expressed in observable, physical terms, such as census tracts, political jurisdictions, streets, rivers, or other man-made or natural demarcations. For example, in referring to a neighborhood, the analyst cannot simply rely on the reader's perception of the neighborhood's boundaries but must actually specify the streets, census tracts, or other observable referents of those boundaries. To the extent that the phenomenon under study is correlated with important spatial features of the investigation, the findings will be of limited application and will require the analyst to be quite specific about these spatial dimensions. The *experiential dimension* of the population refers to the operational expression of the variable under study. A given analysis cannot deal with all forms of unemployment, but may focus on that reflected among persons registered for work at an employment agency; it cannot deal with all forms of mental retardation, but may focus on that reflected by certain levels of IQ.

Once the boundaries of the target population and the sampling frame have been specified, the analyst can determine the boundaries of the study population. When the sampling frame is contained within the target population (see Figure 9-1, diagram 1), the boundaries of the sampling frame become the boundaries of the study population. When the sampling frame overlaps the target population (Figure 9-1, diagram 2), the boundaries of the study population are derived from the boundaries of the sampling frame and those characteristics used to exclude nonmembers of the target population from the frame. When the sampling frame contains the target population (Figure 9-1, diagram 3), the boundaries of the target population become the boundaries of the study population. In the last two instances, the variables that distinguish the two sets of boundaries must be observed in order to identify the study population. These variables will reappear in stage 6 of the research design as data to be collected.

Procedures for selecting units for observation. Once the study population has been defined, the analyst must determine the procedures to be used in selecting units for observation. If all members of the study population are to be observed, no selection procedures are required. However, in most studies, either because of the method required by the research objective or because of costs, only a portion of that population undergoes observation. In such a circumstance the analyst must specify the procedures he or she will use in selecting those units to be observed. Since selection procedures vary significantly from one method to another, they will be discussed in connection with designing the study population for exploratory, descriptive, and explanatory studies.

Number of units to be observed. The final step in designing the study population is to determine the number of units to be observed. This number affects two aspects of the research design: the reliability of the study findings and the cost of conducting the study. On the one hand, the analyst tries to increase the number of observations in order to maximize the reliability of the findings. On the other hand, he or she tries to get by with as few observations as possible in order to minimize costs. Thus, in designing a study the analyst seeks to determine the number of units to be observed to achieve an acceptable level of reliability at an affordable cost. The importance of reliability will vary from one type of study to another, as will become apparent in the material to follow.

DESIGNING AN EXPLORATORY STUDY POPULATION

To recapitulate, the purpose of an exploratory study is to discover some variable that is missing from the conceptual framework or some component of a global concept that has so far gone unspecified. The study population appropriate for such a purpose consists of units of the target population that have contrasting values on some variable that is known and is considered to be causally linked to the missing policy variable. The known variable serves as a criterion by which to judge the suitability of each of the candidates for the missing variable. The criterion variable may be either an antecedent or a consequence of the missing variable, for example, it may be a known intervention that precedes an unknown consequence, or it may be an objective brought about by an unknown intervention. By examining cases which represent contrasting values on the criterion variable, one can discover what other characteristics the cases have in common, and in what ways they also differ. The ways in which the cases differ are the presumed missing variables.

This procedure can be enhanced by using adjunct and constraint variables to further stratify the study population and thus to increase the likelihood of discovering missing variables. In studies of the behavior of individuals, demographic characteristics such as age, sex, and income are used. In studies of social change, the position of persons in the process is used—active versus marginal participants, leaders versus followers, new versus long-term participants. In studies of organizations, structural characteristics such as size, complexity, amount of resources, distribution of power, and decision-making procedures come into play.

The addition of adjunct and constraint variables can be accomplished in either of two ways. The values of the additional variables can be added to those of the criterion variable to form a complex criterion by which to differentiate the cases that make up the study population. Or the criterion variable can be stratified by contrasting values of each of the other variables, creating a study population based on a $2 \times 2 \times 2 \times \ldots$ matrix. This second practice increases the number of cases which an analyst must observe, but provides more specificity in the comparisons to be made, and thus generates a range of missing variables, each of which fits a specific comparison.

Specifying The Population of Units To Be Observed

Determining the study population in an exploratory study is a somewhat complicated procedure. Not only must a sampling frame be found which identifies or lists the units of observation exhibiting the condition specified in the policy objective, it must also identify units for which values on the criterion variable(s) are known. This additional dimension to the boundaries can result in a study population significantly smaller than the target population.

Since the purpose of an exploratory study is discovery and not representativeness, the requirements for a sampling frame are relatively lax. It can take any one of three forms: (1) the findings of a previous survey of the target population which lists each unit of observation by its value on the criterion variable, for example, a national study of the local public housing authorities which identified the occupancy rates of individual authorities; (2) the selection by expert judges who have intimate knowledge of the target population, for example, the selection by officials in the state office of education of various school systems that have been successful, or unsuccessful, in school desegregation; and (3) systematic sampling of various spatial locations of the target population at different times in order to select units of observation that have contrasting values on the criterion variable, for example, the analyst may sample various times of operation and locations on a public playground to identify satisfied and unsatisfied users of a municipal recreation program (Schatzman and Strauss 1973, McMahon and Pugh 1970).

Procedures for Selecting Units for Observation

Procedures for selecting units for observation in an exploratory study are usually based on purposive rather than random sampling (Chein 1976, pp. 517–521). Units are selected on the basis of their contrasting values on a variable that the analyst knows is highly correlated with the type of variable that is missing. Using one of the sampling frames just discussed, the analyst may select one or more units from the extreme categories of the criterion variable on the basis of his or her subjective judgment as to their representativeness, or on the basis of randomness or of convenience.

When the analyst does not have enough concrete knowledge of the criterion variable to form distinct categories or values, a process called "snowball sampling" is useful (McCall and Simmons 1969, pp. 64-67). For example, the analyst may know that the ethnic content of the curriculum is an important variable in determining relative academic achievement, but not know what alternative forms it might take; or he/she may know that the way doctors relate to patients is important in determining the effectiveness of health care, yet not be able to categorize doctor-patient interaction. In snowball sampling the analyst draws units from the sampling frame one at a time and observes them sequentially. As the sample builds up, the distribution of cases with respect to the criterion variable will be quite varied, suggesting tentative categories for classification. As the sampling continues, additional observations begin to reinforce established categories. When no new classes are suggested, that is, when each new observation replicates the existing classification scheme, the analyst closes out the sample. Thus the sampling procedure is analogous to the building of a snowball. There is no predetermined quota or size to be achieved—the sample size simply evolves from the sampling process.

Number of Units To Be Observed

Exploratory studies generally have small study populations. However, since the discovery of properties, rather than their distribution is the major purpose to be achieved, the number of units observed is a relatively unimportant issue. Furthermore, the open-ended nature of the method makes it difficult to specify at the outset the number of units to be observed. The analyst must often pursue the study case by case until a pattern emerges in the variables or relationships being observed. In this sense, size emerges as an outcome of the study. However, some limits to the size of the study population can be indicated. When the study is longitudinal, involving change in the criterion variable over time, the population can be as small as one. When the study is cross-sectional, that is, when observation of differences occurs at one point in time, at least one case must be selected from each category of the criterion variable(s). The number of cases will depend on the homogeneity of the category. As a general rule, an exploratory study population would not exceed 20 cases. Otherwise it would incur excessive costs that result from using an open-ended and relatively unstructured method with a larger population.

An Example

Returning to our study of school desegregation, let us assume that the U.S. Office of Education (USOE) has as its objective to equalize academic achievement among racial and ethnic groups in desegregated schools. The Office seeks to determine what policies or programs might lead to this objective. Since relatively little knowledge exists about this policy problem, USOE turns to exploratory research to discover alternative courses of action. In this study the unit of observation is a school system, and the target population is all school systems in the United States undergoing desegregation as of the date on which the study was requested. The sampling frame for such a target population is the records kept by the Office of Civil Rights in the Department of Health, Education and Welfare (HEW) of school systems which are or have been under court order to desegregate. The preliminary statement of the study population, therefore, would be *U.S. school systems under court order to desegregate as reported by HEW as of (date of the report).*

To commence the exploratory study, the study population must be delimited further in terms of values on a criterion variable that allows it to be stratified into contrasting groups. In this case that criterion is the dependent variable (the objective of policy), "relative academic achievement." We must compare schools which have achieved near equality with schools that have obviously failed in order to identify programs or policies associated with the former and not the latter. This criterion requires us to move the temporal dimension of the study population back far enough in time so that such outcomes might have occurred. A sampling frame based on such a criterion exists in the form of a study recently completed for USOE of academic achievement among schools receiving funds from the Emergency School Assistance Program (ESAP) to enable them to implement court-ordered desegregation. Thus the study population becomes further defined as *U.S. school systems participating in the USOE study of ESAP funds as of (date of study).* Since our conceptual framework identifies relative social class as a constraint variable affecting relative academic achivement, we might choose to include median family income of students of each race as a second criterion variable. Because this information is available for each school in the ESAP study, its inclusion does not further restrict our study population.

There remains the question of how units are to be selected from this population for observation. We have, in essence, four groups to sample: (1) those relatively equal on achievement and relatively equal on family income, (2) those relatively equal on achievement and unequal on family income, (3) those relatively unequal on achievement and equal on family income, and (4) those relatively unequal on achievement and relatively unequal on family income. Since both criterion variables are quantitative, the units of the study population can be arrayed with respect to these two variables, and the units picked from the extreme ends of each array. Since the observation of a school system is a very complex process, the availability of resources will largely determine the size of the study population. Five schools from each of the four groups would make a feasible sample for observation.

DESIGNING A DESCRIPTIVE STUDY POPULATION

The purpose of a descriptive study is to generate a quantitative estimate of the size or distribution of known variables in the target population, or the degree of association among them. To accomplish this purpose requires a study population that closely approximates the target population and from which representative samples can be drawn to produce accurate estimates at a minimal cost.

Specifying The Population of Units To Be Observed

The boundaries of the study population in a descriptive study are simply the overlap between the boundaries of the target population and those of the sampling frame, as discussed earlier in this chapter. When the phenomenon to be described is *not* the dependent variable, the boundaries of the target population must be further specified in terms of those units of observation that exhibit the variable in question. The requirement for a sampling frame in a descriptive study is much more constricting. It must be a list in which all units of observation have an equal or known probability of appearing. If the total population is to be observed, such a list will assure the analyst that all units have indeed been observed; if samples are to be observed, it will allow the analyst to measure the accuracy of his or her estimates. If no sampling frame exists, one must be developed by enumerating the target population, a process that can be quite expensive.

Procedures for Selecting Units for Observation

Before deciding on a procedure for selecting units for observation, the analyst should determine whether sampling is in fact economical under the circumstances. We defined a descriptive study as one in which the analyst maximizes the reliability of the estimate of a characteristic of the study population while minimizing the observations made. It is difficult to obtain a reliable estimate, except under ideal conditions, with a sample of less than 100 cases. Given the attrition due to error in the sampling frame and to nonresponses, the analyst would have to observe well over 100 cases in order to assure the desired number of successful observations. In fact, it probably would be uneconomical to sample a study population of 200 cases or less. In view of this, the costs of drawing the sample and of observing extra cases would be outweighed by the increase in accuracy derived from observing the total population. Consequently, after computing the sample size required to derive the estimate (see next section), the analyst should compare this with the relative costs and benefits of observing the entire study population.

Given a decision to sample, the analyst is faced with choosing the sampling procedure best suited to the research objectives and to the conditions most likely to be encountered during the data collection stage. There is a variety of standard procedures for probability sampling, so called because each unit of a population has an equal or known probability of being selected for the sample. This characteristic permits an application of the laws of probability, and the computation of quantitative measures of the representativeness of the resulting sample. These procedures and the formulas for measuring their accuracy are well discussed in the literature, and the reader who lacks a basic familiarity with the subject should consult that literature.* We will discuss briefly the advantages and disadvantages of three of the more commonly used forms: (1) simple random, (2) stratified, and (3) multistage cluster (area) sampling.

Simple random sampling, and its variant, *systematic sampling,* represent the prototypal model of probability sampling. These procedures are practical for relatively small populations that have readily available sampling frames. They are ideal for the study of the clientele of a service agency such as a school or a health program, or for the membership of a formal organization. Simple random sampling becomes relatively impractical for studies of large populations or geographically dispersed populations, however, because the absence of any clustering among sampling units necessitates a good deal of traveling between units.

A more complicated but more efficient procedure is *stratified random sampling.* The study population is first classified according to some characteristic correlated with the variable under study and then simple random samples are drawn from each class. Although stratified random sampling has the practical limitations of simple random sampling, it has two distinct advantages. One is greater efficiency. By classifying the study population into relatively homogeneous classes, the size of the overall sample can be reduced. Stratified random sampling has the additional advantage of permitting the use of different sampling ratios (the proportion of the sample to the sampling frame) for different classes. By so doing, it is possible to "oversample" a particular class that constitutes a proportion of the larger population too small to show up in a simple sample. Such a procedure is also useful in studies with multiple research objectives, one

*Lazerwitz (1968) provides a well-written and easily understood overview providing necessary operational formulas; a nonmathematical treatment is presented by Chein (1976); a very detailed and practical discussion of sampling including a particularly good discussion of sample size is provided by Parten, (1950).

of which is descriptive and one of which is exploratory or explanatory. The overall sampling frame permits the analyst to make accurate estimates of a population characteristic at least cost, and the classes enable him or her to conduct studies of contrasting cases by oversampling on relevant variables. For example, a simple random sample may produce too small a black subsample to allow any analysis of the effect of race on the dependent variable. However, by stratifying the population by race, the black stratum can be oversampled in order to produce a subsample comparable in size to that of whites.

The third procedure for probability sampling is *multistage cluster* or *area sampling*. Such sampling takes place in more than one stage. The ultimate sampling units, for example, individuals or organizations, are conceived of as clustered together geographically into larger sampling units, which in turn may be clustered into still larger sampling units. The largest clusters are sampled first; and those that are selected constitute the sampling frame for the second stage of sampling, from which those selected constitute the sampling frame for the third stage of sampling, and so on until the ultimate sampling unit is reached. For example, in a national three-stage cluster sample, the United States may be divided into a sampling frame of Standard Metropolitan Statistical Areas (SMSAs) which can be randomly sampled as stage one. Each of the selected SMSAs may be divided into a sampling frame of census tracts, which are then randomly sampled as stage two. Finally, each selected census tract can be broken down into a listing of all dwelling units, and these randomly sampled as the third and last stage.

Such a sampling procedure permits considerable savings in the cost of sampling and data collection in study populations that are geographically dispersed. It is particularly useful in planning studies of national, state, or metropolitan populations. In the previous example, not every household in the United States needed to be listed in the sampling frame, a task which would have been enormously expensive, only those in the cluster of ultimate sampling units. Furthermore, ultimate sampling units are geographically clustered, making the cost of travel to collect data much less than if they were randomly scattered around the country. However, the savings are achieved at the expense of a larger sample size, because the probability of selection for the ultimate sampling unit is conditional on the probabilities of selection of clusters at each level of the sampling process.

Number of Units To Be Observed

The number of units to be observed in a descriptive study is a critical factor in determining the reliability of estimates of characteristics in the study population. The rationale for how large a sample should be rests on probability theory. The basic propositions in this theory indicate four principal determinants of reliability: (1) the absolute size of the sample, and not its size relative to that of the study population;* (2) the homogeneity of the population, the extent to which all units are alike with respect to the variable being observed; (3) the degree of precision or amount of error the decision maker is willing to tolerate in estimating the value of the variable in the study population; and (4) the degree of certainty or level of significance required by the decision maker, that is, the probability that the estimate is correct (expressed as the number of standard error units corresponding to that probability).

In calculating the sample size necessary to meet the requirements of sampling theory, the analyst can use standard formulas (Parten 1950, Chapter 9; Lazerwitz 1968, pp. 285ff; Sudman 1976). Since the homogeneity of the population and the probability of any of its units being selected will vary with different sampling procedures, the appropriate formula must be used. If the analyst is unfamiliar with such statistical procedures, he or she can turn for technical assistance to sampling statisticians who are readily available through market research agencies, university research centers, or state and federal research offices. Some prepared tables show sample sizes required for different decision conditions. For example, Parten shows sample sizes needed for degrees of precision (limits of error), different degrees of certainty, and different levels of homogeneity under conditions of simple random sampling (Parten 1950, pp. 313–318). Thus a sample of 100 would be reliable within 7 percentage points of error, with a probability of $\geqslant 95$, in a population exhibiting the characteristic among 85 percent of the units. If population homogeneity were decreased to 50 percent, the required sample size would increase to 196. If, in addition, the degree of acceptable error were decreased to 5 percentage points, the required sample size would increase to 384. Multistage cluster sampling requires the largest sample size. For metropolitan areas under comparable decision criteria, sample size can run to 1,000; in the case of national studies it can run to several thousand.

Once the sample size has been determined on the basis of probability theory, three additional requirements must be taken into consideration: (1) the number of subsamples to be analyzed, (2) the expected response rate, and (3) the relationship of the sampling frame to the study population. If a sample is to be divided into subsamples for analysis, the overall sample size must be increased accordingly so that the data produced at the smallest subsample level are also reliable. For example, to analyze the popular vote for a presidential candidate by race *and* region, given four regions of the country and two racial groups, the total sample size would be the sum of the appropriate sizes of the eight subsamples.

The size of the sample also depends on the rate of response expected. It is rare indeed when every individual selected by the sampling procedure actually

*The size of the study population does not determine the reliability of the size of the sample. A sample large enough to be reliable for a population of 10,000 persons need be no larger for a similar population of 1,000,000 persons, given identical sampling procedures.

participates in the study. A certain amount of attrition can be expected due to faulty listings, individuals who have left the study population, or the refusal to participate once individuals are contacted. Most studies strive for an 80 percent response rate; that is, they expect an attrition during data collection of up to 20 percent of the selected sample. For this reason, the sample size must be increased at the outset by the amount of expected attrition. Thus, if it has been determined that a sample of 100 is needed to meet the requirements of probability theory, and an attrition of 20 percent is expected in the course of data collection, the actual sample size to be drawn should be $n - .20n = 100$, or $n = 125$.

Lastly, the size of the planned sample must take into account any discrepancy between the sampling frame and the target population. When the sampling frame overlaps or exceeds the target population, that is, the actual study population is something less than the enumerated units in the sampling frame (diagrams 2 and 3 in Figure 9-1), the planned sample size must be increased by that ratio so as to end up with the statistically desired sample size. If, for example, the target population is high-school-age youths in a low-income area, the sampling frame is households, the census reports that 60 percent of the households in the area have high-school-age youth, and the required sample size is 100, then the planned sample size must be $.60n = 100$, or $n = 167$. Estimates of such discrepancy can be made on the basis of a pilot study or secondary data.

To recapitulate, the planned sample size must be based on four conditions, as in the following example.

Conditions	Size
1. Statistical significance	100
2. Four subsamples	400
3. A response rate of 80 percent	500
4. A sampling frame discrepancy of 20 percent	628

It should be recognized that this discussion of sample size is an over-simplification of a complex topic, and our quantitative examples are crude. However, it will serve as an introduction to the logic of sample size so that the analyst will at least be able to translate more precise results obtained from sampling experts into implications for his or her research design.

An Example

Let us assume that the city of Knoxville, Tennessee, is considering a range of programs to be adopted in an effort to enable unemployed persons to get jobs. The city council has given priority to neighborhoods exhibiting a high level of unemployment. The objective of policy, therefore, is to reduce unemployment among those between the ages of 14 and 65 (the normal age for participation in the labor force) in neighborhoods with high unemployment. Previous studies indicate high levels of functional illiteracy as well as lack of industrial skills among the unemployed that can be attributed to migration into the city of large numbers of persons from the surrounding mountains and agricultural areas. Two programs have been designed: one, teaching basic academic skills leading to a high-school diploma; the other, training in industrial skills needed by new industries moving into the area. The research objective formulated by the analyst is

> What proportion of unemployed persons between the ages of 14 and 65 are functionally illiterate and/or lack industrial skills, in neighborhoods with a level of unemployment that exceeds that of Knoxville as a whole, as of January 18, 1979?

The unit of observation in this study is an unemployed person between the ages of 14 and 65. The target population is

> unemployed persons between the ages of 14 and 65, living in neighborhoods with a level of unemployment that exceeds that of greater Knoxville, as of January 18, 1979.

Note that this definition of the target population specifies spatial and temporal dimensions but that an experiential dimension cannot be identified since the dependent variable, unemployment, has yet to be operationally defined. Using the U.S. Census to determine the level of employment in a given neighborhood, the analyst chooses as his sampling frame dwelling units in census tracts with a rate of unemployment which exceeds that of Knoxville as a whole. The adult head of household or spouse is to be asked to report on the employment status of all persons between the ages of 14 and 65 living in each dwelling unit. Therefore, the study population is

> unemployed persons between the ages of 14 and 65, living in dwelling units in census tracts with a rate of unemployment which exceeds that of Knoxville as a whole, as of January 18, 1979, as reported by head of households.

Notice that the sampling frame greatly exceeds the study population. Those characteristics which distinguish the study population from the sampling frame will be picked up in stage 6 of the research design process as data to be collected.

The procedure adopted by the analyst for selecting units from this sampling frame is a two-stage area cluster sampling, stage one being a simple random sample of blocks selected from the combined census tracts, and stage two being a systematic random sample of dwelling units selected from each block.

In determining the number of units to observe, the analyst calculates a minimal sample size of 284 given his sampling procedure and reliability requirements. Since the level of literacy and the level of industrial skill are to be analyzed as a proportion of the total study population, no subsamples are called for; and since relatively simple household interviews are to be used to collect data, an 85 percent response rate is expected, raising the planned sample size to 334. Based on census data, the average rate of unemployment in the census tracts involved is 20 percent, indicating a large discrepancy between the sampling frame and the target population, which thus raises the planned sample size to 1670.

DESIGNING AN EXPLANATORY STUDY POPULATION

The purpose of an explanatory study, as discussed in Chapter 4, is to verify the conditions of causality: the time order of the independent and dependent variables, their concomitant variation, and the elimination of rival hypotheses. It is this last condition that is of principal concern here, for only through the proper design of the study population can rival hypotheses be eliminated.

In Chapter 3 we noted that there are three types of explanatory studies: the pure, the natural, and the ex post facto experiment. (The last two are often referred to as quasi-experiments.) The pure experiment is one in which the analyst can control exposure to the independent variable, either by manipulating the independent variable or by assigning individuals to groups that will vary in their exposure to it. This characteristic permits the analyst to eliminate the maximum number of alternative hypotheses. The pure experiment is also prospective. This characteristic allows the analyst to know, from his or her own observation, which individuals were exposed or not exposed to the independent variable. The analyst is present during the experiment and can monitor participation in it.

In the natural experiment, the analyst cannot control exposure to the independent variable. He or she must take as the study population groups of individuals whose exposure or nonexposure was determined by the natural course of events. For this reason, such an experiment is limited in the number of alternative hypotheses that can be eliminated. However, the natural experiment is also prospective, so that the analyst can ascertain participation in the experiment by direct observation. In the ex post facto experiment, the analyst again lacks control over exposure to the independent variable, and the ability to eliminate rival hypotheses is similarly limited. An additional limiting condition, however, is that the ex post facto study is retrospective. It is designed after exposure to the independent variable, and the members of the target population available to the analyst are those present at the conclusion of the experiment, rather than at its outset. Thus, in order to proceed in the verification from cause-to-effect (see pp. 36f.) the analyst must reconstruct through the collection of data a study population that was present before as well as after exposure to the independent variable.

Although the principal consideration in designing the study population of an explanatory study is the control of those variables that represent alternative hypotheses, additional considerations will enter into the design depending on the nature of the circumstances under which the study is conducted. In natural and ex post facto experiments, whether or not members of the target population will be or have been exposed to the independent variable becomes a factor in selecting units for observation. In an ex post facto study the population to be observed must be further defined as those who were present both before and after change in the independent variable.

At this point it is necessary to elaborate the process of eliminating rival hypotheses, or variable control. A variable can be said to be controlled when it operates uniformly on all units under observation. This permits the analyst to observe the effects of variations in the independent variable without having these effects confounded by those of the extraneous variable. Control can be achieved in either of two ways: by designing the study population so that all units of it have the same value on the variable to be controlled, or by designing the subgroups of the study population so that the distribution of their values on the variable to be controlled is comparable. The first method involves defining the boundaries of the study population; the second, selecting units from the population for observation. For example, in controlling for social class in our study of academic performance under school desegregation, we could either confine our study to students of the same social class, or we could have the same proportion of students from each social class in each group undergoing a specific level of desegregation. Equalizing the value of the variable to be controlled allows the analyst to have fewer cases to observe. Because of the greater homogeneity, any effect of the independent variable will be more apparent. On the other hand, having a similar distribution of values has the advantage of allowing greater generalizability of the study findings, because the hypothesis is tested under a wider range of circumstances.

Specifying The Population of Units To Be Observed

The definition of the study population begins, as in exploratory and descriptive studies, with the target population referred to in the policy objective, namely, the population of persons, objects, or events exhibiting the condition which is the objective of policy making. However, in an explanatory study other dimensions may be added in order to verify causality. If the analyst is to eliminate a rival hypothesis by equalizing the value of an extraneous variable, that value becomes an added dimension to the boundaries distinguishing the study population. For example, if, in a study of the effectiveness of manpower training, age is to be controlled by limiting the study to trainees between the ages of 20 and 35, that age range is added to the dimensions defining the study population.

Since the purpose of an explanatory study does not require making generalizations to some larger population, any of the sampling frames mentioned previously can be used—a list that permits probability sampling, a list generated by a panel of experts, or a list of the spatial and temporal locations of the target population. When the sampling frame chosen permits probability sampling, the resulting study population can serve both explanatory and descriptive purposes. By dividing the frame into strata based on exposure to the independent variable, the strata can be sampled disproportionately to meet the requirements of the explanatory study, but the results can be combined proportionately by means of their respective sampling ratios to meet the requirements of a descriptive study.

The sampling frame is more constricted in an explanatory study than in a descriptive study. In order to control variables reflected in rival hypotheses, a sampling frame must be found which not only lists members of the target population, but also identifies each member's values on the variables to be controlled. For example, in studying neonatal mortality the analyst may wish to control for the effects of age, prior pregnancies, and prior medical care. To do so would require a sampling frame that identifies the age, prior number of pregnancies, and prior level of health care of a population of pregnant women. If the study is a quasi-experiment, whether or not the unit of observation was or will be exposed to the independent variable under study is another datum that must be reflected in the sampling frame. Because of the costs of collecting such information it is most likely that such a frame, if available, will include only a portion of the target population. When such a frame is used, the population available for observation is further restricted.

When the data necessary to eliminate rival hypotheses are not present in the sampling frame, or when the analyst chooses not to restrict the study to such a frame, the collection of these data must be provided for elsewhere in the research design. In doing so the analyst has two choices. The data can be collected during the process of selecting units for observation, in a sense creating a second sampling frame prior to the main process of data collection. Or the data on variables to be controlled can be collected along with the data on all other variables to be observed. Under this second option, variable control is accomplished by use of statistical techniques carried out during the analysis of data, rather than by the design of the study population. In actual practice both procedures are often used. Those variables for which it is feasible to do so are controlled through the design of the study population. The remainder are controlled statistically during the data analysis stage of the study.

Procedures for Selecting Units for Observation

The elimination of rival hypotheses or variable control through the selection of units for observation involves two steps—group design and group composition. *Group design* refers to the number of groups to be observed and their respective exposure to the independent variable. *Group composition* refers to the process by which groups are formed. The alternative designs that result from variations in each step control different types of variables. Therefore, before discussing procedures that can be applied at each step, let's differentiate five types of variables that may need to be controlled in an explanatory study.

The first type is the *awareness of being studied,* sometimes known as "the Hawthorne effect." It is usually precipitated by some kind of pretest measure that leads the subject to think about the issues reflected by the dependent variable before he or she has been exposed to the independent variable.

A second type are *environmental events* over which the analyst has no control within the context of his or her study; for example, the enactment of legislation, a court ruling, or a change in the level of public taxation or expenditures. Most studies in the public policy area are susceptible to such environmental changes.

A third type consists of *individual characteristics which are dynamic* in nature and cannot be assumed to be stable for any length of time, for example, human maturation or the natural tendency of human beings to change over time. Children tend to learn with age irrespective of formal education; the elderly tend to deteriorate in spite of the beneficial effects of intervention programs.

A fourth type consists of *characteristics of individuals which can be considered fixed* or unchangeable during the life of the study being designed; for example, demographic characteristics such as sex and race, or prior experience such as number of previous arrests or length of prior treatment.

A fifth type is *self-selection,* which refers to the tendency of people to volunteer for programs or elect to live in environments that are consistent with their own values or goals. It is because of this last set of variables that the analyst cannot summarily conclude that changes in the dependent variable necessarily reflect the effect of the policy being tested. Personal disposition plays a large part; for example, mothers who have personal habits that in themselves may prevent neonatal fatality may seek out prenatal care; and persons who favor racial equality may attend desegregated schools.

In general it can be said that the first three types of variables can be controlled through group design, and the latter two through group composition. We will discuss each of these steps in the design sequence.

Variable Control Through Group Design

Variable control through group design involves dividing the study population into comparison groups based on whether or not the units of observation will be or have been exposed to the independent variable. In this way the effect of the independent variable is measured by change in the dependent variable. The literature on group design is extensive and should be consulted for each alternative discussed (Ross and Smith 1968, Campbell and Stanley 1963). Our summary discussion will focus on the implications of alternative designs for achieving research objectives.

The simplest alternative is the *one-group design,* in which a single group is observed both prior to and after being exposed to the independent variable. Such a design is the most efficient way of controlling for fixed individual characteristics (type 4). Since the control group (before) and the experimental group (after) consist of the same individuals, no more perfect control of such variables is possible. However, the one-group design cannot control for the effects of prestesting (type 1), environmental changes (type 2), or dynamic individual characteristics (type 3) (see Figure 9-3). Nonetheless, the one-group design may be the only feasible alternative in a given policy context. The acceptability of this situation is eased by evidence of reasoning that the variables left uncontrolled are static or not operable in the research context under consideration.

By contrast, the *two-group design,* in which both groups are comparable with respect to fixed individual characteristics, provides a means of controlling for the effect of pretesting (type 1), environmental changes (type 2), and dynamic individual characteristics (type 3). The relative effect of the independent variable is indicated by the difference between the groups in their respective "gain scores"—their posttest minus their pretest measures. However, this design does not permit the analyst to estimate the absolute effect of the independent variable nor the separate effects of the variables controlled. The analyst knows whether or not the independent variable has an additive effect,

Figure 9-3 Alternative experimental group designs

NUMBER OF GROUPS	VARIABLES TO WHICH GROUPS ARE EXPOSED			
	Pretest	Independent	Environmental and dynamic individual	Posttest
1	X	X	X	X
2a.	X	X	X	X
b.	X	. . .	X	X
4a.	X	X	X	X
b.	X	. . .	X	X
c.	. . .	X	X	X
d.	. . .	. . .	X	X

Source: Adapted from John Ross and Perry Smith, "Orthodox Experimental Designs," in METHODOLOGY IN SOCIAL RESEARCH, ed. Hubert M. Blalock, Jr., and Ann B. Blalock (New York: McGraw-Hill Book Company, 1968), pp. 355ff.

but he or she does not know the size of that effect apart from its interaction with other variables present in the design.

For this reason, the analyst may wish to turn to the *four-group design*. This alternative allows the analyst to derive separate estimates for the effect of the independent variable and for the effect of pretesting (type 1), and a combined estimate for environmental changes (type 2), and dynamic individual characteristics (type 3). These estimates are derived by a series of intergroup comparisons of the gain scores for each group (Ross and Smith 1968, pp. 360–366). This alternative is based on the assumption that fixed individual characteristics have been controlled through the assignment of units of observation to groups.

In choosing among alternative group designs, the analyst will have to decide the relative importance of each type of variable. For example, pretesting may not need control when the interventions being tested do not have as their primary purpose a change in subjects' attitudes but some objective change, such as in housing conditions, job opportunities, or financial resources; or when subjects are observed unobtrusively. On the other hand, the analyst may control for the separate effect of additional variables by adding to his or her design a group for each additional variable to be tested.

Variable Control Through The Composition of Groups

The way in which groups are composed controls for fixed individual factors (type 4) and self-selection (type 5). There are three alternative ways of composing groups—by means of precision control, frequency distribution control, or randomization (Greenwood 1945).

In *precision control* all units of observation are individually matched on the variables being controlled in each of the groups in the design. The extreme example of this procedure is the use of twins. Because of the demand for simultaneous matching on several dimensions, such a procedure obviously requires a very large pool from which to draw units of observation. Furthermore, precision control controls only those factors that enter into the matching process. In *frequency distribution control* all groups in the design are matched with respect to one factor at a time; that is, all groups have the same distribution by age and race, but the two factors are not identical in the same unit of observation. Frequency distribution control requires a much smaller pool of units of observation and is therefore less costly. However, it results in less rigorous control of the variables involved. Under *randomization* groups are composed by some random process, so that the resulting distributions of variables to be controlled can be attributed to chance, and so tested. Randomization can be achieved by (1) drawing each group of units as a random sample from the same study population prior to their exposure to the independent variable, (2) randomly assigning units of observation to the respective groups in the design, and (3) randomly assigning exposure to the independent variable to groups formed on the basis of precision or frequency control.*

Randomization has two distinct advantages: It controls for self-selection (type 5) and for additional individual fixed characteristics beyond those controlled through a matching procedure. The disadvantage of randomization is that each group in the design is heterogeneous, so that differences in response are less likely to occur between those groups exposed and those not exposed to the independent variable. For this reason the most efficient procedure is to combine randomization with precision control. Units of observation are either matched or stratified in terms of one or two key variables to be controlled. The members of each match or stratum are then randomly assigned to the respective groups to control for all other individual characteristics, including self-selection. This procedure provides greater precision in the control of known individual characteristics while at the same time controlling unknown ones.

The alternative procedures for group composition constitute a means for distinguishing so-called pure from quasi-experiments. In the pure experiment, some form of randomization must be used, either in composing groups for observation or in assigning groups to be exposed to the independent variable. In policy research, however, such procedures rarely can be used. Most public programs or policies apply to all units of the target population, making it legally or politically impossible to withhold the program from some and not others. In such cases precision or frequency distribution control can be combined with any one of the group designs to create quasi-experiments. However, matching or frequency distribution control in quasi-experiments is no easy task. It involves finding groups formed by some process other than that initiated by the analyst and that are reasonably comparable with respect to the variables being controlled. Three alternatives are available: (1) the selection of comparable units outside the target population that will not be exposed to the intervention, (2) the selection of those waiting to be served by the program, (3) the use of a time series of observations during the life of the program (Weiss 1972, pp. 67–68; Nunnally 1975).

Number of Units To Be Observed

As has been noted earlier, an explanatory study can involve only one unit of observation, in the case of a one-group design, or as few as two units, in the case of a two-group design. Such designs are called a "case study" and a "com-

---

*Where randomization is not possible, an alternate approach to controlling for self-selection is to select a study population in which exposure to the independent variable is non-volitional, for example, persons experiencing a natural disaster, inmates of a correctional institution, or students in a public school. Deutsch and Collins (1965) provide a good example of this approach.

parative study," respectively. However, increasing the number of units to be observed allows the analyst to control for a larger number of alternative hypotheses and hence to generalize the study findings to a larger set of circumstances. In addition, the technique to be used to analyze the data will generate requirements for the number of units to be observed (see Chapter 8). The design of an explanatory study should strive, at a minimum, for a sufficient number of units in each group to allow the elimination of the null hypothesis that chance accounts for the difference found among the groups. Such a number depends on a variety of factors, including the mathematical properties of the data, the amount of difference between the groups in the design, and the degree of certainty (the confidence interval) required by the analysis. For a precise determination the analyst should seek advice from a statistical expert. A minimal number which fits many situations is 20 units in each group. As the number of groups in the design increases, the number of units to be observed increases accordingly. Thus, in a four-group design, requiring 20 units per group, the minimal population to be observed would be 80.

An Example

The New Jersey Negative Income Tax Experiment (NITE) (Pechman and Timpane 1975) provides a good example of the design of a population in an explanatory study that comes close to being a pure experiment. In relating this example, we shall depart from the real case in order to illustrate the procedures outlined in this chapter, all of which were not followed in NITE. The research objective is to determine the effect of a variety of negative income tax rates on the incentive to work among low-income persons in the labor market. The unit of observation is the low-income household (one having an income not exceeding 150 percent of the official poverty level), with a male member in the labor force (one between the ages of 18 and 58 who is neither a student, a ward of an institution, nor a member of the armed services). The target population as defined by the client in this study, the U.S. Office of Economic Opportunity, is all such households in the U.S. However, since it is infeasible to conduct such an experiment on a national scale, this particular study is confined to urban areas in New Jersey. (Additional studies were subsequently conducted in other regions to provide a more representative national picture.)

We can identify a number of variables that must be controlled. For one thing, it is possible that marked increases or decreases in the supply of jobs in the local labor market due either to seasonal fluctuations or the relocation of employers, could affect incentive to work. This variable will be controlled by observing only units of the target population who reside in similar labor markets. For this purpose the cities of Passaic, Paterson, Jersey City, and Trenton are chosen.* Controlling this first variable results in further restricting the target population in this study to

> low-income households with a male member in the labor force in Passaic, Paterson, Jersey City, and Trenton, New Jersey.

A second variable that must be controlled is ethnicity. It is possible that households of different ethnic groups may respond to the labor market differently, depending on perceived or experienced barriers to job finding. Ethnicity will be controlled by using a comparable distribution in all groups in the research design. Lastly, since incentive to work is a mental process, it is conceivable that any inquiry about a respondent's efforts to obtain or maintain employment might substantially affect that variable. Therefore, pretesting will be controlled by adding groups to the design that will not be pretested.

The target population in this study cannot be observed directly because it does not coincide with any available sampling frame. In this type of study a two-level sampling frame is appropriate. The first level consists of those census tracts in the three cities that have the highest percentage of income-eligible households and the highest percentage of each ethnic group. The second level of the sampling frame consists of all households in the above tracts that are income eligible and of the appropriate ethnic group. These households are identified by interviews conducted in each tract, starting with tracts with the highest proportion of income eligibles in each ethnic group and continuing until a list of such households has been obtained large enough to accommodate the group design. (In the actual study, 29,000 such interviews were conducted.)

The design required to test four levels of negative income tax and control for ethnicity and pretesting calls for 30 groups. The number of units of observation needed to fill this design is estimated to be 1320 (see Figure 9-4). (In the actual study 1216 households were used.) This number was arrived at by inflating the minimum number of households required for each group to allow for attrition during the life of the study. The rate of attrition is expected to vary from one intervention to another, for example, the group experiencing intervention 4 is expected to have twice the attrition rate as that exposed to intervention 1. Units from each ethnic group in the sampling frame will be randomly assigned to the respective groups in the design.

For the purpose of illustrating how variable control is carried out in quasi-experiments, let us turn to a hypothetical example of a natural experiment. Let us assume that the City of Chicago has decided to undertake a program that provides low-interest loans for home improvement to families below a certain income level. The objective of this program is not only to improve the

---

*We will assume similarity of labor markets even though the designers of the original study do not comment on this variable in selecting these cities.

Figure 9-4 Group design and associated sizes for explanatory study of negative income tax (pure experiment)

| | CONTROL VARIABLE | | | | | | |
| | Black | | White | | Puerto Rican | | |
Intervention	pretest	no	pretest	no	pretest	no	Total
1	30	30	30	30	30	30	180
2	30	30	30	30	30	30	180
3	40	40	40	40	40	40	240
4	60	60	60	60	60	60	360
none	60	60	60	60	60	60	360
Total	220	220	220	220	220	220	1320

quality of the housing stock directly affected, but also to produce a "spillover" effect of stimulating improvements to residential structures by proximate owners who do not participate in the program. The program is to be confined to neighborhoods designated by the planning commission as having a high potential for rehabilitation, that is, the majority of structures are reasonably sound and no major change in land use patterns is foreseen. In this example, the option of using matching neighborhoods not participating in the program as a means of variable control is unavailable. By definition, neighborhoods not designated by the planning commission as part of the program are not comparable. To use comparable neighborhoods from some other city would leave other important variables uncontrolled. In this particular case, however, the City is planning to stage the program over a three-year period, starting it in only a third of the neighborhoods each year. This procedure provides a waiting list of comparable neighborhoods as a control group. Those neighborhoods for which the program is scheduled to start in the first year can be taken as the experimental group, and those for which the program is scheduled to start in the third year can be taken as the control group.

In an ex post facto experiment an additional problem arises in designing the study population. In such a study the analyst has immediate access to those members of the target population who have already been exposed to the independent variable. What is needed is access to those who were also present before exposure to the independent variable. Such a study population must be defined as a cohort, that is, those individuals who were present prior to exposure to the independent variable, during exposure, and at the same point in time after exposure. To illustrate, let us return to our study of the effects of school desegregation on academic achievement. Since the U.S. Office of Education wants results during the current fiscal year in order to provide policy guidance during the next fiscal year, an ex post facto design is required. In this study we want to observe students who were in a school system before as well as after the adoption of the particular desegregation plan. In addition, we want to observe students who were exposed to the intervention for the same amount of time. To do this we must observe a cohort of students (those enrolled in the same grade level), rather than a sample of students currently enrolled. For purposes of this study we will select a cohort who were in the system two years prior to desegregation, and who remained in the system two years afterward.

SUMMARY

In describing the study population to be used in the research design, the analyst should discuss the following points:

1. *The prototypal person, object, or event that constitutes the unit of observation.* When the unit of observation is complex, both the constituent sub-unit and the ultimate unit of observation should be specified.
2. *The population of units to be observed.* In its specification the analyst should distinguish between the target population to which the policy action ultimately applies, the sampling frame which provides access to that population, and the resulting study population which is subject to observation. The population of units to be observed should be defined in terms of its temporal, spatial, and experiential boundaries.
3. *The procedures to be used for selecting units for observation.* In descriptive studies the sampling procedures are described. In exploratory and explanatory studies the group design and procedures for composing groups are described.
4. *The number of units to be observed.* The criteria for arriving at this number should be specified in terms of the reliability and the validity of the expected findings.

REFERENCES

BOGUE, DONALD. *Skid Row in American Cities.* Chicago: University of Chicago, Community and Family Study Center, 1963.

CAMPBELL, DONALD T. and JULIAN C. STANLEY. *Experimental and Quasi-Experimental Designs for Research.* Chicago: Rand McNally and Co., 1963.

CHEIN, ISIDOR. "An Introduction to Sampling," in *Research Methods in Social Relations,* Selltiz, Wrightsman, and Cook, pp. 512–549.

DEUTSCH, MORTON, and MARY EVANS COLLINS. "Interracial Housing," in *American Social Patterns,* ed. William Petersen. Garden City, N.Y.: Doubleday and Company, Inc., 1965.

GREENWOOD, ERNEST. *Experimental Sociology*. New York: Kings Crown Press, 1945.

HYMAN, HERBERT. *Survey Design and Analysis*. New York: Free Press, 1955.

LAZERWITZ, BERNARD. "Sampling Theory and Procedures," in *Methodology in Social Research* eds. Hubert M. Blalock Jr. and Ann B. Blalock. New York: McGraw-Hill Book Co., 1968, pp. 278–332.

McCALL, GEORGE J., and J. L. SIMMONS, eds. *Issues in Participant Observation*. Reading, Mass.: Addison-Wesley, 1969.

McMAHON, BRIAN, and THOMAS F. PUGH. *Epidemiology: Principles and Methods*. Boston: Little Brown and Co., 1970.

NUNNALLY, JUM C. "The Study of Change in Evaluation Research: Principles Concerning Measurement, Experimental Design, and Analysis," in *Handbook of Evaluation Research, Vol. 1*, eds. Elmer L. Struening and Marcia Guttentag. Beverly Hills, Calif: Sage Publications, 1975, pp. 101–138.

PARTEN, MILDRED. *Surveys, Polls and Samples*. New York: Harper & Brothers, Publishers, 1950.

PECHMAN, JOSEPH A., and P. MICHAEL TIMPANE, eds. *Work Incentives and Income Guarantees, the New Jersey Negative Income Tax Experiment*. Washington, D.C.: The Brookings Institution, 1975.

ROSS, JOHN, and PERRY SMITH. "Orthodox Experimental Designs," in *Methodology in Social Research*, eds. Hubert Blalock, Jr., and Ann Blalock. New York: McGraw-Hill Book Co., 1968, pp. 333–389.

SCHATZMAN, LEONARD, and ANSELM L. STRAUSS. *Field Research: Strategies for a Natural Sociology*. Englewood Cliffs, N.J.: Prentice-Hall, Inc., 1973.

SELLTIZ, CLAIRE, LAWRENCE S. WRIGHTSMAN, and STUART W. COOK. *Research Methods in Social Relations* (3rd ed.). New York: Holt, Rinehart, and Winston, 1976.

SUDMAN, SEYMOUR. *Applied Sampling*. New York: Academic Press, 1976.

WEISS, CAROL H. *Evaluation Research*. Englewood Cliffs, N.J.: Prentice-Hall, Inc., 1972.

chapter 10 / stage 6:
data to be
collected

This chapter deals with specifying those data to be collected in order to achieve the research objective(s). This process involves defining the concepts contained in those objective(s) operationally and determining where in the research design those definitions are to be implemented. Considerable interaction exists between stage 6 and stage 7, selecting procedures for data collection. The way in which concepts are defined will depend partially on how the corresponding data can be collected, and so the reader may wish to carry out these stages simultaneously. However, there is a danger in doing so. It is not uncommon for the analyst inadvertently to specify the data to be collected on the basis of techniques that are personally familiar to him or her or are readily available, rather than on the basis of the concepts contained in the research objectives. To guard against this possibility we advocate treating these stages separately.

Specifying the data to be collected involves three steps: (1) identifying the guiding concepts in the research objective(s), (2) defining those concepts operationally, and (3) specifying the stage in the research process at which data required by those definitions will materialize. If the prior stages of the design have been adequately executed, carrying out these steps should be a relatively straightforward task. That is, *if* the concepts in the conceptual framework have been clarified, *if* the research objective(s) has been precisely specified, and *if* the study population has been carefully delimited, specifying the data to be collected is relatively simple. It may be time-consuming, for the development of operational definitions is often tedious. But such specification should engender no major conceptual problems at this stage in the research design. Before proceeding to the steps involved in this process, we will turn our discussion briefly to the nature of data and the various forms they can take.

THE NATURE OF DATA

The nature of data can be grasped by means of the triangle of reference, illustrated in Figure 2-1 (p. 23) in which a concept is depicted as a triangle connecting an idea (or mental image), a referent (or objective reality), and a term (or verbal symbol). Data are recorded observations of referents. They are, therefore, the means by which concepts are measured. In Chapter 3 we noted that the concepts dealt with in policy research are often highly abstract or global and, in and of themselves, not amenable to research. They must first be broken down into subconcepts or variables, which in turn must be broken down into indicators. If a concept is simple, it will have only one indicator or referent and will be measured in terms of the corresponding datum. However, most concepts in social policy research are global concept—that is, have multiple variables—and often have multiple indicators or referents. In this case a datum is a measure of an indicator and must be combined with other data to form a measure of the guiding concept. This process will be described in detail in Chapter 12. Thus a referent is some aspect of reality, an observation is a sensate experience of that referent, and a datum is a recording of that experience. While there is a tendency in the literature to use the term *datum* when refering to any of these three phenomena, the reader should be aware of the distinctions among them.

The principal task at this stage of the research design is to specify the indicators by which the guiding concepts in the research objective(s) are defined, which in turn determine the data that can be collected. However, data can take many different forms. It is important to be aware of these alternative forms lest the analyst be unnecessarily restricted in his or her selection of indicators and consequently limited in defining the guiding concepts.

Data vary on the basis of their mathematical properties. *Quantitative data* refer to those that can be expressed as values on a ratio, interval, or ordinal measurement scale. *Qualitative* or *categorical data* are those that can only be expressed on a nominal measurement scale, that is, as one of the respective categories of a classificatory system. A qualitative datum can take the form of a dichotomous attribute to indicate either the presence or absence of a referent, or of a manifold attribute, where three or more categories of a referent are involved. The development of sophisticated statistical techniques for the analysis of data has tended to encourage the confinement of research observations to quantitative data. This tendency should be resisted, as many of the indicators important to policy making can only be measured in terms of qualitative data. For example, age and income can easily be measured in terms of "number of years lived," or "amount of wages received." However, one's self-concept of being "young" or "old," or "rich" or "poor" may be more relevant to the problem at hand.

Data also vary with respect to the level of human behavior to which they pertain. A datum can pertain to a property of an *individual,* to the *distribution* of such a property among a group of individuals, or to the property of an *organization* or institution. For example, poverty can be measured in terms of an individual's level of income. However, an equally valid measure of poverty is the distribution of income among the group of persons with whom the individual interacts. Group poverty has an important bearing on the individual's self-concept as a person, as well as on the availability of social resources for dealing with his/her poverty. Of course, policy research should be equally concerned with the properties of organizations or institutions responsible for executing policies and carrying out programs. Data about organizational characteristics that are particularly relevant to policy research include the nature of organizational goals, the administrative regulations that govern an organization's behavior, the processes by which policies and programs are carried out, and the resources allocated to those processes.

Finally, data vary in terms of their source. *Primary* data are those collected first hand by the analyst; *secondary* data are those collected for some other purpose but reused by the analyst in a new research design. Primary data have the advantages of being uniquely suited to the objective(s) of the proposed research and of being collected by procedures established and controlled by the analyst. However, gathering such data often exceeds the cost in time and money that are available to the policy-making process. For these reasons secondary data may be more useful. Such data include the *U.S. Census* with its wealth of information on population, housing, and business; the data banks of large survey research centers; the published results of previous studies; and the public records of official events. Public records contain a rich source of readily available information which is particular relevant to policy research. They include the recording of births, deaths, accidents, crimes, and contacts of communicable diseases, to name a few. The sources in which these events are reported were identified in Chapter 6. A second type of public records are the official proceedings of public organizations, in which pronouncements of public goals and policies often appear—for example, the minutes of governing bodies, the enactments of legislatures, the regulations of administrative agencies, and the rulings of regulatory agencies and the judiciary. Enunciation of public goals and policies also may be reflected in the statements of public officials reported in the news media.

A third type of public records are the service statistics of public agencies which reflect the degree of participation in or utilization of the services they provide. Considerable resentment has been expressed in recent years, and rightly so, against the use of confidential records on clients of public service agencies for purposes other than those for which the records were originally intended. We feel that confidential information collected by public agencies to fulfill their statutory mandate should not be used for research without the advice and/or consent of the individuals involved (see pp. 60ff.). What we do condone is the use of aggregate data on the number and distribution of persons participating in such programs, which is a matter of public interest. Such uses are consistent with holding agencies accountable to their constituencies.

A fourth type of public records are statements of the distribution of material and personnel resources within organizations and between organizations that act in the public interest. They include organizational charts that outline the authority and responsibility allocated to each division or member of an organization, contracts that specify the respective functions which the contracting organizations agree to carry out, incorporation papers or enabling legislation that delimits the responsibilities of a given organization or governmental agency, and budgets or financial statements that reflect the way in which an organization spends its financial resources.

Having discussed the various forms of data in which the analyst might ultimately cast his or her operational definitions of guiding concepts, we are now in a position to examine the steps in that process.

IDENTIFYING GUIDING CONCEPTS

Specifying the data to be collected begins with identifying the guiding concepts of the proposed research. The concepts in the statement of the research objective(s) are of two types: those which identify the population under study, and those which represent the properties of that population to be observed and analyzed. Each major word in the statement of research objectives is a concept that guides the research design. However, identifying such concepts involves some judgment. Therefore, we will examine an example of how this process takes place for each of the three methods of research.

First, let us look at an exploratory study in which the research objective is to identify a variable missing from a conceptual framework. Using one of our examples from the previous chapter, let us assume that the objective has been stated as follows

> What policies or plans are associated with successful school desegregation in school systems of different size and ethnic mix in the U.S. between 1970 and 1978?

The unit of observation in this study is a *school system*. The study population is *systems in the U.S. that attempted to desegregate between 1970 and 1978*. The variable to be identified is *policies or plans* that lead to desegregation. Two constraint variables assumed to be associated with success or its absence, the *size* and *ethnic mix* of a system, are used to facilitate the identification of the missing variable.

Next, let us consider a descriptive study in which the research objective is to measure the size of a variable in a given population. Let us assume a policy problem in which the decision maker wishes to ascertain the impact of a federal housing program in terms of the extent to which central city residents have been able to take advantage of housing opportunities in the suburbs. The research objective has been stated as follows

> What is the rate of migration to suburban communities of central city households who received federally subsidized housing assistance in 1978?

In this example, the unit of observation is a *central city household*. The study population is *all such households which received federally subsidized housing assistance in 1978*. The variable to be observed, in this case the objective of policy, is *rate of migration to suburban communities.*

Finally, let us consider an explanatory study in which the research objective is to test a causal relation between the institution of a policy and an unintended consequence. We will use as our example the negative income tax experiment described in the previous chapter. Let us assume that the research objective has been stated as follows

> The rate of negative income tax will not be associated with a disincentive to work among labor force participants in low-income families, controlling for size of family, number of members in the labor force, age of head, and ethnicity, in four New Jersey cities in 1976.

In this example, the unit of observation is a *labor force participant*. The study population is *such participants in low-income families in four New Jersey cities in 1976*. The policy (independent variable) being evaluated is *rate of negative income tax*. The variable whose association with the independent variable is being observed is *incentive to work*, which in the context of this policy problem is an unintended consequence of the policy. Four constraint variables are included to eliminate rival hypotheses: *size, number of members in the labor force, age of head,* and *ethnicity* of the respective families.

Thus the concepts contained in the statement of research objectives refer either to the unit of observation, the boundaries of the population being observed, the variables being observed, or the variables being controlled.

OPERATIONALLY DEFINING CONCEPTS

Now that each guiding concept has been identified in the statement of the research objective(s), it must be defined operationally. The concepts pertaining to the study population will have been operationally defined in stage 5 if the procedures set forth in that chapter were followed. We can therefore proceed to define those concepts which are the subject of the investigation, together with any variables which are to be controlled during the study.

As noted earlier, the process of conceptual clarification occurs in two steps: (1) reducing a global concept to variables, resulting in a connotative definition; and (2) reducing each variable to its indicators, resulting in an operational definition. Except for exploratory studies, which we shall discuss presently, the first step has already been accomplished during the construction of the conceptual framework. Therefore, the guiding concepts in the statement of research objective(s) will in all likelihood be expressed as variables. The step remaining at this point is to reduce each variable to its indicator(s) by which it can be analyzed.

Types of Definitions

The reader will recall our brief discussion of an operational definition in Part I p. 25. It is appropriate at this point to elaborate on that discussion. We indicated there that an operational definition specifies the procedures whereby the analyst might identify or reproduce the referents of a concept. Hence, an operational definition of a variable must specify some observation(s) or measurement(s) of that variable which can be obtained by a systematic procedure. The test of the adequacy of the definition is whether or not someone else, who may or may not be familiar with the research, can conduct the relevant observations and derive comparable results solely by following the directives furnished by the definition. If this cannot be done, the definition is probably not operational; or if it is, it is faulty and requires refinement.

As our definition of operationalization implies, there are two kinds of operational definitions: the *identifying* and the *generating*. An identifying definition specifies the referents of the concept in the form of empirical or sensate features whereby we can recognize the phenomenon to which the concept refers whenever and wherever it exists. For example, if we were to define a poverty-stricken family in terms of the amount of income required to purchase a subsistence level of food, shelter, and clothing for a family of four, two of which are children within a specified age range, and living in an urban area, we would be providing an identifying definition of that condition. Aided by that definition even someone who had never known a poverty-stricken family could recognize one when he or she encountered it.

A generating operational definition specifies the mental and/or physical manipulations whereby we can generate (that is, reproduce) the referents of the concept, and thereby recognize the phenomenon to which the concept refers. The procedure is best understood by considering a property concept. To repeat, a property is a characteristic exhibited by a series of subjects, objects, or events. Some properties are manifest, others are latent. For example, a man's height or complexion is manifest; it is readily recognizable. But his attitude toward certain political or economic events is latent; it is recognizable only if he chooses to manifest it by words or deeds. An attitude is a disposition, a psychic state. It is a tendency to behave in a certain manner in reaction to certain situations. Its nature can be determined only by its verbal and/or behavioral manifestations. Behavioral scientists are concerned with many such properties. They include, in addition to attitudes, personality traits, intelligence, aptitudes and so forth.

Hence, to determine the existence of such properties, it is necessary to create situations that will generate their manifestations. For example, to be able to categorize persons as either racially prejudiced or tolerant, we must somehow elicit from them reactions, verbal or behavioral, whereby we can make the appropriate judgment about them. Perhaps they are asked to indicate their agreement or disagreement with an inventory of items, each one describing a hypothetical interracial situation. Such a inventory would, in essence, be a generating operational definition of the property concept "racial attitude." In effect, then, test or questionnaire items generate responses which serve as indicators of the respondents' attitudes toward other races. Similarly, an intelligence test is a generating definition of intelligence.

There are some problems attached to the use of generating operational definitions. Compared to the identifying, the generating definition is more difficult to formulate and to administer. Then, too, the behaviors involved are only indirect indicators of the latent property or psychological state being measured. Thus the validity of generating definitions is much more difficult to establish. In an identifying definition the indicators represent a direct expression of the variable in question, making their validity self-evident. In a generating definition the indicators represent only an indirect expression of the variable. Establishing its validity requires more elaborate procedures. The implications of these respective definitions for the validity of the measures they generate will be discussed in more detail in Chapter 12.

Which of the two types of operational definitions should the analyst employ and when? Concepts with easily observable referents call for an identifying definition, whereas concepts whose referents are not directly observable call for a generating definition. Poverty, mixed racial enrollment, unemployment, interracial faculty, these would require the identifying type. But when we deal with individual psychic states, such as emotional adjustment, or states of social groups, such as organizational cohesion or effectiveness, then the generating type may be required. Among policy analysts identifying definitions are preferred because they are more easily understood and their validity is more readily apparent. Since policy research deals with variables that are manipulable and objectives that are manifest, these advantages can usually be realized. However, there are occasions when the objective of policy involves a psychological state, or when the focus of research is a bridging variable, such as the attitude of service providers toward clients, clients' understanding of a service, or consumers' satisfaction with a public good or service. In such cases the use of generating definitions is necessary.

Constructing a Definition

In constructing an operational definition, one uses much the same deductive process as in constructing a connotative definition. The analyst identifies—either by direct observation, by perusing past research reports, or by inquiring of knowledgeable others—all the referents that distinguish the variable to be operationalized. These referents become conceptualized as indicators of the variable in terms of which he or she will gather data.

Having established the referents, the analyst must determine the units in which they will be measured, so that the instrument to be constructed in stage 7 will yield data in units appropriate to that measurement. This determination must be based on the type of scale to be used in measuring the indicator, whether it be nominal, ordinal, or interval. When a nominal scale is involved, a classification scheme must be adopted which specifies the number and definition of the categories to be used. Let us assume, for example, that the analyst is to measure the ethnicity of members of a study population. The concept "ethnicity" could be treated as a dichotomous attribute, that is, one having two categories; native born and foreign born. On the other hand, it could be treated as a manifold attribute, each category representing one country of origin in the study. If an ordinal scale is used, the number of rank orders must be indicated. Single ranks may be used, one for each unit of observation, or ranks may be grouped into quartiles, deciles, or percentiles. For example, the sizes of cities is usually measured in single ranks because the number of cities is relatively small. However, the crime rate of census tracts in large metropolitan areas may be more conveniently measured in deciles. Performance on standardized academic achievement tests is usually measured in percentiles to be most useful in individual guidance. When an interval scale is used, the size of the interval must be specified. For example, income may be measured in individual dollar amounts. However, the *U.S. Census* usually reports income in $1000 intervals. Having so operationalized a variable, each indicator represents a datum that must be collected to obtain a measure of a given variable.

When the indicators are few, as in the case of the variables of income or age, the task is simple. Age can be operationalized as the number of years lived as of one's last birthday, and income as the dollar value of all monies coming in, both earned (such as salary and wages) or unearned (as dividends, interests, rents, and so forth) during a given year. When the indicators of a variable are many, the process of formulating an operational definition is a bit more complicated. The analyst must specify what values or categories of each indicator combine to form the unique variable under study. In order to arrive at such a definition, the analyst should diagram all possible combinations of values or categories so that he or she will not overlook any relevant combinations. The process of combining multiple indicators into a measure of a variable will be elaborated in Chapter 8. We will merely illustrate that process here with an operational definition of the concept "unemployment."

The U.S. Bureau of Labor Statistics defines as unemployed anyone 14 years of age or older who (a) did not work at all during a given week, (b) was available for work, and (c) was looking for work (*BLS Handbook of Methods* 1971, p. 8). Such a definition is not operational in that it would not lead to consistent observations without considerable elaboration or interpretation. What constitutes working? What does it mean to be available for work? What constitutes looking for work? The definition can be thought of as a set of subconcepts or variables which need to be broken down into indicators. The variables can be so defined as follows:* (a) "did not work" refers to anyone who worked less than 10 hours during a given week for a wage or salary; (b) "available for work" refers to anyone who is not a housewife, retired, or a full-time student; (c) "looking for work" refers to anyone who looked through want ads or made an inquiry about a job during a given week, *or* who would have been looking except that he or she was suffering from an illness that had not lasted more than 30 days, *or* was waiting to begin a new job or to return to a job from which he or she had been laid off. Thus we have operationally defined a global concept by breaking it down into variables, and the variables in turn into indicators, as illustrated in Figure 10-1.

As can be seen from this example, operational definitions are much more cumbersome than connotative ones. The original definition conveys the fact that unemployment is defined by three variables. However, in operationally defining these variables, one of them, "looking for work," is defined by three alternative indicators. In arriving at such a complicated definition it is often

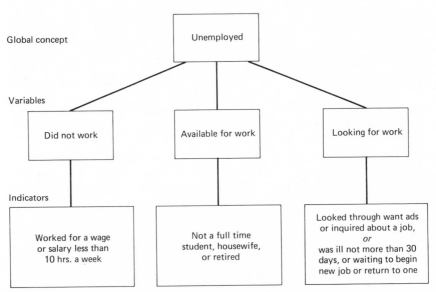

Figure 10-1 Operational definition of the concept "unemployed"

*This definition represents a modification of that reported in *BLS Handbook of Methods*. Some labor force analysts would make further modifications, classifying as "underemployed" those who work less than 35 hours a week, who work for less than the minimum wage, or who are housewives.

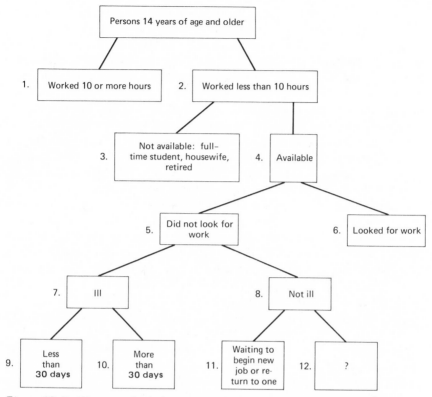

Figure 10-2 Diagram of relations among indicators of unemployment*

possible to overlook relevant indicators or combinations of indicators. To avoid this the analyst is advised to diagram, either in a matrix or a branching tree, all of the possible combinations of the values or categories of the respective indicators. This we have done in Figure 10-2, treating each indicator as a dichotomous attribute.** Boxes 2, 4, and 6 in this figure represent indicators that are necessary in defining unemployment. This fact is reflected in their hierarchical relationship in the diagram. That is, one cannot get to box 6 without going through boxes 2 and 4. Box 9 (by way of 5 and 7) and box 11 (by way of 5 and 8) represent alternative indicators in defining unemployment. This fact is reflected in their lateral relationship to box 6 in the diagram, that is, one can go from box 4 to box 5 (and then to 9 or 11) or one can go to box 6.

---

*In the interest of simplifying the diagram, some boxes express variables rather than indicators.

**In so doing we recognize that "unemployed" is a category of a larger variable (or more accurately, a manifold attribute), "status in the labor force," of which the other two categories are "employed" and "out of the labor force."

Box 12 represents an indicator about which considerable controversy exists in the definition of unemployment. It refers to persons who do not work for a wage or salary, are available for work, are not looking for work, are not ill, and do not have a job they are waiting to go to. Presumably such persons have become discouraged about finding work and have dropped out of the labor force. Some labor economists urge their inclusion in measures of unemployment. The advantage of operational definitions is reflected in this controversy. *The phenomena which are or are not to be included in the operational definition of a given variable are explicit, allowing other observers to redefine the variable and account for any differences in their resulting observations.*

In developing operational definitions in descriptive studies, the analyst must be alert to the need for norms by which to judge the policy significance of research findings. The need for such norms is most likely to arise in studies referred to as needs assessment, the purpose of which is to assist in specifying the objective(s) of policy making. For example, the rate of unemployment can easily be measured, but in the absence of a specific policy objective it is difficult to determine whether a given rate is high or low. Norms can be derived from three sources: (1) data from other populations that serve as a standard, (2) standards established by some authoritative body, or (3) data on subgroups within the study population. When the norm is derived from a source external to the study [(1) and (2)], the analyst must use the equivalent of the operational definition by which the norm was derived in defining the variable in question. For example, the U.S. Census contains data on education, housing, labor force participation, and income. When using census data as a norm, the analyst should consult the definition of terms published by the Census Bureau in order to maintain consistency among terms. (U.S. Bureau of Census 1970). Adhering to such comparability will make the analyst's findings infinitely more useful to policy making.

Operational Definitions in Exploratory Studies

Up to this point we have been discussing guiding concepts or variables which by nature can be operationally defined. By contrast, an exploratory study attempts to identify variables missing from the conceptual framework or to break down global concepts into their indicators. These tasks would not seem to require data collection, but if we refer to our model of conceptual clarification, the role of operational definitions in this type of study will become clearer.

The conceptual framework in the exploratory study indicates what type of policy variable is missing; it may be a policy action, an implementation variable, a bridging variable, an adjunct variable, or a constraint. Knowing the type of variable that is missing allows the analyst to limit the range of phenomena to be examined. For example, if one's research objective is to identify a relevant implementation process, one could look at funding levels, types of personnel employed, operating procedures, equipment, and facilities. If type of personnel is identified as the missing variable, further exploration may be necessary in order to identify the indicators that differentiate personnel. Again, a number of alternatives exist to provide a framework for such exploration. Personnel can be differentiated on the basis of formal training, length of experience, attitudes, age, sex, and so forth.

Thus in an exploratory study investigation moves through three levels of conceptual clarification, from global concepts to sub-concepts or variables, and from variables to referents or indicators. At each step, observation is guided by a set of categories suggested by the higher level of conceptualization. However, such a set is treated as an open system; the analyst uses it as a place to begin the investigation, but always remains open to new categories not previously anticipated. Thus, although the analyst cannot use operational definitions of guiding concepts in an exploratory study, he or she can use a set of categories to represent those variables or indicators whose presence must be verified.

SPECIFYING THE RESEARCH STAGE
IN WHICH DATA WILL BE COLLECTED

Operational definitions of the guiding concepts may come into play in any one of three stages in the research process: (1) the selection of the study population, (2) the manipulation of the independent variable, and (3) the observation of the study population. The selection of the study population refers to the use of a sampling frame to select units from the target population for observation. The manipulation of the independent variable occurs in explanatory studies and refers to an alteration in the independent variable in an effort to determine its impact on the dependent variable. Observation of the study population refers to an act by the analyst to observe the state of variables in the study population at a given point(s) in time. Operational definitions used in the first two stages may require data to be collected by the analyst; those used in the third stage always do.

As was discussed in Chapter 9, the boundaries of the study population may be conterminous with the sampling frame. In such a case, the operational definition of those boundaries is an integral part of the sampling frame and no additional data need be collected in order to select the study population. When the two boundaries are not coterminous, the missing indicators are used to select from the sampling frame those members which fit the definition of the study population. This *screening process* involves the collection of data and must be planned for in the research design. It can be carried out in either of two ways. The analyst can collect such data as a separate step in the process of selecting the study population. For example, in a study of school dropouts the analyst may begin with a list of all nongraduates who are no longer enrolled in school.

To eliminate those who may have transferred to another school, the analyst may examine the school record of each student on the list to see whether they contain a request for a transfer. A second approach is to add the missing indicators to the list of data to be collected during the observation stage of the research. Here, for example, an item could be added to the questionnaire being sent to all members in the sampling frame, asking the respondent to indicate if he or she is currently enrolled in another school. Then, at the stage of data analysis, the analyst can separate from the total responses those that conform to the definition of the study population.

The choice of procedure to follow depends on a trade-off between the availability of the missing data and the relative size of the study population. If the missing data are reflected in the sampling frame or appear as readily available secondary sources, screening of the sampling frame prior to observation may be relatively easy. If the data must be obtained directly from the units of observation, their collection may be more economical as part of the observational phase of the research. However, the advantage of direct observation must be weighed against the size of the study population relative to that of the sampling frame. If the sampling frame contains only a few members of the study population, it would be more economical to gather the missing data by means of a screening process.

Manipulation of the independent variable is a stage unique to explanatory studies. In pure experiments it does not involve data collection, because the analyst has control over the manipulation of the independent variable or exposure to it. However, as a check on this exposure some analysts elicit from the subject the degree of alteration in the independent variable that he/she actually experienced. Such a step requires data collection. In quasi-experiments the analyst does not have control over the independent variable, neither can he/she determine which members of the study population will be exposed to it. Consequently, exposure must be determined in either of two ways—either in selecting the study population or in observing it. Thus the operational definition of the independent variable in such studies comes into play either in determining the boundaries of the study population or in determining data to be collected while observing it.

In specifying the data to be collected, the analyst should bring together in one chart the variables that express the guiding concepts, the indicators by which they are defined, and the stage in the research process where those indicators will be observed. Such a chart will serve as a check on the completeness with which the research objective(s) has been operationally defined and will also facilitate presenting the plan for data collection to the decision maker. To illustrate this step, we will use the research objective of the negative income tax experiment discussed earlier in this chapter. In using this example two precautions are in order. Although the example is inspired by what is known as the New Jersey Negative Income Tax Experiment it does not conform completely to it. Therefore, the reader should not expect our exposition to be an accurate reflection of what actually occurred. Furthermore, in operationally defining the variables in this research objective, we have not attempted to ascertain their feasibility nor their validity. Our intent is simply to illustrate. Therefore, in using this example the reader should focus on the relationships among guiding concepts, indicators, and research stages rather than on their substance.

In the first column of Figure 10-3 we have entered each of the guiding concepts, or variables, that appear in the research objective. To facilitate determining the research stage where data will be collected, we have divided the column between variables that reflect the boundaries of the study population and variables that reflect the policy problem. In the second column we have entered the indicators by which each variable is operationally defined. For the most part they are self-explanatory or drawn from previous discussion. A few warrant comment. The independent variable in this example, "rate of negative income tax," refers to seven different tax programs. Each program consists of a level of income guaranteed each family relative to the official poverty level and a rate at which income earned beyond that level will be taxed. For example, 50/30 means that a family will be guaranteed an income of 50 percent of the poverty level, and the rate at which additional income will be taxed is 30 percent. The dependent variable, "incentive to work," is equally difficult to interpret. Presumably incentive to work can be indicated by the number of hours worked. However, the experiment should not be evaluated by changes in hours worked that are beyond the control of the worker, such as those due to a layoff or reduction in the amount of work offered by the employer. However, unless such actions reflect general changes in the local labor market, they could be compensated by seeking job opportunities with another employer, given an unimpaired incentive to work. Thus the average hours worked are related to the prevailing unemployment rate as an indicator of incentive to work.

Finally, in the third column we indicate the stage in the research process where each operational definition will be applied: In this particular example, as is true with most pure experiments, most of the definitions will be used in connection with selecting the study population. If the indicators involved are reflected in an existing sampling frame, the amount of data collection will be small. If, however, a sampling frame must be constructed, a considerable amount of data collection will be required before the experiment can get under way.

SUMMARY

Specifying the data to be collected involves three steps: (1) identifying the guiding concepts in the statement of the research objective(s), (2) developing operational definitions of those concepts, and (3) determining the stage in the

Figure 10-3 Summary of operational definitions: the negative income tax experiment

CONCEPT/VARIABLE	INDICATORS	RESEARCH STAGE WHERE OBSERVED
Study population boundaries		
1. labor force participant	a. 14 years of age or older b. worked at least 10 hours per week, during month prior to study, for wage or salary	selection of study population
2. low-income family	a. two or more persons living under the same roof who are related by blood or marriage b. total household income not to exceed 150 percent of poverty level	selection of study population
3. four New Jersey cities	a. the incorporated areas of Passaic, Paterson, Jersey City, and Trenton	selection of study population
Policy variables		
4. rate of negative income tax	a. ratio of income guarantee as percent of poverty level to tax rate: 50/30, 75/30, 50/50, 75/50, 100/50, 75/70, 100/70	manipulation of independent variable
5. incentive to work	a. any change in the ratio of the annual average of hours per week worked to the employment rate in the respective cities	observation of study population
6. size of family	a. number of family members living under same roof	selection of study population
7. number of members in labor force	a. number of family members who worked at least 10 hours a week, in month prior to study, for wage or salary	selection of study population
8. age of head of household	a. age on last birthday of person in family having the highest income	selection of study population
9. ethnicity	a. self-report of head of household as to whether family is white, black, or Spanish-speaking	selection of study population

research process at which those definitions will be applied. Those concepts that pertain to the study population will have been operationally defined in stage 5. If this is not the case, the analyst should return to that stage and develop such definitions.

The statement resulting from stage 6 of the research design should consist of a chart which accounts for all of the guiding concepts in the research objective(s), their indicators, and the stage in the research process where those indicators will be observed. The chart should be accompanied by a justification of the operational definitions used, when this is deemed necessary.

It should be recognized that there is an arbitrary separation between operational definitions of guiding concepts as determined in this stage, and procedures for data collection specified in the following stage. At this stage the analyst should be as precise as possible in the selection of indicators and the units in which they are to be measured. If, in the subsequent stage, the construction of the actual instruments requires some modification, the analyst should be prepared to revise his or her operational definitions accordingly. In cases where the operational definition consists of a measure on an established instrument, such as a score on the Stanford Achievement Test, the instrument need only be mentioned here. In stage 7 it can be discussed in terms of its substance and administration.

REFERENCES

BLS Handbook of Methods, Bulletin 1711. Washington, D.C.: U.S. Government Printing Office, 1971.

U.S. Bureau of the Census, *1970 Census User's Guide.* Washington, D.C.: U.S. Government Printing Office, 1970.

chapter 11 / stage 7: procedures for data collection

Our primary concern at this stage of the research design is to specify the procedures to be used in collecting data. Of course, the operational definitions of guiding concepts imply these procedures. However, in stage 6 the analyst's primary concern is to select the observations that will be the most valid indicators of the guiding concepts, while in this stage he or she is concerned with selecting the actual techniques and instruments with which to make those observations. Of course, the adoption of particular procedures may require the analyst to modify the definitions of certain concepts to conform to what is actually measured. Because of this interdependency, these two stages should be considered simultaneously. They are presented sequentially so that substantive decisions which flow from the research objectives are not overshadowed by measurement techniques. Technical feasibility should be allowed to modify the operational expression of research objectives, not predetermine them.

Before proceeding it will be helpful to define some terms associated with this stage of research design. We consider a data collection procedure to consist of two elements: a *technique* and an *instrument*. A data collection *technique* is a set of behaviors, or series of acts, engaged in by the analyst to collect a set of data. The behaviors constitute an interrelated sequence which together produce an outcome, for example, an interview or participant observation. Techniques are relatively standardized in that their use is not confined to a particular study. They constitute a set of skills that often are associated with a social science discipline. The reader should be aware that some authors use the term *method* to refer to what we have defined as technique. In this book the term *method* has a larger meaning. It refers to the type of reasoning (exploratory, descriptive, explanatory) that characterizes the research design and is required to achieve the research objective(s).

A data collection *instrument* refers to a device, material in nature, which is used to determine the data to be elicited and to record them. An instrument is usually specific to a given study, although some instruments have become standardized; an example is an interview schedule or an intelligence test. Thus the terms *method, technique,* and *instrument,* as used in this book, constitute hierarchical relationship. A method is the type of reasoning which underlies the research design, techniques are behaviors which carry out that method, and instruments are devices used to execute a technique.

A few other terms should be defined for clarity. In Chapter 10 we used the term *datum* to refer to a specific piece of information recorded in an instrument. It follows, therefore, that to observe refers to the process of collecting data. By contrast we use the term *measure* to refer to a datum that has been converted into some value on a quantitative scale or some category in a classification system that is used to measure a variable. To measure, therefore, refers to the process of collecting *and* transforming data into measures of guiding concepts. The second part of that process, transforming data into measures, will be taken up in the next chapter.

The purpose of this chapter is to review alternative techniques and instruments available for data collection, and to describe the criteria the analyst should use in choosing among them. We do not intend to be comprehensive or detailed in this review. The literature on the subject is profuse, and the reader will be referred to more fully developed sources where appropriate. Our objective is to provide detail sufficient to discuss the decisions that must be executed at this stage of the design process.

ALTERNATIVE PROCEDURES FOR DATA COLLECTION

In the literature on research methodology, the discussion of techniques and instruments of data collection is usually integrated around three or four types of observation: field research or case studies, secondary data analysis, survey research, and experiments (Babbie 1975). This typology is not very useful for selecting observational procedures for a given study. In the first place, there is only a rough correspondence between this typology and the research methods we have advocated in this book. While so-called field research procedures are most frequently associated with exploratory studies, their use is not so confined. Second, the typology is too general to fit the design requirements of a particular investigation. For this reason, we have disassembled these types into their associated techniques and instruments, so that the analyst has greater flexibility to tailor data collection procedures to the objectives and circumstances of a particular research.*

ALTERNATIVE TECHNIQUES

We will discuss alternative techniques of data collection in terms of four general types. Two of these are direct in that the analyst observes the phenomenon in question either through the use of mechanical or electronic devices—which we will call *hardware*—or through individual perceptions, what we term *direct observation by the analyst.* The other two types are indirect in that the analyst relies on the observations of others, either through the *use of secondary data* such as public records or through perceptions elicited by the analyst, which we will call *respondent observation* (Selltiz, Wrightsman, and Cook 1976).

Use of Hardware

Hardware refers to mechanical and electronic devices for monitoring human behavior. They range from the polygraph, used by psychologists to measure galvanic skin responses, to the camera used by anthropologists to record social life in a cultural context (Collier 1967, Heider 1976). The use of electronic devices such as audio and video recorders has received increasing attention in recent years. Such devices have been used to observe interactions between doctors and their patients in a clinic, the participation of individuals in a public meeting, and traffic and parking behaviors of individuals on a city street. Webb and his collaborators (1970, pp. 142-171) give an extensive account of the uses of hardware in social science research.

Hardware may be thought of as an instrument for data collection. At times, however, it actually supplants the observer, and the process becomes an observational technique, as, for example, with the use of audiovisual devices. When every sound and image is recorded on audio or video tape, a plethora of data confronts the analyst from which the relevant items must be selected. For this reason, the analyst using audiovisual equipment must have an additional means by which to select from the recorded observations those that are pertinent to his or her research objectives.

The use of hardward involves some planning. The analyst must decide whether the technique is to be overt or covert, that is, whether or not the subjects of observation are to be made aware of the use of the equipment. The

---

*Probably the widest variety of data collection techniques is conveyed in recent textbooks on anthropological research methods (Crane and Angrosino 1974, Pelto and Pelto 1978).

decision involves the location of the devices and the information given the subjects about the nature of the investigation. The analyst must also decide whether the observation is to be natural or contrived. Will the device record whatever events occur naturally, or will the analyst intervene in those events to trigger a response on the part of the persons observed? The popular television show *Candid Camera* is an example of planned intervention. Additional factors to be considered are the mobility of the procedure, that is, whether the equipment is to be used in single or multiple locations; the timing of the observations, whether total or sampled; and the manpower and training needed to operate the equipment.

Direct Observation by The Analyst

Any form of observation in which the analyst is present to observe the phenomenon in question may be termed *direct observation*. This technique of data collection ranges from the simple act of counting discrete objects, persons, or events in a given environment, to more subjective and complicated forms of observation as a participant in the event under study. Such observation is as old as science itself, and is often referred to as naturalistic.

Direct observation by the analyst can be described in terms of the role he or she assumes, or the degree of involvement between the observer and the observed. As involvement increases, the process more nearly approaches what has been termed "participant observation" (McCall and Simmons 1969, Schatzman and Strauss 1973, Spradley and McCurdy 1972). Four types of roles can be distinguished (Gold 1969). At one extreme is the *complete observer,* one who is not a participant in the event or group of people being observed and whose identity and presence are unknown to them. This role is exemplified by studies in rooms equipped with one-way mirrors through which the analyst observes the behavior of individuals or groups while hidden from view. It is also exemplified by studies of public places or events at which the analyst is inconspicuous. Thus the analyst may record the number of pedestrians who violate traffic signals on a city street, or the number and type of individuals who speak at a public hearing. The *observer as participant* is one whose presence and identity are known to the persons being observed but who does not actively participate in the phenomenon under study. For example, the analyst may attend a classroom in a public school to observe the interactions between pupils and teacher. While the analyst may try to make his or her presence as inconspicuous as possible, it is still a factor of which the pupils and teacher are likely to be aware.

The *participant as observer* is one whose presence and identity as an analyst are known and who also becomes a regular participant in the phenomenon under study. Numerous examples exist, as this role is most frequently used in participant observation. One such study is *Tally's Corner,* in which the observer took up residence in a neighborhood of young unemployed black males to find out how they coped with unemployment (Liebow 1967). Finally the *complete participant* is one whose presence is known to the group being observed but not his or her identity as an analyst. Participation is complete in that the analyst must adopt a role (known as a "cover") natural to the persons being observed and become an active part of the phenomenon being studied. This covert form of observation may be necessary in the study of illegal or taboo behavior, where knowledge of the analyst's identity would seriously distort the events being observed (Humphreys 1970). For example, the analyst may become an applicant for service at a public welfare agency in order to observe how a client is treated when filing an application.

Use of Secondary Data

As discussed in Chapter 10, secondary data refer to any observations made by someone other than the analyst for purposes other than those underlying the study at hand. If such data were gathered as part of a formal research process, their use poses few problems for the research design. The analyst must simply familiarize him or herself with the data collection procedures used and then determine how the specific procedure would affect the attainment of the research objectives. The use of public records requires more caution. Such records contain data that were collected to facilitate governmental decision making and administration, and the techniques used do not always conform to the requirements of scientific observation.

The inexperienced analyst may assume that the use of public records eliminates this stage in the research design—that the data can be taken simply as given. However, a number of factors enter into the way in which public events are recorded that severely limit their reliability and/or validity. One such factor is the *completeness* of reporting procedures. Completeness refers to the extent to which every instance of the phenomenon in question has an equal probability of being recorded. Births are uniformly reported in the U.S. by the hospital in which they occur or by the attending physician. Only a small number of such events, primarily births occurring at home, go unreported. However, the receipt of unemployment compensation reflects only certain kinds of employment and industries that are covered by state unemployment insurance programs and is, therefore, a relatively incomplete record of unemployment.

A second factor that can plague the reliability of record systems is their *consistency*. On the one hand, consistency can be affected by the persons designated to fill out public records. For example, if some records are filled out by office personnel and others by treatment personnel, the resulting set of records may be inconsistent. Consistency also refers to the procedures for recording public events. Crime records are notorious in this regard. Considerable discretion is allowed police officers in determining when to make an arrest or issue a citation and what particular illegal acts to record. Lastly, public records of the occurrence of events may contain *judgments* about the nature of such events, and these of course go beyond the pale of observation. For example, the cause of death reported on a death certificate is the attending physician's judgment as to the probable cause. However, in the absence of an autopsy, all other conditions of the deceased cannot be ruled out as possible causes. Thus, although the fact of death may be a reliable record, its cause may not be.

When using public records as a form of observation the analyst should build safeguards against such factors into the research design. In the first place the analyst should undertake a thorough examination of the reporting system to determine its completeness and consistency. He or she should find out the basis on which an event comes to the attention of public officials, who records the event, and the process by which it is recorded. In the case of some reporting systems, such as the U.S. Vital Statistics, reporting procedures are well documented. In the absence of such documentation, the analyst should interview the officials operating the system to become familiar with reporting procedures and should also examine a sample of records to determine their consistency and the nature of systematic omissions. The discovery of incompleteness or inconsistency need not deter the analyst from using such records. If estimates of the extent and nature of error can be made, those estimates can be used to make appropriate corrections in analyzing the data drawn from such records.

Another safeguard is for the analyst to establish his or her own systematic procedure for extracting the necessary data from such records. In this manner each record is reviewed and any inconsistencies corrected or omissions filled in by the analyst. Such a procedure involves constructing an instrument to specify the precise items which the observer is permitted to collect, the basis on which inconsistencies can be reconciled, and the procedure for securing items that are missing. Instructions and training may be required for the use of such instruments.

Respondent Observation

We turn now to data collection techniques that involve respondent observation. By respondent observation we mean any procedure by which the analyst elicits the observations of persons who have direct knowledge of the phenomenon under study. Next to the use of public records, respondent observation is the most frequent form of data collection in policy research. It is carried out by use of a schedule of standardized questions addressed to each respondent in the study.

Respondent observations can be elicited in either of two ways—through an *interview* or through the *self-administration of a questionnaire*. The interview is a technique in which the analyst addresses a set of questions verbally to the respondent, who in turn gives his or her replies verbally to the analyst by whom they are recorded. Thus an interview involves personal interaction between the analyst and the respondent, either face-to-face or by telephone. The interview technique permits the analyst to elaborate questions and to probe the respondent for further information. In the self-administration of a questionnaire, the respondent replies in writing to questions that appear on a written instrument that has been prepared by the analyst. This technique involves no personal interaction between the analyst and the respondent. It also does not allow for any variation in the format of the questions.

These two techniques can be further categorized according as they are administered *singly* or to a *group*. Interviews are usually conducted with respondents one at a time so as to eliminate any bias which one person's reply might have on another's. However, group interviewing may be appropriate when the data to be collected depend on group interaction. The observations to be made may require either a collective decision or interaction among respondents in order to facilitate recall of past events. In group interviewing, the analyst will have to distinguish between replies that are primarily consensual or of majorities and replies that reflect great diversity or the views of significant minorities. Group interviewing requires more skill than individual interviewing. The analyst must not only ask the questions properly but also facilitate group interaction in order to generate the full range of replies.

The distinction between an individually and a group administered questionnaire is more procedural than substantive. Group administration involves the simultaneous response to a questionnaire by two or more respondents at a single place and time under the supervision of the analyst. Since questionnaires involve only written communication, presumably no interactive effect occurs when the technique is group administered. Individually administered questionnaires are used when respondents are geographically scattered. Questionnaires are group administered when respondents are clustered into a "captive audience," such as students in a classroom, clients in the waiting room of a service agency, or persons attending a public function.

ALTERNATIVE INSTRUMENTS

An instrument can be defined as a device used by the analyst to systematize the collection of data. In social research an instrument consists of a written set of instructions about what variables to observe and how to observe them. It also provides a format for recording those observations. Instruments can be classified according to their degree of structure. An *unstructured* schedule is one which identifies a general class of variables to be observed and does not specify the indicators by which individual variables are to be measured. A *structured* instrument specifies both the variables to be observed and the indicators by which they are to be measured.

Unstructured Instruments

The extreme form of an unstructured instrument is a *log,* a technique commonly used in participant observation. A log is a written narrative of what the analyst observes over regular time intervals. It provides a way of making observations systematically over time without specifying who or what to observe. A log customarily consists of two parts: The first is a description of observations, and the second is a statement of tentative conclusions about the types of variables and indicators reflected in those observations or the relations among them. This separation of accounts assists the analyst in maintaining a distinction between describing and hypothesizing about the phenomenon under study.

A more structured instrument is the *interview guide,* so called because it specifies a set of topics or a class of variables to be covered in an interview without indicating how the interview is to be conducted. Such a guide permits the analyst flexibility in phrasing questions to be asked on a common set of topics. It allows the analyst to take advantage of the unique perspective of each respondent. No presumption is reflected in such a guide about the indicators by which specific variables are to be measured.

Finally, there is the *schedule of open-ended questions.* This type of instrument specifies the variables to be observed in terms of standardized questions to be addressed to all respondents. However, it does not specify the indicators to be used in measuring those variables, that is, a specific form the answers are to take. For example, "Why did you move?" and "What do you like about this program?" are open-ended questions because the respondent is allowed to choose the type of reason or program characteristic with which to formulate his or her reply. Thus the respondent determines the indicators by which the variables are measured.

Structured Instruments

A fully structured instrument is one which specifies the particular variables to be observed and the indicators by which they are to be measured. One type of structured instrument is the *schedule of closed-ended questions,* usually referred to as an interview schedule or questionnaire. Examples of closed-ended questions are

1. Which of the following factors affected your decision to move?
   ( ) increase in income
   ( ) dislike of neighborhood
   ( ) change of job
   ( ) increase in family size
   ( ) other _____

2. Do you like this program?
( ) a lot ( ) a little ( ) not at all
3. How old are you? _____

Questions 1 and 2 are obviously closed-ended because the schedule specifies the format in which the respondent must answer the question. Question 3 is also closed-ended because, even though the instrument does not so specify, there is only one indicator, time, by which age is commonly measured.

Another form of structured instrument is the standardized *paper-and-pencil test* frequently used to measure psychological states such as attitudes, aptitudes, and values. These instruments usually consist of statements, rather than questions, with which the respondent is asked to specify his or her degree of agreement according to some predetermined format. Examples of such test items are

1. Most politicians are untrustworthy.

1	2	3	4	5
Agree Strongly			Disagree Strongly	

2. Persons on public assistance should be required to work.
agree _____ disagree _____ no opinion _____

3. I would be willing to have a member of another race
____ marry a member of my family
____ be a close friend
____ live on my street
____ work at my place of employment

A variety of systematic approaches has been developed for the construction of such instruments, as exhibited in a rich body of literature (Sellitz, Wrightsman, and Cook 1976; Edwards 1957; Dawes 1971). Such instruments can be constructed so that the statements, called items, collectively constitute a valid scale, thus combining data collection and data analysis in one step.

It should be remembered that each question or item on a structured instrument refers to a particular indicator by which a variable is measured and a guiding concept of the research objective(s) is operationalized.

SELECTING PROCEDURES FOR DATA COLLECTION

We have summarized the range of data collection techniques and instruments discussed in the previous section in Figure 11-1. This list is by no means exhaustive. It can be thought of, rather, as a classification of major types within which any specific procedure can be located. By means of this classification we

Figure 11-1 Classification of techniques and instruments

TECHNIQUES

Use of hardware
  audio-visual recording
  filming
  physiological monitoring
Direct observation by analyst
  complete observer
  observer as participant
  participant as observer
  complete participant
Use of secondary data
  review of public records
Respondent observation
  interview
  self-administration of questionnaire

INSTRUMENTS

Unstructured
  log
  interview guide
  schedule of open-ended questions
Structured
  schedule of closed-ended questions
  paper-and-pencil tests

---

can now proceed to discuss the general principles involved in selecting data collection procedures without limiting our discussion to the specific techniques or instruments listed here.

In selecting those procedures best suited for the proposed research, the analyst must consider a number of factors: (1) the method of research to be employed, (2) the field conditions under which the research is to be carried out, (3) the relative reliability and validity of alternative procedures, and (4) their relative cost (Dillman 1978). Whether a study is exploratory, descriptive, or explanatory will have a bearing on the choice of procedure. However, the procedures we have discussed do not have an exclusive relationship with any one method. The conditions under which the study is to be conducted, such as the length of time, the size and dispersion of the population, and certain characteristics of the persons to be observed, will also affect the choice of procedure. In addition, techniques and instruments are not always equally reliable and valid, so that the analyst may be forced to make a trade-off between these related qualities in the attainment of the research objectives. Finally, the analyst must choose among alternative procedures on the basis of their relative cost, selecting the one most reasonable in cost in relation to the policy objective to be achieved.

Method of Research

The exploratory method least restricts the choice of data collection procedures to be employed. In fact, multiple techniques are typically employed in such studies to discover a greater range of relevant variables and indicators.* Because they are small in size, exploratory studies lend themselves to the use of techniques that are more time-consuming and costly such as the use of hardware and participant observation. However, secondary data and respondent observation may also be employed to good advantage in such studies. Exploratory studies are restrictive with respect to instrumentation. Unstructured instruments, such as logs, interview guides, and open-ended questions, are typically used in order to permit the analyst to discover missing variables, indicators, or relations among them.

Because the descriptive method requires greater precision in observational procedures, it consequently restricts the choice of data collection techniques. When it is used in the study of large populations, as is usually the case, the alternatives are narrowed even further. Consequently, secondary data or some form of respondent observation are typically employed in descriptive studies. However, when such studies involve a small population, for example, the clients of a service program, some form of hardware or direct observation by the analyst is feasible. The descriptive method requires that all instruments be completely structured. Only in this manner can the analyst draw valid conclusions about the distribution of a set of indicators in a given population. For example, if the analyst should ask a group of 20 persons, "Why did you move?" there may be 20 different responses. Each answer may reflect a different indicator of the respondent's motivation to move—one psychological, one economic, one environmental, and so on. From these responses the analyst would be in error to conclude that the reasons people moved were equally distributed among the 20 indicators. In order to draw a valid conclusion regarding their distribution, the analyst would have to question each respondent about each indicator mentioned.

Explanatory studies, since they also require precision, are restrictive in observational procedures. But as they are usually smaller, a wider range can be employed than in descriptive studies. Hardware as well as secondary data and respondent observation can be used in explanatory studies. With respect to direct observation, the analyst is more likely to adopt the role of complete observer than participant observer. Explanatory studies also require instruments that are fully structured.

---

*This use of multiple techniques is referred to by Webb et al. as the "triangulation of measurement processes," the use of more than one measurement technique to verify a fact (1970, p. 3).

Field Conditions

The conditions under which data collection is to occur are an important determinant of the choice of procedure to be used. A number of conditions applicable to any study can be identified: (1) the time available for collecting data, (2) the complexity of the phenomenon being observed, (3) the size of the population to be observed, (4) its spatial distribution, (5) the motivation and/or sensitivity of the population to participation in the study, and (6) the capacity of the population to generate the data to be collected (Goode and Hatt 1952, pp. 170-176; Selltiz, Wrightsman, and Cook 1976, pp. 294-299). The relations between these field conditions and the various data collection procedures are summarized in Figure 11-2. The reader should keep in mind that our discussion is only suggestive. The conditions we identify are not exhaustive nor are they always applicable to specific situations. Furthermore, the relations we depict between the respective conditions and the procedures are *tendencies* not invariants. The reader will have to extrapolate from these general relations in making decisions about a specific situation.

In terms of the amount of time available for the collection of data, the use of hardware and various forms of direct observation by the analyst are the

Figure 11-2 Relations between field conditions and data collection procedures

1. least	*Time Available*		most
secondary data	questionnaire	interview	direct observation hardware
2. least	*Complexity of Phenomenon*		most
secondary data	questionnaire	interview	direct observation hardware
3. small	*Size of Population*		large
direct observation hardware	interview	questionnaire	secondary data
4. concentrated	*Spatial Distribution of Population*		dispersed
direct observation hardware	interview	questionnaire	secondary data
5. low	*Motivation of Population*		high
direct observation hardware	interview	questionnaire	secondary data
6. low	*Capacity of Population*		high
direct observation	interview	hardware questionnaire	secondary data

most taxing. The use of both audio or video recorders and participant observation require that data be collected while the phenomenon under study is occurring and that the recording follow certain predetermined procedures. The interview is more time-consuming than the self-administered questionnaire, both because of the time required to contact the respondent and the time taken up by interviewer-respondent interaction. The use of secondary data is least time-consuming because observations have already been made and recorded.

When the phenomenon under study is rather complex—for example, the interaction among members of an organization or between professionals and clients in a service program—some form of direct observation or hardware is most appropriate. This affords the analyst better overall coverage of the different behaviors of each actor. The interview is usually more appropriate than the questionnaire because the interviewer can assist the respondent in following the line of inquiry about a complicated set of events. Secondary data are apt to be least appropriate because reporting systems tend to be confined to simple events.

As the size of the population to be observed increases, the use of secondary data becomes the most appropriate procedure. The cost in time and money of collecting original data from very large samples can become prohibitive. The questionnaire is more appropriate than the interview because it reduces the resources needed to make contact with the respondent and eliminates personal interaction between interviewer and respondent. Direct observation and the use of hardware are appropriate with relatively small study populations. A similar relationship exists between the spatial distribution of the study population and the appropriateness of the various data collection procedures. The use of secondary data is the most feasible procedure for studying populations that are widely dispersed. Questionnaires are more feasible than interviews because they eliminate the need for personal interaction. Direct observation and the use of hardware are feasible only with populations that are relatively concentrated in space.

When the focus of investigation is human behavior, the motivation of the persons involved to participate in the study and/or their sensitivity to being observed become important considerations in the choice of data collection procedures. When motivation is high (and sensitivity low), secondary data are presumably appropriate. Since it can be assumed that such persons would give freely of information to public reporting systems, the analyst can resort to questionnaires rather than interviews in the expectation of a high rate of return. However, when the respondents are likely to withhold information or be sensitive about being observed, some form of direct observation by the analyst or the use of hardware is more appropriate. Thus in the study of illicit or deviant behavior, the analyst is often a participant-observer, and one-way mirrors and videotapes are commonly used to study the interactions between service providers and their clients.

Similarly, in each of the procedures certain assumptions are implied about the capacity of persons to supply the necessary information without assistance from the analyst. The use of public records assumes the highest capacity because such records usually involve the least supervision in filling them out. The use of hardware or questionnaires assumes more capacity than does an interview because the respondents themselves must interpret the nature of the information desired. When it is necessary to stimulate the memory of the respondent, or to probe psychological states, the interview is more appropriate. Participant observation assumes the least capacity, because the analyst makes the various observations based on personal experience.

In discussing the merits of the various procedures, certain trade-offs become readily apparent. A data collection procedure that may be most appropriate with respect to one condition may totally miss the mark in terms of another. For example, if the phenomenon under study is extremely complex, the analyst is advised to use some form of direct observation. However, if the time available to collect the data is very short, the analyst would do well to use secondary data or a questionnaire. Similarly, if the population being observed is geographically dispersed, the most appropriate procedure is the use of secondary data or a questionnaire. However, if the motivation to respond is very low, direct observation or an interview would produce better results. Thus, the scheme we presented in Figure 11-2 for relating field conditions to data collection procedures cannot be used prescriptively—it will not indicate to the reader what trade-offs to make. But it does make one more aware of the existence of trade-offs, and can be used to help the analyst discover the implications of the more specific decisions he or she must make.

Validity and Reliability

Data collection procedures must also be chosen on the basis of their anticipated validity and reliability. Validity refers to the degree to which the data collected by the technique or instrument correspond to the indicators sought by the analyst. Reliability refers to the degree to which repeated application of the same procedures under the same conditions will yield the same data. It is commonly assumed that the analyst will choose procedures that are high both in validity and reliability. However, it is less commonly recognized that a procedure high in validity may be low in reliability, and vice versa.* The relationship be-

*The traditional view holds that a measurement device that is high in validity is necessarily high in reliability, but that the reverse is not necessarily so. This view is derived from work on highly structured instruments and is not applicable to comparisons among data collection procedures. Some procedures are more valid because they are less likely to distort the phenomenon being measured, yet they are less reliable because of their unstructured nature, allowing for more random error. Even highly structured instruments can yield measures that are high in validity and low in reliability (internal homogeneity) when the phenomenon being measured is multidimensional or variable over time. For a fuller discussion of the validity-reliability continuum see Selltiz, Wrightsman, and Cook (1976, pp. 194-197).

Figure 11-3 Relation between reliability, validity, and techniques of observation

low	Validity		high
hardware secondary data complete observer	questionnaire	interview	complete participant
low	Reliability		high
complete participant	interview	questionnaire	hardware secondary data complete observer

tween these qualities and the data collection procedures we have been discussing is summarized in Figure 11-3.

When studying human behavior, direct observation by the analyst in the role of complete participant or participant-observer is considered the most valid technique of data collection. Such roles allow the analyst to observe the symbolic or subjective meaning of behavior through his or her own experience. By the same token, the interview is considered to be a more valid technique than the questionnaire, because it allows the analyst to assist the respondent in grasping the intended meaning of the questions, and to probe or inquire about the meaning of the respondent's answers. The use of hardware and forms of direct observation in which the analyst is a complete observer are considered to be least valid, because of the lack of any opportunity to tap subjective meanings. Secondary data may also be considered least valid when they consist of public records of events the respondent is reluctant to disclose. For example, records of the Internal Revenue Service are probably the least valid means of collecting data on personal income.

These techniques, by and large, have a reverse relationship with reliability. The use of hardware, secondary data, and the role of the analyst as complete observer probably yield the most reliable data. They either eliminate the analyst in the observation process or allow the use of highly standardized procedures that are not altered by interaction with the respondent. Similarly the questionnaire can be considered more reliable than the interview, because it eliminates personal interaction between the observer and the observed, a source of variation in procedure. The role of complete participant is the least reliable, because it tends toward total subjectivity on the part of the observer.

Again, disclosing this general trade-off between the validity and reliability of various data collection techniques does not constitute a prescription about which technique to use in a given situation. The reader will have to determine whether or not symbolic or subjective meaning is a significant aspect of the phenomenon under investigation. For example, in studying traffic accidents or the incidence of diseases, the trade-off may not be present; in the study of attitudes about driving or illness it may be quite significant. Once the existence of a trade-off has been established, the analyst must seek out evidence that will help in judging the relative validity or reliability of the various techniques under consideration.

Up to this point there has been relatively little said about what criteria to use in selecting an instrument(s) for data collection. A significant relationship exists between the degree to which instruments are structured and their validity and reliability. (See Figure 11–4.) The log and other forms of less structured instruments are likely to be more valid than closed-ended questions and paper-and-pencil tests. That is, they allow a better fit between the indicators by which the respondent views the phenomenon and those chosen by the analyst to represent its significant properties. On the other hand, the more structured instruments, because they are explicitly systematic, are likely to be more reliable. This relationship is reflected in the fact that less structured instruments are appropriate in exploratory studies, in which validity is of primary importance, and tightly structured instruments are appropriate in descriptive studies, in which reliability is of primary importance. Thus structured instruments can be both reliable *and* valid when they are based on the results of an unstructured exploratory study in which the respondent has specified the indicators he or she uses to identify a given phenomenon (Harding and Clement 1979).

Our characterization of paper-and-pencil tests as relatively invalid may seem unjustified, particularly since they figure so heavily in psychological research. However, further reflection should clarify the point. The controversy over the validity of intelligence tests is a good example. It is probably accurate to say that responses to a standard set of questions provide a less true picture of a person's intelligence than a detailed log of how that person responds to a variety of situations calling for problem-solving behavior. Yet a log is a highly individualized set of observations that is of doubtful reliability in comparing the performance of many persons. The point to be made is not that paper-and-pencil tests are inherently invalid but that greater care must be used to establish their validity. As indicators of psychological states they are, at best, indirect. For this reason psychologists go to great length to establish the validity of such tests by

Figure 11–4   Relations between validity, reliability, and observational instruments

low	*Validity*	high
paper-and-pencil tests	interview guide	low
closed-ended questions	open-ended questions	
high	*Reliability*	low

determining the correlation between their results and the behaviors they are intended to predict.

Cost

Finally, the various data collection procedures must be evaluated in terms of their cost. The use of hardware and the various forms of direct observation by the analyst are probably the most expensive observational techniques. Their high cost derives from the fact that either equipment or personnel must be present throughout the duration of the events being observed. In addition, when such techniques are used in an unstructured manner, they generate an enormous amount of data that must be recorded and reviewed for relevance. The interview is more costly than the questionnaire because personnel must be hired to conduct the interview, and because travel is often required to bring the interviewer and interviewee together. The use of secondary data is by far the least costly data collection procedure. This characteristic alone probably accounts for its widespread use. However, in evaluating alternative data collection procedures, cost must always be weighed against other criteria one is trying to maximize. Obviously the low cost of using secondary data that turn out to be relatively invalid does not compensate for the failure to achieve the analyst's research objectives. The cost of data collection must also be weighed against the cost of policy execution. For it is a cardinal rule that the cost of research undertaken on behalf of policy making should constitute only a small proportion of the cost of executing that policy. Were this not the case, the benefits obtained from the policy might be outweighed by the cost of obtaining them.

PLAN FOR FIELD WORK

The results of this stage of the research design process should be expressed in a plan for field work. Such a plan is simply a statement of the techniques and instruments the analyst has selected and a description of the steps involved in their use. A field work plan is important for two reasons. It conveys to the person whose administrative approval is necessary, or whose monetary support is being solicited, that the analyst's understanding of the actual procedures is sufficient for their successful execution. In addition, such a plan is necessary for estimating, in stage 9 of the design process, the resources needed to carry out the study.

The field work plan should describe each major step involved in using the selected technique. These steps involve the procurement of equipment and/or the hiring of personnel, training in use of the technique, the actual process of observation, the recording of observations (where this is not built into the instrument), and the preparation of the data for storage and retrieval. Each step should be described in terms of the personnel or equipment required, the amount of time it will take, and where it will occur. The analyst may need to consult the references cited in this chapter for the particular technique being described.

For example, a field work plan may call for the hiring of 20 interviewers to conduct 20 interviews a piece, each interviewer to receive three hours of training by the analyst. It may further specify that each interview is to last one hour, to take place in the respondent's home, and to require one-half hour of travel time by the interviewer. In addition, the interviewer is to make three attempts to contact a prospective respondent. Information is to be recorded on the interview schedule and edited by the interviewer, a process expected to take one-half hour. Five coders are to be hired to code the data for keypunching, which is expected to take one hour per schedule. Data are to be stored on computer tape for analysis.

The analyst may choose an instrument for data collection that has already been constructed. Inventories of existing instruments are available (Miller 1970; Bonjean, Hill and McLemore 1967). In addition the analyst may find readymade instruments in the periodical and book literature as discussed in Chapter 2. In such an event, the plan need simply refer to the instrument and cite the source in which it is described and evaluated. Of course, the analyst may also wish to append a copy of the instrument to the research design.

However, since most policy research deals with unique situations, the analyst may have to construct the appropriate instruments to implement the study design. Although their actual construction may be undertaken later as part of the research process, their completion at this stage will facilitate the analyst's projections in the remaining stages of the research design. In any event, the field work plan should describe the type of instruments and include a sample of items to be used in order to convey to the reader the nature of the instruments to be developed. Guidance in the construction of instruments is provided in several good references (Schatzman and Strauss 1973; Babbie 1975; Goode and Hatt 1952; Selltiz, Wrightsman, and Cook 1976).

It is helpful if the fieldwork plan is accompanied by a chart which specifies the data collection procedure to be used for each indicator identified in Chapter 10 (see Figure 11-5). For each indicator or datum listed as an operational definition of a guiding concept (1), the chart should specify the technique to be used (2), the source of that datum (3), and the instrument and item number by which it will be elicited (4). By means of such a chart, the analyst can ascertain that every datum called for by the research objective(s) has a procedure by which it will be collected, and that only those procedures will be used which are required to attain those data. If all the data are to be collected from the same source and by the same technique, columns (2) and (3) will be super-

(1) Indicators of guiding concepts/ variables	(2) Technique of observation	(3) Source of datum	(4) Instrument/ Question no.

Figure 11-5 Techniques and instruments to be used in data collection (continuation of Figure 10-3)

fluous. However, in some studies, multiple sources, multiple techniques, or multiple instruments may be required. For example, in a study of the health practices of elderly persons, some data may come from elderly respondents, some from the respondents' spouses, some from the respondents' doctors, and some from medical records. In such a case, a chart such as that in Figure 11-5 can prove quite useful in keeping track of the relevant procedures to be used.

SUMMARY

Our outline of the steps involved in designing this stage of research has brought to light several criteria for selecting one set of procedures rather than another. The procedures should be selected on the basis of (1) the method of research, (2) the conditions under which the study is to be conducted, (3) their anticipated validity and reliability, and (4) their cost.

The results of this design stage should be presented in a plan for field work which consists of three elements:

1. a description of the technique(s) to be used in terms of the steps to be carried out, the personnel and equipment required, the time to be consumed, and the location of its execution
2. the instruments to be used, or a description sufficient to indicate their nature once constructed

3. a chart linking the techniques and instrument items to each indicator of guiding concepts identified in Chapter 6.

REFERENCES

BABBIE, EARL R. *The Practice of Social Research.* Belmont, Calif.: Wadsworth Publishing Co., Inc. 1975.

BONJEAN, CHARLES M., RICHARD J. HILL, and S. DALE McLEMORE. *Sociological Measurement: An Inventory of Scales and Indices.* San Francisco: Chandler Publishing Co., 1967.

COLLIER, JOHN JR. *Visual Anthropology: Photography as a Research Method.* New York: Holt, Rinehart and Winston, 1967.

CRANE, JULIA G., and MICHAEL V. ANGROSINO. *Field Projects in Anthropology.* Morristown, N.J.: General Learning Press, 1974.

DAWES, R. M. *Measures and Indicators of Attitudes.* New York: Wiley, 1971.

DILLMAN, DON A. *Mail and Telephone Surveys.* New York: John Wiley and Sons, 1978.

EDWARDS, ALLEN L. *Techniques of Attitude Scale Construction.* New York: Appleton-Century-Crofts, 1957.

GANS, HERBERT J. *The Urban Villagers,* New York: Free Press, 1962.

GOLD, RAYMOND L. "Roles in Sociological Field Observations," in *Issues in Participant Observation,* eds. George J. McCall and J. L. Simmons. Reading, Mass.: Addison-Wesley, 1969, pp. 30–38.

GOODE, WILLIAM J., and PAUL K. HATT. *Methods in Social Research.* New York: McGraw-Hill, 1952.

HARDING, JOE. "Heuristic Elicitation Methodology and FRM Acceptability," paper presented at WHO Conference on Cross Cultural Research Methods and Instruments and FRM Acceptability, May 13–15, 1974, Geneva, Switzerland.

HARDING, JOE, and DOROTHY C. CLEMENT. "Regularities in the Continuity and Change of Role Structures, the Ixil Maya," in *Predicting Sociocultural Change,* eds. Susan Abbott and John Van Willigen. Athens, Ga.: University of Georgia Press, 1979.

HEIDER, KARL G. *Ethnographic Film.* Austin, Texas: University Press, 1976.

HOWELL, JOSEPH T. *Hard Living on Clay Street.* Garden City, N.Y.: Anchor Books, 1973.

HUMPHREYS, LAUD. *Tearoom Trade, Impersonal Sex in Public Places.* Chicago: Aldine Publishing Co., 1970.

LIEBOW, ELLIOT. *Tally's Corner.* Boston: Little, Brown, 1967.

McCALL, GEORGE J., and J. L. SIMMONS, eds. *Issues in Participant Observation.* Reading, Mass.: Addison-Wesley, 1969.

MILLER, DELBERT C. *Handbook of Research Design and Social Measurement* (2nd ed.). New York: David McKay Company, Inc., 1970.

PELTO, PETTI J., and GRETEL H. PELTO. *Anthropological Research.* Cambridge, England: Cambridge University Press, 1978.

SCHATZMAN, LEONARD, and ANSELM L. STRAUSS. *Field Research: Strategies for a Natural Sociology.* Englewood Cliffs, N.J.: Prentice-Hall, Inc., 1973.

SELLTIZ, CLAIRE, LAWRENCE S. WRIGHTSMAN, and STUART W. COOK, *Research Methods in Social Relations* (3rd ed.). New York: Holt, Rinehart and Winston, 1976.

SPRADLEY, JAMES P., and DAVID W. McCURDY. *The Cultural Experience.* Chicago: Science Research Associates, Inc., 1972.

WEBB, EUGENE J., DONALD T. CAMPBELL, RICHARD D. SCHWARTZ, and LEE SEECHRIST. *Unobtrusive Measures: Nonreactive Research in the Social Sciences.* Chicago: Rand McNally & Company, 1970.

chapter 12 / stage 8:
techniques of
data analysis

We come now to the final stage dealing with the substance of the research design, a description of the techniques to be used in analyzing the data to be collected. The specification of these techniques permits the analyst to anticipate whether or not the findings that can be derived from the data will answer the question(s) of fact with which the study began. In other words, this stage brings the technical steps in research design together into a final demonstration of their adequacy.

The analysis of data can be conceptualized in four steps: (1) combining data into measures of the guiding concepts; (2) aggregating those measures for the study population as a whole (for descriptive studies); (3) verifying relations between concepts when they are at issue; and (4) determining the limitations on inferences that can be drawn based on the research design. The analyst's first task is to organize the data into appropriate measures of the guiding concepts specified in the research objective(s). However, such measures apply to individual units of observation. Therefore, in descriptive studies the measures for each unit must be combined into some summary measure for the study population as a whole. Clearly, it is the experience of the study population as a whole (or its appropriate parts) that meets the research objective(s), not the experience of individual units. The third step is applicable to studies in which relations between variables are at issue. It involves identifying those relations and determining how they will be measured or verified. Lastly, the analyst is obligated to indicate the extent to which inferences can be made from the data as analyzed. It is at this point in the design process that the analyst is able to review the implications of the decisions made at each prior stage for meeting the research objectives.

CONSTRUCTING MEASURES OF GUIDING CONCEPTS

In constructing measures of guiding concepts the analyst returns to the process of conceptual clarification executed in stage 3 of the research design. It will be recalled, from our discussion of that process, that a highly abstract or global concept is first reduced to one or more subconcepts or variables, and then each variable in turn is reduced to one or more indicators by which it is measured (see Figure 7-3). Constructing a measure of a guiding concept is simply a reversal of that process. When the guiding concept refers to a unidimensional phenomenon—that is, one represented by a single variable—and which in turn is represented by only one indicator, the process is simple: The indicator is the measure of the guiding concept. Thus, for example, a score on a standardized achievement test is a measure of academic achievement. However, when the concept refers to a multidimensional phenomenon involving several variables, each of which in turn is represented by several indicators, the process becomes more complicated. The analyst begins by combining the indicators into a single measure of each variable, and then combines each of those measures into a higher-level single measure.

Unfortunately the terminology used in the literature to refer to measures involving more than one indicator is inconsistent (Babbie 1975; Selltiz, Wrightsman, and Cook 1976). In keeping with what we believe to be common sense and prevailing practice in policy making, we use the term *scale* to refer to a measure involving a single indicator and the term *index* to refer to a measure involving multiple indicators or variables. Thus an index can be thought of as a composite of two or more scales. A well-known example is the Cost of Living Index, which combines changes in the cost of various consumer items (scales) into a single measure of change in the cost of living. Similarly it is possible to construct indexes of employability, housing quality, and health status.

The process of constructing a measure of a guiding concept can be recapitulated through a modification of Figure 7-3 as has been done in Figure 12-1.

An index implies that the composite measure is at least ordinal if not interval in nature. The counterpart for composite measures that are qualitative or nominal in nature is a *typology*. A typology can be thought of as a composite of two or more classification schemes, each of which reflects individual indicators or variables. Therefore, in discussing techniques for combining multiple indicators into an overall measure we shall discuss index and typology construction. In this discussion we use the term *measure* in a generic sense to refer to whatever quantitative or qualitative measurement is arrived at to represent a guiding concept. It may be represented by a scale or classification of a single indicator; or it may consist of an index or typology that combines several indicators or variables.

It should be recognized that it is not always necessary to combine all

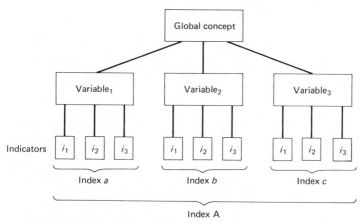

Figure 12-1 Constructing a measure of à guiding concept through recombining indicators

indicators of a given variable into a single measure. Sometimes no reasonable basis exists for their combination. In such a case, the data for a given concept are reported as a series of individual indicators, as in a profile, or grouped into several indexes or typologies. For example, the concept "quality of life" of residential neighborhoods may be operationalized in terms of 30 indicators. To combine them into a single measure is difficult to justify conceptually. However, it is possible to conceive of three indexes that reflect the physical, the economic, and the social aspects of the environment.

The process of combining individual scales or classifications into composite ones requires planning on the part of the analyst. While the process of conceptual clarification specifies what indicators are related to a variable, and how those indicators are related through variables to the guiding concept, it does not tell us what relative weight to give each indicator. For this the analyst must turn to appropriate quantitative or qualitative techniques. Because the literature on this subject is relatively sparse, we will describe the range of techniques available before discussing the bases on which the analyst may choose among them.* For the purpose of simplifying this discussion we will assume

*There is a long tradition in social science research of developing techniques for constructing composite measures out of multiple items on a questionnaire or interview schedule (Babbie 1975; Selltiz, Wrightsman, and Cook 1976; Edwards 1957; Dawes 1971). However, these techniques are not directly relevant for our purposes. In the first place they usually are based on the assumption that the underlying phenomenon is unidimensional. In this sense they are more appropriate to the construction of what we have defined as scales. In addition, they were developed to measure psychological states rather than behavior or other objective phenomena, thus creating special problems regarding their validity. Therefore, we will discuss techniques that, though related to this tradition, grow directly out of experience with policy research. However, the reader should consult this literature when it may be appropriate to his or her measurement problem.

that a given concept is represented by only one variable, so that only one step will be required to construct the overall measure. If the reader is dealing with a concept represented by multiple variables as well as multiple indicators, he or she should be able to extrapolate a two-step process from this discussion.

Deductive Techniques

Deductive techniques for combining multiple indicators into a measure of a guiding concept involve decisions about their relative importance prior to the collection of data. These decisions are arrived at through reasoning from some assumption that is deemed valid by the analyst. The simplest of such techniques is to sum the values of the individual indicators. Such a technique can be used with indicators measured on nominal as well as ordinal and interval scales. Nominal-scale indicators are treated as a dichotomy in which the presence of the property is given a score of 1, and its absence a score of 0. The assumption underlying such an approach to index construction is that all indicators are of equal importance in measuring the variable in question.

For example, an index of housing quality could be constructed based on the presence or absence of the following properties

missing window pane	_ yes _ no
no hot water	_ yes _ no
no flush toilet	_ yes _ no
crack in foundation	_ yes _ no
leak in roof	_ yes _ no

The score on such an index for an individual house would be computed by summing the number of items checked "yes." The index yields a range of scores from 0 to 5.

This technique of index construction can be refined if the analyst has a reasonable basis for assuming that one indicator is more important than another in contributing to the overall value of the variable being measured. Such an assumption could be based on prior evidence, subjective judgment, or the value preferences of the decision maker. In this case numerical weights are attached to the value of each indicator according to its relative importance in the index. It should be noted that the numerical weight does not necessarily reflect the size of this difference, merely that one indicator is relatively more important than another. Most analysts are agreed that weighting should be done only when there is a clear basis for assuming a substantial difference. In the absence of a compelling reason, indicators should be treated as of equal importance in the construction of an index.

Returning to our previous example, the analyst may have a reasonable basis for assuming that the absence of hot water or a flush toilet is a significantly more critical factor in housing deterioration than the other three indicators. As a result, these two indicators may be given a weight of 2. The revised procedure for computing the index of housing quality is

Indicator	Raw score			Weight		Weighted score
missing window pane	_ yes	_ no	X	1 =		___
no hot water	_ yes	_ no	X	2 =		___
no flush toilet	_ yes	_ no	X	2 =		___
crack in foundation	_ yes	_ no	X	1 =		___
leak in roof	_ yes	_ no	X	1 =		___

A score for an individual house on this index is computed by summing the weighted scores for all indicators. The scores on such an index range in value from 0 to 7.

In combining indicators into an index, one must ascertain that the respective scales have the same range of values. If they do not, the scales should be standardized to the same range. Failure to do so results in the application of implicit weights in the construction of the index. Let us suppose, for example, that the analyst wishes to construct an index of the potential for housing rehabilitation which combines our weighted index of housing quality with two other indicators—the age of the house and its value. Now the analyst is faced with three scales which have quite different ranges. To standardize them the analyst decides to convert them to a scale of 10 for ease of interpretation (any scale can be used as the standard), as follows

Indicator	Range of scale	Units in scale	Correction factor	Units in standardized scale
index of housing quality	0–7	8	1.25	10.0
age of house (in years)	0–50	51	0.20	10.2
value of house (in $1000s)	10–100	91	0.11	10.0

In addition to standardizing each scale, the analyst must make sure that all have the same starting point. To do this in our example, we add -1 to the score for the value of a house to bring that scale in line with the beginning value of the other scales. Thus, in computing the index of the potential for housing rehabilitation, the score of an individual house on each scale is multiplied by its respective correction factor, adjusted to the same starting value, and summed, as in the following formula

index - (1.25 X quality) + (0.20 X age) + [(0.10 X value) –1]

An index requires that the data from which it is constructed be either interval or ordinal. The data collected by the analyst do not always meet this requirement. Frequently he or she is confronted with classificatory data that fall into distinct categories, whether nominal or ordered. From such data the analyst must then construct a typology. A typology consists of a series of types, each of which is a special combination of the variables into which a guiding concept has been broken down. That is, each type is a unique combination of the properties or dimensions of the phenomenon under study. A typology differs from a classification. In a classification the units of observation are arranged into groups on the basis of a single dimension. In a typology, however, the units are arranged on the basis of several dimensions, because a typology is derived by combining or relating two or more classification schemes. This technique has been codified by Lazarsfeld and Barton (1951, Barton 1955), on whom the subsequent discussion relies heavily.

The reader is doubtless familiar with the graphic technique of relating two quantitative variables, each representing a property, as coordinates or axes to form a two-dimensional space or plane. On this plane are plotted the values of the units of observation with respect to these variables, so that every unit has its location in such a property space. A graph of this kind is called a scattergram of a bivariate distribution. A somewhat similar property space can be constructed from classificatory data when the two variables are qualitative.* Thus, we can combine or relate two dichotomies, one on each coordinate, the result being a grid of four cells, wherein every unit of observation has its location in one or another. This is the familiar fourfold table. To be sure, there is a difference between a scattergram and a fourfold table. The axes of the scattergram, and the space they form, are contiguous. The axes of the fourfold table, on the other hand, are segmented into distinct categories which intersect and thereby cut up the property space into an array of distinct cells. The value of each cell is indicated by the respective values of the intersecting categories. Hence another difference between the two property spaces is that each unit of observation in a scattergram has its own point-specific value, but the units located within a given cell of a fourfold table all share the cell value.

In a similar manner, the analyst can relate three variables representing

---

*The plane formed by two coordinates, each representing a variable, is referred to by Lazarsfeld and Barton generically as a property space. However, when the coordinates represent qualitative variables ("attributes" is the term used by them), then Lazarsfeld and Barton refer to the plane as an attribute space.

as many properties, one to the others. This would result in a three-dimensional property space which, if all three variables were dichotomized, would enclose eight cells. Graphic portrayal would require a cube, a bit difficult to achieve on flat paper. However, we could convey the same idea were we to divide the categories of one of the coordinates of a fourfold table into two subcategories each, which would represent the third variable, thereby resulting in eight cells. And were we to do this on both coordinates, we could relate four variables in a property space of 16 cells on a plane. The technique may be demonstrated by means of the following illustration.

Let us assume that the analyst is dealing with the policy problem of how to reduce unemployment. The research objective is to discover barriers to employment among the current jobless which might be addressed by remedial programs. An exploratory study of the phenomenon utilizing interviews with counselors at the state employment service discloses that certain workers encounter much greater difficulty than do others in finding employment. The counselors reveal that the two groups of job seekers are distinguishable in terms of the properties of (1) age, (2) education, (3) skill, and (4) work history. More specifically, the unemployed person who eventually enters the job market is more successful if he or she is under forty-five years of age, has completed high school, has a specific job skill, and has a stable work record (that is, no more than two jobs in the last five years). Conversely, the opposites work to the person's disadvantage. Note that this information does not come in interval form, because it is obtained indirectly from employment counselors rather than directly from the unemployed themselves.

We can now relate these four properties of the phenomenon of chronic unemployment in the form of a property space of 16 cells as shown in Figure 12-2. Note that each property has been dichotomized into alternatives which serve either as a plus or as a minus in seeking employment. The values of the cells are indicated by the combinations of plus and minus signs that symbolize the categories of the variables of age, education, skills, and work history in that order. The table is so set up that the values of the cells decrease from positive to negative going from left to right and going from top to bottom. Thus cell 1 represents the most favorable combination and cell 16, the least favorable combination of properties from the viewpoint of employability.

The next step in typology construction is to reduce the property space from 16 cells to a smaller number of clusters or types. The more numerous the cells, the more difficult the reduction process. One approach to the task is a commonsensical or pragmatic one. Returning to Figure 12-2 we might reason as follows: (1) Job seekers who have more factors working for than against them are sufficiently alike and should, therefore, constitute one subgroup; (2) those who have more factors working against than for them should, for the same reason, constitute another subgroup; and (3) those who have as many factors working for as against them should constitute a third subgroup. In other words,

Work record	Skill level	Age: (+) Under 45 years — Years of education: (+) 12 or less	(+) Under 45 years — (−) More than 12	(−) 45 years and older — (+) 12 or less	(−) 45 years and older — (−) More than 12
(+) 2 jobs or less in 5 years	(+) skilled	*a* + + + +	*b* + − + +	*c* − + + +	*d* − − + +
	(−) unskilled	*e* + + + −	*f* + − + −	*g* − + + −	*h* − − + +
(−) more than 2 jobs in 5 years	(+) skilled	*i* + + − +	*j* + − − +	*k* − + − +	*l* − − − +
	(−) unskilled	*m* + + − −	*n* + − − −	*o* − + − −	*p* − − − −

Figure 12-2 Property space relating the four barriers to employment treated as dichotomies

cells *a, b, c, e,* and *i* (where pluses outnumber minuses) should be combined to comprise the "highly employable" type; cells *h, l, n, o,* and *p* (where minuses outnumber pluses) should be combined to comprise the "difficult to employ," and cells *d, f, g, j, k,* and *m* (where pluses equal minuses) should be combined to comprise the "moderately employable" type. The results of these combinations are shown in Figure 12-3. Like any pragmatic approach, this one also raises questions regarding the proper allocation of borderline cells; in this instance cells *i* and *h.* That is, can we place a floater who has an unstable work history (cell *i*) in the same type as a steady, stable worker (cell *a*) simply because both are young, high-school educated, and skilled? Similarly, can we place a person with a stable work history (cell *h*) in the same type as a floater (cell *p*) simply because both are older, uneducated, and unskilled? The answer is that in allocating borderline cells some arbitrariness is unavoidable.

Before embarking on reduction, the analyst is advised to return to the conceptual framework and reexamine the purpose and orientation of the investigation. The combinations of cells and hence the typology, should serve the ends of the research and ultimately that of policy. In view of this, perhaps a different typology or a more elaborate one of employability might be more useful for the policy maker than that shown in Figure 12-3. In addition, the analyst should consider that certain cells represent specific combinations of properties

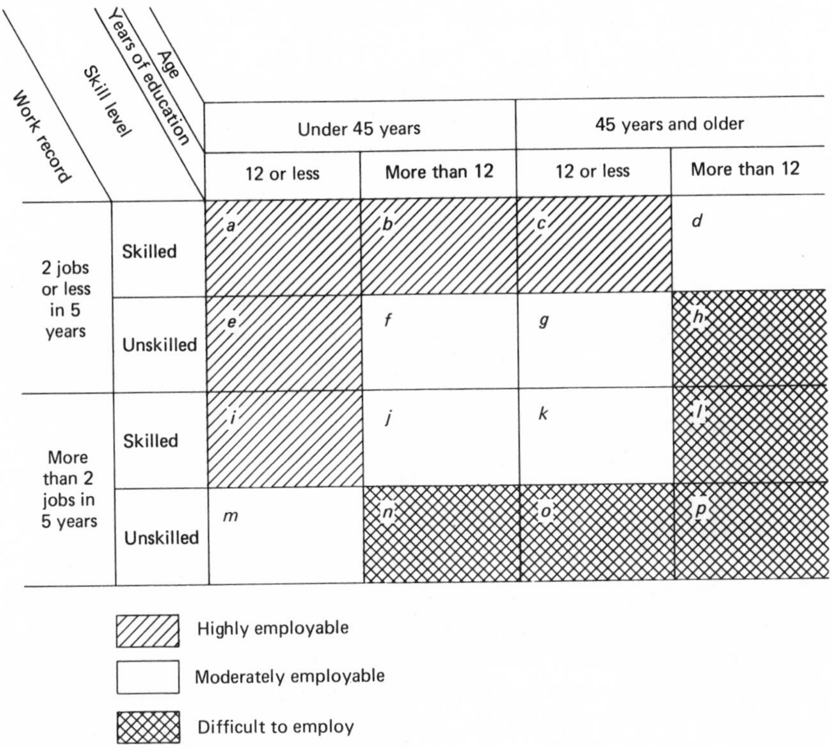

		Under 45 years		45 years and older	
		12 or less	More than 12	12 or less	More than 12
2 jobs or less in 5 years	Skilled	a	b	c	d
	Unskilled	e	f	g	h
More than 2 jobs in 5 years	Skilled	i	j	k	l
	Unskilled	m	n	o	p

(Axis labels: Work record, Skill level, Years of education, Age)

Highly employable

Moderately employable

Difficult to employ

Figure 12-3 Typology of employability

which probably never or rarely ever occur in real life. Such a nonfrequency cell might be eliminated from the property space at the outset. Cells *e* and *g* (Figure 12-2) are cases in point. Thus, it is improbable that a high-school educated worker with a stable job history would also be lacking in any skill, since skill is a function of both education and job tenure. However, unless a cell represents a combination of properties that is obviously illogical and unreal, the analyst is cautioned against its hasty elimination on a priori grounds. The analyst should first use the scheme in an investigation to see whether indeed the questionable cell remains empty, because not one case in the study sample has that value.

The reader's attention is called to the fact that the typology of employability depicted in Figure 12-3 is ordinal in character. That is, the relation of the three types of job seekers is that of a gradient from the most to the least employable type. Thus it should be noted that from classificatory data one can construct a typology ordinal in its structure, and this in turn can be converted into an index. Thus, by assigning numerical values to its constituent types, we can convert the employability typology into an index of employability. Assuming that a three-point index serves our needs, it would assume the following form.

Employability type	Combination of properties shown in cells of Figure 12-3	Index value
Highly employable	cells *a, b, c, e, i*	3
Moderately employable	cells *d, f, g, j, k, m*	2
Difficult to employ	cells *h, l, n, o, p*	1

An index constructed from an ordinal typology has a distinct advantage over an index constructed from the summed scale values of its constituent variables, as described earlier. Index values derived from an ordinal typology can be operationally defined by the precise combination of properties to which they correspond. Those derived from summed scale values only tell the analyst that one index value is higher than another.

Inductive Techniques

The previous techniques entail some prior knowledge of the phenomenon under study or some other reasonable basis upon which to justify the combination of multiple indicators into an overall measure. Such techniques are adopted before the data are collected or analyzed. However, when such a basis does not exist one must turn to a posteriori techniques, techniques that are applied after the data have been collected and are based on the nature of the distribution of those data or their interrelatedness in the population under study. Such techniques are inductive in nature.

The simplest of these approaches is based on the distribution of the values or categories of the various indicators within the study population. An index score is determined by a given unit's position vis-à-vis the other units of observation, with respect to the covariation of the various indicators. For this reason we will call such techniques *positional*. They result in indexes or typologies in which the observed population is evenly divided among the values or types of the composite measure. The assumption underlying positional techniques is that incidents of the phenomenon being measured are evenly distributed in the real world, and that the data in question are a reasonably accurate reflection of that distribution. It follows, therefore, that any positional slicing of the data into thirds or quartiles or percentiles will represent valid differences in the phenomenon in question.

With indicators that are at least ordinal in scale, one sums the scores on all scales (or rank orders) for each unit of observation. Next, the units are arrayed by the rank order of their summed scores. This rank order is then converted into an index by slicing the array into equal segments (number of units) depending on the number of index values desired, and assigning the corresponding index value to each segment. For the purpose of illustration, let us assume in our previous example of the index of housing quality that ten houses have been observed. We add the score (0,1) on all five indicators for each house, and array the ten houses according to their summed scores. Assuming that we want a five-scale index, we divide the array into fifths, assign a value of 1 through 5 to each fifth, and end up with the following index scores for each house

House	Summed score	Index value
A	0	
B	0	1
C	1	
D	1	2
E	2	
F	3	3
G	7	
H	8	4
I	9	
J	9	5

When the indicator scales being combined are interval in nature, a more sophisticated approach can be used. The data on the respective indicators can be displayed in two-dimensional scattergram. Then, on the basis of the least squares line of regression, the units of observation can be assigned an index based on the number of σ's in which they fall from that line. For the purpose of illustration, let us assume that we wish to combine age and amount of education into an index of employability. (See Figure 12–4.) We would prepare a scattergram and compute the least squares line of regression. Then we would draw through the scattergram two bands on eitherside of the line of regression, one representing $\pm.5\sigma$, and the other representing $\pm1\sigma$. To all the units falling within the first band above and below the line we would assign an index value of 1; to those falling within the second band, an index value of 2; and to those falling outside the bands, an index value of 3 (Dyer 1970).

Finally, in the case of an overall measure that is nominal in nature, a typology can be constructed on the basis of equal frequencies among the constituent types. This is done by constructing a matrix formed by the indicators to be combined, and displaying the distribution of the units of observation in that matrix (see Figure 12–5). These steps can be accomplished easily by means of a computer cross-tabulation program (Nie, et al. 1970). Then, in keeping with the

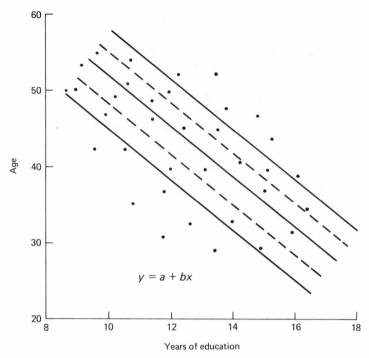

Figure 12-4 Use of scattergram to construct an index of employability

Work record	Skill level	Age →	Under 45 years		45 years and over	
		Years of education →	12 or less	More than 12	12 or less	More than 12
2 jobs or less in 5 years	Skilled		a $n = 0$	b $n = 5$	c $n = 0$	d $n = 5$
	Unskilled		e $n = 0$	f $n = 10$	g $n = 10$	h $n = 5$
More than 2 jobs in 5 years	Skilled		i $n = 5$	j $n = 0$	k $n = 10$	l $n = 10$
	Unskilled		m $n = 5$	n $n = 10$	o $n = 5$	p $n = 20$

Figure 12-5 Frequency distribution within property space relating the four barriers to employment as dichotomies

policy interests of the analysis, one combines adjacent cells so as to create types roughly equivalent in size. Thus, for example, in constructing our typology of barriers to employment, we might combine the cells in Figure 12-5 to create the following types.

Types of barriers	Cells	n
no structural barrier	b, d, i	15
educationally deficient	f, n	20
lacks marketable skill	g, h, m	20
unsuitable work habits	k, l	20
not capable of competitive employment	o, p	25

Similarly, when the matrix is collapsed to create an index, the cells of the matrix can be arrayed in rank order and then combined on the basis of segments of equal frequency. Finally, index values are assigned accordingly. In constructing an index of employability, the cells of Figure 12-5 could be combined as follows.

Types	Cells	n	Index value
highly employable	b, d, f, g	30	1
moderately employable	h, i, k, m, n	35	2
difficult to employ	l, o, p	35	3

Another set of inductive techniques can be identified based on some evidence of the interrelatedness of the various indicators in the observed population. For this reason we will call such techniques *correlational.* The assumption underlying correlational techniques is that any clustering in the values or categories of the respective indicators signifies a unique value or category in the phenomenon being measured. Such clusters can therefore be assigned unique index values.

The simplest way to identify natural clusters in the values or categories of the indicators to be combined is through visual inspection. The analyst arrays the units of observation according to each indicator and looks for patterns among the rankings. The point in the array at which the pattern shifts is considered the boundary between values on the corresponding index. Thus Hollingshead and Redlich (1958), in constructing an Index of Social Position, arrayed the census tracts in the City of New Haven by their scores on each of three indicators of social class. Where there was similarity in the rankings from one indicator to another, they assigned a common index value ranging from 1 to 5. Marked dissimilarities in rankings were interpreted as transitional areas between social classes and were therefore used as cutting points on the Index (pp. 395ff.).

Alternately, the data can be displayed in a multiple cross-tabulation, and the analyst need only look for the cells with the highest frequencies to determine underlying types. Cells with a small frequency can be either combined with those of a large frequency, treated as a category of deviant cases, or dropped from the typology. Thus, on the basis of Figure 12-5, the cells or combinations that suggest basic types of barriers to unemployment are *f-g, k-l, n*, and *p*.

A variety of statistical methods exists for identifying clusters among the values of a group of indicators, including factor analysis (Gorsuch 1974, Harmon 1967), cluster analysis (Wallace 1968), and latent structure analysis (Lazarsfeld 1959). These methods prove quite useful when a large number of indicators is involved. For example, factor analysis is a technique whereby commonalities among a group of indicators, suggestive of some underlying variable, are identified on the basis of intercorrelations among indicators. The outcome of factor analysis is the identification of such commonalities, called factors, and the correlation of each indicator with each factor, resulting in a statistical unit called factor loadings. In this technique the factors can be used as the basis for indexes in a large set of indicators and the factor loadings, as weights by which to combine indicator values into index values.

The most valid of inductive techniques for combining indicators into a single measure is based on their respective correlation with an indicator external to the group being combined, and judged to be superior in measuring the concept in question. The external indicator is called a criterion. Of course, if one had such a superior measure one would not need to construct an index. However, even when such measures are available, they are impractical to use in the observation of a large population or on a repeated basis. Under such circumstances a pilot study is conducted to establish a correlation between the indicators that are to serve as the basis of the index and the indicator that is to serve as the criterion. This correlation is then used in a larger study as the basis for weighting the indicators when combining them into an index of the concept in question. Of course, when such weights are established through the findings of a previous study, the technique is no longer inductive by our definition. It constitutes a deductive process in which prior empirical evidence is used to select weights for the construction of an index in the study being designed.

In constructing their index of social position, Hollingshead and Redlich used the judged social class position of census tracts, made by a panel of experts, as their criterion. Against it they regressed their three indicators of social position: (1) mean educational level, (2) mean occupational rank, and (3) mean land value of each census tract. Using as weights the beta values from the resulting multiple regression equation, they combined the score on each indicator into an index score of social position for each census tract.

Choosing a Technique

Having reviewed a number of techniques, both deductive and inductive, for combining multiple indicators into a single measure of a guiding concept, we will now discuss some criteria for choosing the most suitable technique. We will focus our remarks on criteria that are particularly relevant to policy research, trusting that the reader will turn to other sources for a fuller discussion of mathematical and other more technical considerations where necessary.

A primary consideration is the research method being used. In exploratory studies the analyst is interested in achieving as much variation as possible in the distribution of values in a given population; in this way he/she will improve the chances of discovering the missing policy variable. For such purposes positional techniques will prove most useful in constructing measures of guiding concepts. However, such techniques should not be used in a descriptive study. Here the objective is to obtain a representative picture of the distribution of a given variable in the study population. If all the units of observation end up on one value or in one category, so be it. Therefore, in combining multiple indicators the choice of technique should be concerned primarily with the validity of the distribution of values it generates. In an explanatory study the aim returns again to diversity in the distribution of values with respect to the independent variable. In order to establish the effect of the presumed cause, it is necessary to have maximum variability in the independent variable. Once again, positional techniques are appropriate.

For a variety of reasons, deductive techniques are generally more suited to policy research than are inductive ones, except in the cases just described. Deductive techniques force the analyst to make his or her best judgment, or to seek out the best evidence relating one indicator to another. Deductive techniques also "smoke out" the decision maker's real preferences. To avoid either of these judgments is to weaken the impact of the research on the policy problem. Furthermore, deductive techniques provide a conceptual link between the complex measures being constructed and the phenomenon they purport to measure. Because the combinations of values are based on explicit assumptions about the nature of the phenomenon being investigated—rather than on statistical uniformities—the connections between these values and the indicators with which the decision maker must ultimately deal can be more easily established. Finally, deductive techniques provide greater assurance that analysis will focus on what is manipulable rather than on what is mathematically demonstrable. For this reason, factor analysis has limited utility in policy research. The factors or indices so generated do not necessarily have referents within the context of the policy problem.

Beyond these general consideration, there are some criteria related to more specific choices. One is procedural parsimony. The analyst should choose the technique that gets the job done in the simplest manner. In policy research, interest lies in problem solving rather than procedural elegance. Reliance on overly sophisticated techniques not only increases the cost of decision making but creates a barrier to democratic participation. Another criterion is reproducibility. The analyst should choose the technique that is most explicit about the basis on which indicators are combined. To do so facilitates the ability to replicate the process or to alter it on the basis of new evidence or alternative value assumptions. For this reason, indexes constructed on the basis of typologies are preferable to those resulting from the arithmetic summation of indicator scores. Last but not least is the criterion of cost. Policy making endeavors to provide the greatest benefit at the lowest cost. Therefore, the analyst should not use techniques that are so time-consuming as to prevent their actual use in the decision-making process, or so costly as to reduce significantly resources that might otherwise be translated into direct policy benefits.

AGGREGATING INDIVIDUAL MEASURES

Having specified or developed measures of the guiding concepts, the analyst must indicate, for the descriptive study, how he or she will aggregate those measures into some kind of summary statistic for the study population as a whole. It is the aggregate experience of the study population that is at issue in a descriptive study, not the experience of its individual units.

Measures pertaining to individual units can be aggregated in a variety of ways. They can be expressed as a frequency distribution—that is, a table or graph showing the absolute or percentage frequency in each category, rank, or interval of the scale involved. Or they can be summarized in terms of their central tendency by a mode, median, or mean; or by a rate, ratio, or proportion. They can also be summarized in terms of their dispersion, such as their semi-interquartile range or standard deviaion. Such procedures are adequately described by the literature on descriptive statistics (Dornbusch and Schmid 1955). It should be noted that in transforming individual data or measures into group statistics, nominal-scale data may be converted into interval-scale data by means of rates, ratios, or proportions. For example, we can measure the incidence of heart disease (a nominal datum) in terms of the proportion of the population which has contracted it (an interval datum). The conversion of nominal- into interval-scale data permits the use of more powerful quantitative techniques of analysis.

VERIFYING RELATIONS BETWEEN VARIABLES

In studies that are exploratory and explanatory, and in some that are descriptive, the objective of research is to determine the nature and extent of relations between two or more variables. For example, in an exploratory study the analyst is looking for variables that are related to or associated with criterion variables—it is this relationship whereby missing policy variables are identified. In descriptive studies, the objective may be to establish the degree of association or correlation between alternative policy interventions and the policy objective. The extent of this relationship is the basis on which the potential for success is estimated. In explanatory studies the analyst seeks to verify the relationship between the independent variable (the presumed causal agent) and the dependent variable (the presumed effect), which is one of the conditions that must be met in testing a causal hypothesis. The other two conditions, time order of the independent and dependent variables and the elimination of rival hypotheses, are dealt with in the design of the study population. However, if they have not been included in stage 5, they must now be tackled in the data analysis stage of research.

The various techniques for verifying relations between two or more variables are adequately described in an abundant literature. We shall, therefore, attempt merely to characterize the different types of techniques available, as a prelude to discussing the bases on which the analyst should choose among them. We shall distinguish between two basic types: *qualitative* techniques and *quantitative* techniques. The second category may be further subdivided into measures of *bivariate association, multivariate association,* and *statistical significance.*

Techniques of Verifying Relations

In the rush to make the social sciences more rigorous through the development of quantitative techniques for the analysis of large data bases, the fact that relations can be verified and hypotheses tested through qualitative techniques has almost been overlooked (McCall and Simmons 1969, Glaser and Strauss 1967, Schatzman and Strauss 1973). The essential process involved in such techniques has been referred to by Robinson (1969) as *analytic induction.* After intensive examination of a particular case or cases of the phenomenon under investigation, the analyst develops a hypothesis about the joint occurrence of two or more variables. This hypothesis is then verified by examining additional cases one by one to see if the relationship still persists. If contrary evidence is found, the analyst can either adjust the hypothesis through reformulation or reject it in favor of a new hypothesis.

For example, Jane Jacobs (1961) conducted a study to discover what makes some neighborhoods safe for pedestrian use while others are plagued with various forms of street crime. After examining a number of neighborhoods in major cities on the East Coast, she hypothesized that a mixture of land uses prevents street crime. She cited the North End of Boston, an old ethnic neighborhood, as an example of this phenomenon. In subsequent years, Boston newspapers reported that a group of "hippies" had moved into that neighborhood and were subject to harassment by the very residents who, according to the hypothesis, were to be the guardians of the public peace. Presumably this incident refuted Jacobs' hypothesis regarding the association between land use patterns and street crime. However, on closer inspection the incident can be seen as a modification rather than a negation of her hypothesis, because it represents an alteration in the basic conditions, not their replication. In this instance, the users of the city street were not neutral with respect to the values of neighborhood

residents. Rather, they were perceived as a direct threat to those values. Therefore, the original hypothesis held true only when users of neighborhood streets
were neutral with respect to prevailing values, not "invaders" introducing a contrary life style.

To complete the verification of a relationship, the technique of analytic
induction must be supplemented by what is called *the search for negative cases*.
Armed with supporting evidence for his or her hypothesis, the analyst now
undertakes a search for situations in which the presumed independent variable
is *absent* to see if the presumed dependent variable is also absent. For example,
Jacobs went on to examine large public housing projects that represented a
segregated use of land, namely, for residential use only. In such neighborhoods
she found a high incidence of street crime and vandalism. In using both techniques the analyst is operating on the basis of the canons of induction discussed
in Part I (pp. 54ff.).

When analytic induction is employed in explanatory studies, a third
element, the *examination of plausible rival hypotheses,* must be used along with
the other two. Once the analyst has developed an hypothesis to explain the
recurrence of two or more variables in a causal sequence, alternative rival
hypotheses are introduced in an effort to explain the same phenomenon. If any
of these does offer a viable explanation, the first hypothesis is inadequate. In
testing her hypothesis with a public housing project, Jacobs raised the possibility
of social class or income as an alternative explanation of street crime. Street
crime and vandalism are known to be much higher in poor neighborhoods than
in working- or middle-class neighborhoods (Seeber 1973). However, her analysis
did not examine the association between the income of a neighborhood and the
level of street crime, and thus failed to eliminate a relevant rival hypothesis.

Quantitative techniques for verifying relations are numerous and well
documented in the literature. The simplest technique is to compare the summary
measures or statistics on two or more variables among subgroups in the population under study. For example, two or more groups that vary in terms of their
mean or standard deviation on one variable can be examined to see if they also
vary with respect to their mean or standard deviation on another variable. The
covariation can be described in terms of the size of the difference in such measures between any two groups.

Techniques exist for calculating standardized measures of covariation.
They are referred to as measures of association or correlation. Some are appropriate to bivariate analysis, and others for multivariate analysis. Bivariate measures reflect the degree of association between two variables. They range from
measures for nominal-scale variables, referred to as coefficients of contingency;
to measures for ordinal-scale variables, referred to as coefficients of rank order
correlation; to measures for interval-scale variables, referred to as coefficients of
product moment correlations. Techniques also exist for ascertaining an association when the two variables are measured by different types of scales. Freeman

(1968) and Siegel (1956) present comprehensive and well-organized discussions of such options.

Multivariate measures reflect the degree of association among three or more variables (Tufte 1974, Kleinbaum and Kupper 1978). Of particular importance to explanatory studies are measures of partial correlation. A partial correlation refers to the association between two variables when the impact of other variables upon that pair is held constant or controlled. Measures of partial correlation are obviously important in eliminating rival hypotheses when this has not been accomplished through the design of the study population. Partial correlations among nominal-scale variables can be calculated by using a computer program to create multiple cross-tabulations and then using contingency coefficients to measure the association within the tables of the partials (Nie et al. 1970). This technique is described by Hyman (1955) and Rosenberg 1968). Measures of partial correlation exist for ordinal-scale variables (Siegel 1956) as well as for interval-scale variables (Blalock 1972).*

The most sophisticated procedure for multivariate relations is multiple regression analysis. Techniques, such as path analysis (Borgatta 1969, Heise 1975, Kerlinger 1973) allow the analyst to compute the separate effect of each variable of a multivariable causal model on the dependent variable. Such techniques can be used in descriptive studies. The partial regression coefficients indicate the number of standard units of change in the dependent variable attributable to each independent variable. They thus enable the analyst to predict the amount of the policy objective that might be attained by each proposed intervention. Multiple regression analysis is also very useful in explanatory studies. A partial regression coefficient reflects the effect of a single variable on a dependent variable, holding constant the effects of alternate variables. Such coefficients thus permit the testing of more than one causal hypothesis at a time. By means of such analysis the analyst can verify his or her entire conceptual framework.

Lastly, there are tests of the statistical significance of relations, sometimes referred to as tests of the null hypothesis. A test of statistical significance measures the probability that the amount of association measured by a coefficient of correlation might have occurred by chance. It adds extra weight to the plausibility of causality by ruling out chance as a factor accounting for the relationship between variables. There are some who argue that such tests should only be used when chance has been introduced into the generation of the data being analyzed, that is, through the random assignment of units of observation to the respective groups in a pure experiment (Selvin 1957). Others argue that every observation is a sample of a hypothetical universe of observations and can therefore be thought of as random (Hagood 1970). In any event, it should be

---

*A comparable technique for controlling the effect of a third variable is standardization, used with rates, ratios, and proportions (Fleiss 1973).

remembered that a test of statistical significance does not establish the substantive significance of the relation, which can only be conveyed by a measure of association or correlation (Morrison and Henkel 1970). Every measure of association has a test of significance appropriate to it (Siegel 1956, Blalock 1972). The more common ones are the "t" test and the "F" test used in connection with the analysis of variance.

Choosing among Techniques

A number of criteria should be considered in choosing among the many techniques for verifying relations: (1) the method of research, (2) mathematical properties of the data, (3) the size of the study population, and (4) the design of the study population.

In exploratory studies analytic induction and the comparison of subgroup statistics are well suited because their flexibility allows for the dynamic process of discovering relations, and because they are adaptable to small samples. In descriptive studies, standardized quantitative measures of association or correlation are needed. Since such studies are not concerned with testing causality, bivariate and multiple correlations will be employed. Explanatory studies, on the other hand, will rely principally on partial correlation techniques, though other techniques can also be used, depending on the design of the study population.

When dealing with quantitative techniques, certain mathematical properties of the data being analyzed must be taken into consideration. One such property is the nature of the scale by which each variable is measured. As noted above, different techniques are required for nominal-, ordinal-, and interval-scale data. In addition, whether the distribution of values is linear or curvilinear must be taken into account. The references cited in this section discuss the mathematical assumptions underlying each technique so that the analyst can select a method compatible with the data being analyzed.

The size of the population being observed is another factor that will influence choice of a technique. When the number of units is very small, analytic induction and the comparison of subgroup statistics are most appropriate. It is nearly impossible to compute any quantitative measures of multiple correlation with fewer than 20 cases. Consequently, in trying to eliminate rival hypotheses, the analyst will have to resort to a series of bivariate correlations from which he or she can only speculate, on the basis of their relative size, what might be the interrelated effect of their respective variables.

The final, determining factor in the selection of a technique is the design of the study population. In general the more the design of the study population approaches a pure experiment (in which the analyst controls exposure to the independent variable so as to eliminate rival hypotheses), the simpler can be the technique for verifying relations. A relation can be verified by a simple comparison of subgroup statistics or by a bivariate measure of association. Where such controls are not built into the design of the study population, techniques involving the measurement of partial correlations must be used, the ultimate being path analysis.

INFERENCES TO BE DRAWN

The last step in the design of techniques for data analysis should be a discussion of the nature of inferences that can be drawn from the expected findings. The research findings of course refer to the actual measures arrived at through the techniques selected in the previous steps. Inferences, on the other hand, refer to conclusions that can be drawn from these findings as they affect the policy maker's objectives. Important limitations on such inferences have occurred at each stage in the design process. These limitations may already have been identified in the course of writing up the design. The purpose is not to reiterate them here, but to identify their probable impact on the utility of the proposed research for resolving the given policy problem. This process forces the analyst to make judgments, however tenuous or hedged they may be. Such a step is crucial to providing the consumer, who may be less knowledgeable about research design, with guidance in applying the study's findings. In policy making one cannot avoid decisions that are made on the basis of imperfect research. Such decisions will be made. It is incumbent upon the analyst to make them as enlightened as technically possible.

The quality of findings in policy research is assessed with respect to four criteria: (1) their generalizability,* (2) their validity, (3) their reliability, and (4) their practical significance.

Generalizability refers to the extent to which the expected findings can be applied to the policy problem at issue. Two factors limit the generalizability of findings—one stemming from the conceptual framework, the other from the study population. The conceptual framework specifies those variables which are known or expected to have a significant impact on the policy problem. To the extent that the framework corresponds to the actual conditions that prevail the findings will be generalizable. However, if after conducting the research the nature of the policy problem has changed, bringing new variables to light, the findings will be correspondingly limited. A more likely source of discrepancy arises from the fact that in any given research it is often infeasible to incorporate all the variables of the conceptual framework into the research design. The cost of doing to may be prohibitive. The generalizability of the study findings is, therefore, explicitly limited by the effects of those variables not dealt with in

*Campbell and Stanley (1963) refer to generalizability as "external validity" and other forms of validity as "internal."

the design. In explanatory studies this limitation refers to the number of relevant variables that were controlled. In such studies conclusions regarding causality are limited to those rival hypotheses which have been eliminated. Thus, in making inferences, *a given set of research findings is applicable only to situations which are characterized by a similar set of variables or conceptual framework.*

The second source of limitations on the generalizability of research findings is the study population. As was discussed in Chapter 9, the study population does not always exactly correspond to the target population reflected in the policy problem. To the extent that a discrepancy occurs, the generalizability of the research findings will be limited. Thus, *the study findings can be applied only to those members of the target population who also fall into the study population.* However, the analyst should not be content simply to note such a limitation. He or she should attempt to bridge this discrepancy by elaborating alternative assumptions under which the leap might be made from the study population to the target population. Is the missing group known to be similar or dissimilar with respect to any of the variables in the conceptual framework? Lacking such information, the analyst should speculate about the impact of this discrepancy on the policy problem. How large a group does the discrepancy represent? How much error (or cost in misspent resources) would ensue by applying the findings to the target population?

Validity refers to the extent to which the study findings are applicable to the research objectives, that is, the extent to which the measures obtained reflect the variables specified in the research objectives. Here the principal source of limitation is the way in which variables are operationally defined, specifically, the indicators chosen to measure the guiding concepts. Two ways of assessing validity are particularly relevant to policy research: face validity and predictive (or pragmatic) validity (Selltiz, Wrightsman, and Cook 1976; pp. 169-181). *Face validity* is used with measures that are presumed to reflect a phenomenon directly. Such validity is determined by a judgment of the degree to which a given measure fully incorporates or is representative of all the possible referents of the given variable. For example, the definition of an unemployed person as somebody who is without a job and looking for work ignores persons without jobs who gave up looking for work out of discouragement. Those referents of the variable which are not reflected in its operational definition need to be carefully noted and their relevance to the study objective discussed. *Predictive validity* is used with measures of indicators that only indirectly reflect the phenomenon in question but are presumed to be closely associated with it. Predictive validity is determined by the degree of correlation between a measure of the indicator and a measure of an appropriate referent of the given variable. In an example used earlier in this chapter, age and level of education were used as indicators of a person's employability. Of course, these are only indirect measures of employability; a direct measure would be the number of job interviews or length of time required for the person to obtain employment. Therefore, predictive validity, in this case, would be determined by the degree of association between age or level of education and the length of time required to obtain a job. The implication for prospective inferences is that the *study findings apply only to those referents of the guiding concepts that are measured, or to the degree that those referents are correlated with the indicators that are actually measured.*

Reliability refers to the degree of confidence that can be placed in the research findings—in operational terms, the extent to which repeated applications of the research design under similar conditions would yield consistent findings (Selltiz, Wrightsman, and Cook 1976; pp. 181-192). Limitations on reliability derive from two primary sources in the design; from sampling the study population and from the procedures used for observation. When units of observation have been selected randomly, measures of the reliability of findings can be easily derived by means of well-established procedures (Lazerwitz 1968, Kueckeberg and Silvers 1974). Unintended variability can also arise from observational procedures, either from the technique of observation, the instrument used to record observations, or the way in which the instrument was actually applied in the field, as discussed in Chapter 11. Such procedures are tested for their reliability by means of coefficients of correlation between two or more repeated or equivalent procedures. Whether measurable or not, the analyst should make an assessment of the amount of variability that can be anticipated from all such sources, and then estimate the effect such variability will have on the decisions to be made by the policy maker. In this connection it is helpful to remember that the objective of any research design is not necessarily to eliminate error but to know its nature and extent. The amount of effort expended to reduce error should always be weighed against the effect of such error on the utility of the study findings. The implication of the assessment of reliability on inference is that *the study findings can be applied to policy making only within a range of variability.*

Practical significance refers to the extent to which the study findings will facilitate action on the policy problem. This quality depends on the adequacy with which that problem was assessed in the justification stage of the design. At this point the analyst should be able to indicate the precise barriers to policy making which the research objective(s) will address. The substance and form of that objective(s) should be relevant to those barriers. Ultimately the practical significance of the research findings depends on the cost of conducting the research relative to the benefits of making policy based on its findings.

THE STATEMENT OF TECHNIQUES FOR DATA ANALYSIS

In writing the statement of techniques for data analysis, the analyst should link each guiding concept with its indicator, and in turn with its measure (where more than one indicator is used); and should indicate any relations with other concepts that are to be verified. Figure 12-6 will facilitate this presenta-

Guiding concept/ variables (1)	Indicators (2)	Measure (for multiple indicators) (3)	Summary measure/ statistic (where applicable) (4)	Relations to be verified (where applicable) (5)	Measures of relations (6)

Figure 12-6 Specification of measures of and analyses of relations among guiding concepts

tion. The analyst begins by listing each guiding concept or variable in column (1) together with its respective indicators in column (2). When more than one indicator is involved, the procedures for combining them into a single measure is entered as a formula or in graphic form in column (3). When summary measures are called for, as in descriptive studies, the form of the statistic is entered in (4).

Having specified the measures of guiding concepts, the analyst should list any relations to be verified, when such is the objective of research, in column (5). In listing relations it is customary to place the dependent variable first, followed by the independent variable. In multivariate relations the dependent variable is followed by the independent variable, which in turn is followed by each variable to be controlled in the order of its importance. For each relation, the analyst should specify the technique or measure to be used for its verification in column (6).

Finally, the statement of techniques for data collection should contain a discussion of the limitations on inferences to be drawn from the study's findings, along the lines discussed in the previous section.

SUMMARY

The process by which data are analyzed can be described in four steps. The process begins with raw data, collected by instruments designed in stage 7, which are transformed into measures of the guiding concepts. When the data constitute multiple indicators of a concept, they must be combined into an index or typology. Whether a single indicator or an index, each measure must be expressed in units appropriate to the research objectives. In the case of descriptive studies, summary measures or statistics must be specified for the study population as a whole. When the units for observation are selected on a probability basis, these summary measures must then be submitted to a test of statistical significance. In order to verify relationships, an appropriate measure of association or correlation is computed, and this in turn may be submitted to a test of statistical significance.

The statement on techniques to be used in data analysis should contain the following specifications:

1. the measure or indicator to be constructed for each guiding construct, indicating the units of measurement in which each will be expressed
2. statistics to be used to aggregate measures across units of observation (in the case of descriptive studies)
3. qualitative or quantitative procedures to be used to verify relations
4. a discussion of the quality of the inferences that can be made from the research findings.

REFERENCES

BABBIE, EARL R. *The Practice of Social Research*. Belmont, Calif.: Wadsworth Publishing Company, Inc., 1975.

BARTON, ALLEN H. "The Concept of Property-Space in Social Research," in *The Language of Social Research*, eds. Paul F. Lazarsfeld and Morris Rosenberg. New York: The Free Press, 1955, pp. 40–54.

BISHOP, YVONNE N. M., STEVEN E. FEINBERG, and PAUL M. HOLLAND. *Discrete Multivariate Analysis: Theory and Practice*. Cambridge, Mass.: MIT Press, 1975.

BLALOCK, HUBERT M. JR. *Social Statistics* (2nd ed.). New York: McGraw-Hill, 1972.

BORGATTA, EDGAR, ed. *Sociological Methodology, 1969*. San Francisco: Jossey-Bass, 1969.

CAMPBELL, DONALD T., and JULIAN C. STANLEY. *Experimental and Quasi-experimental Designs for Research.* Chicago: Rand McNally and Co., 1963.

DAWES, R. M. *Measures and Indicators of Attitudes.* New York: John Wiley and Sons, 1971.

DORNBUSCH, SANFORD M., and CALVIN F. SCHMID. *A Primer of Social Statistics.* New York: McGraw-Hill Book Company, Inc., 1955.

DYER, HENRY S. "Toward Objective Criteria of Professional Accountability in the Schools of New York City," *Phi Delta Kappa, 52,* 4 (December 1970), 206–211.

EDWARDS, ALLEN L. *Techniques of Attitude Scale Construction.* New York: Appleton-Century-Crofts, 1957.

FLEISS, JOSEPH L. *Statistical Methods for Rates and Proportions.* New York: John Wiley and Sons, 1973.

FREEMAN, LINTON C. *Elementary Applied Statistics.* New York: John Wiley and Sons, 1968.

GLASER, BARNEY G., and ANSELM L. STRAUSS. *The Discovery of Grounded Theory.* Chicago: Aldine Publishing Co., 1967.

GORSUCH, R. L. *Factor Analysis.* Philadelphia: Saunders, 1974.

HAGOOD, MARGARET JARMAN. "The Notion of a Hypothetical Universe," in *The Significance Test Controversy,* eds. Denton E. Morrison and Ramon E. Henkel, pp. 65–78.

HARMON, H. H. *Modern Factor Analysis* (2nd ed.). Chicago: University of Chicago Press, 1967.

HEISE, DAVID R., *Causal Analysis.* New York: John Wiley & Sons, Inc., 1975.

HOLLINGSHEAD, AUGUST B. and FREDERICK C. REDLICH. *Social Class and Mental Illness.* New York: John Wiley and Sons, 1958.

HYMAN, HERBERT. *Survey Design and Analysis.* Glencoe, Ill.: Free Press, 1955.

JACOBS, JANE. *The Death and Life of Great American Cities.* New York: Random House, Inc., 1961.

KERLINGER, FRED N. *Foundations of Behavioral Research* (2nd ed.). New York: Holt, Rinehart and Winston, Inc., 1973.

KERLINGER, FRED N., and ELAZAR J. PEDHAZUR. *Multiple Regression in Behavioral Research.* New York: Holt, Rinehart and Winston, Inc., 1973.

KLEINBAUM, DAVID G., and LAWRENCE L. KUPPER. *Applied Regression Analysis and Other Multivariate Methods.* North Scituate, Mass.: Duxbury Press, 1978.

KUECKEBERG, DONALD A., and ARTHUR L. SILVERS. *Urban Planning Analysis: Methods and Models.* New York: John Wiley and Sons.

LAZARSFELD, PAUL F. "The Logical and Mathematical Foundation of Latent Structure Analysis," in *Measurement and Prediction,* eds. S. A. Stouffer, Edward A. Suchman, Paul F. Lazarsfeld, Shirley A. Star, John A. Clausen. Princeton, N.J.: Princeton University Press, 1959.

LAZARSFELD, PAUL F., and ALLEN H. BARTON. "Qualitative Measurement in the Social Sciences: Classifications, Typologies, and Indices," in *The Policy Sciences,* eds. Harold D. Lasswell and David Lerner, Stanford, California: Stanford University Press, 1951, pp. 169–180.

LAZERWITZ, BERNARD. "Sampling Theory and Procedures," in *Methodology in Social Research*, eds. Hubert M. Blalock, Jr., and Ann B. Blalock. New York: McGraw-Hill Book Co., 1968, pp. 278–333.

McCALL, GEORGE J., and J. L. SIMMONS, eds. *Issues in Participant Observation*. Reading, Mass.: Addison-Wesley, 1969.

MORRISON, DENTON E., and RAMON E. HENKEL. *The Significance Test Controversy*. Chicago: Aldine Publishing Co., 1970.

NIE, NORMAN H., C. HODLAI HULL, JEAN G. JENKINS, KARIN STEINBRENNER, and DALE H. BENT. *SPSS: Statistical Package for the Social Sciences*. New York: McGraw-Hill Book Co., 1970.

ROBINSON, WILLIAM S. "The Logical Structure of Analytic Induction," in *Issues in Participant Observation*. eds. McCall and Simmons, pp. 196–205.

ROSENBERG, MORRIS. *The Logic of Survey Analysis*. New York: Basic Books, 1968.

SCHATZMAN, LEONARD, and ANSELM L. STRAUSS. *Field Research: Strategies for a Natural Sociology*. Englewood Cliffs, N.J.: Prentice-Hall, Inc., 1973.

SEEBER, RONALD C. "Research Report: Jane Jacobs on Street Crime, A Cautionary Note," Department of City and Regional Planning, University of North Carolina, Chapel Hill, 1973 (unpublished).

SELLTIZ, CLAIRE, LAWRENCE S. WRIGHTSMAN, and STUART W. COOK, eds. *Research Methods in Social Research* (3rd ed.). New York: Holt, Rinehart, and Winston, 1976.

SELVIN, HANAN C. "A Critique of Tests of Significance in Survey Research," *American Sociological Review*, 22 (October 1957), 519–527.

SIEGEL, SIDNEY. *Nonparametric Statistics for the Behavioral Sciences*. New York: McGraw Hill, 1956.

TUFTE, EDWARD R. *Data Analysis of Politics and Policy*. Englewood Cliffs, N.J.: Prentice-Hall, Inc., 1974.

WALLACE, DAVID L. "Clustering," in *International Encyclopedia of the Social Sciences*, ed. David L. Sills. New York: The Macmillan Co. and The Free Press, 1968, Vol. II, pp. 519–524.

chapter 13 / stage 9:
administration

The final stage of research design involves a consideration of the resources and organization necessary to execute the design. Obviously, the best conceived design will come to naught if adequate financial resources and appropriate manpower are not assembled. Interestingly, the opposite error is also possible. In an effort to survive through grantsmanship, some analysts give primary attention to the organizational and financial aspects of the prospective research, and only sketchy consideration to its substantive and methodological content. Research so conceived can be equally disastrous. There is some validity to the view that research design begins with a budget, because knowledge of the amount of resources available is necessary to design its scope. However, determination of the substance of a research project is independent of the resources and organization necessary for its execution. Nevertheless, a general notion of the amount and kind of resources available is indispensable in clarifying the constraints imposed on the design.

This final stage of research design has three components: (1) the organizational plan, (2) the management plan, and (3) the financial plan. Depending on the specifications set forth by a funding source for the proposed research, these components may constitute separate sections of the resulting proposal. However, since they all involve decisions about essential resources, they can be subsumed under one design stage.

THE ORGANIZATIONAL PLAN

Since policy research takes place in an organizational context that influences both its execution and its utilization, the analyst must take organizational factors into consideration in designing administrative guidelines. The organizational context has two dimensions: an external aspect having to do with the organizational auspices under which the research will be carried out; and an internal aspect, involving the acquisition and deployment of personnel necessary to do the research.

Auspices of the Research

The organizational plan should specify the organization or the respective sub-division(s) that is administratively responsible for carrying out the research. The issue of administrative responsibility is different from the authority to conduct the research. The former refers to control over the decisions regarding the execution of the research, while the latter refers to the authorization or request for the research to be undertaken. Authority for conducting the research was dealt with in the justification stage; administrative responsibility is dealt with here.

As the result of large-scale social experimentation in the 1960s, much has been written on the appropriate organizational location of research activities in program planning and evaluation (Caro 1971, Rieken and Boruch 1974, Weiss 1972a, Weiss 1972b, Wholey 1972). The central issue is whether the administrative responsibility for policy research should be lodged with those responsible for implementing its findings (*inside* research) or with an independent agent (*outside* research). To be more specific, inside research is that which is conducted by an organization or subdivision thereof, for which one or more of the courses of action under consideration is its sole or major function. Outside research is that which is conducted by an organization that either does not carry on any of the activities under investigation, or engages in such activities only through one of its several subdivisions. For example, research carried on by the office of planning within a state government would be outside with respect to any of the policies or programs carried out by the state's department of human resources. Similarly, research carried out by the secretary of human resources would be outside with respect to policies or programs carried out by one of that department's bureaus. It should be recognized that the analyst in an outside research project is independent only in the sense that once the research has been satisfactorily completed, he or she is not subject to sanctions regarding the substance of the work. Independence in a pure sense never exists, of course. Even the self-employed analyst, presumably a free agent, often selects findings to report that will please the decision maker and thus ensure future contracts. And the analyst whose independence derives from affiliation with a university is not immune to such distortions. The academician needs acceptance by some wider audience in order to further his or her career (National Academy of Sciences 1969, p. 193).

Hiring an independent agent to conduct policy research, it is argued, will assure the freedom to critically examine alternative courses of action. Inside research, on the other hand, has the advantage of greater collaboration between the analyst and those responsible for implementing the research findings. Such collaboration should lead to greater insight into the operation of policies or programs and thus increase the likelihood that research findings will be utilized. Clearly, conflicting benefits are posed by the choice of auspices for policy research.

In order to resolve this dilemma we must return to our earlier discussions of the nature of the policy-making process and of alternative courses of action faced therein (see Chapter 5). Sometimes the alternative actions refer to the actual policy concept(s); that is, whether or not to adopt (continue) policy X, or whether to continue policy X or to adop policy Y. We refer to such considerations as policy planning (also known as summative evaluations). At other times, the alternative actions refer to the implementation of a policy or the administration of a program, for example, whether to implement policy X through means x or means y. We refer to such considerations as program planning (also referred to as formative evaluations).

Returning to our dilemma, there are those who argue that research having to do with policy making (summative evaluations) should be conducted outside the organization for which one or more of the alternatives are its major function (Riecken and Boruch 1974, pp. 224ff.). Such an arrangement is necessary, it is believed, to avoid the interests vested in continuing the policy or program from biasing the conduct of the analysis. Research having to do with program planning (formative evaluations), lacking such vested interests, may be conducted inside. However, this position is not completely consistent with reality. On the one hand, it ignores the fact that policy makers on occasion are capable of considering radical shifts in the policies or programs with which they are identified (Mayer 1978). It also ignores the fact that administrators may have interests vested in one or more ways of implementing a given policy (Berube and Gittell 1969).

We believe that a more precise resolution of the dilemma lies in the following position: Administrative responsibility for policy research should be lodged with that decision maker who is willing and able to adopt any of the courses of action under investigation. We believe that this position gives recognition to the human willingness and ability to change as well as to those structural factors that facilitate change. If the organization sponsoring the investigation is not free to take any one among the range of actions under consideration, then either the alternatives have been incorrectly assessed or the research is lodged under the wrong auspices. If the justification stage has been properly executed, the policy problem will be phrased within a range of actions that is within the decision maker's discretion. Our position is that administrative responsibility for carrying out research should not be delegated to anyone who is less free to engage in such alternatives.

The second element in the organization plan is specification of the various personnel needed to carry out the research together with their respective responsibilities. The personnel plan is expressed as a set of job descriptions that can be used in hiring and supervision, and as an organizational chart which shows the flow of authority for carrying out the research.

In order to identify the personnel needed, the analyst should review the tasks involved in carrying out the procedures for selecting the study population as described in stage 5, for data collection as described in stage 7, and for data analysis as described in stage 8. A listing of theses tasks will enable the analyst to identify the type of personnel needed to carry them out. Thus the analyst arrives at a set of job descriptions based on the personnel needed to carry out the various research tasks. For example, a set of summary job descriptions for a moderate-sized study might be as follows:

1. *Research director.* Designs research, supervises construction of instruments, integrates work of consultants, supervises research associate, interprets data and disseminates findings
2. *Research associate.* Assists in research design, instrument construction, and interpretation; supervises field supervisor; coordinates field work and data analysis; analyzes data
3. *Field supervisor.* Assists in instrument construction; supervises field workers; assists in data analysis
4. *Field workers.* Collect data, assist in editing and coding
5. *Consultants.* Provide technical assistance in sampling procedures, computer manipulation of data, and statistical analysis.

These personnel and their accompanying responsibilities can be diagramed in the form of an organizational chart. The chart should indicate the organizational context of the study, the different personnel to be employed, and the chain of responsibility that links them. In preparing such a chart, the analyst needs to keep in mind the span of responsibility, that is, how many persons can be supervised by a given position; the level at which different tasks must be integrated; and the relative amount of time to be expended by respective personnel. For example, in Figure 9-1 it is assumed that a part-time field supervisor can supervise the work of six field workers. It is further assumed that the tasks of data collection need to be coordinated with data storage and data analysis. And finally, it is assumed that a full-time research associate can administer the daily operations of the research with only limited assistance from a research director to provide the initial design, advisory supervision of operations, and dissemination of research findings.

The job descriptions can be translated into a set of qualifications to be used in hiring and deployment of staff. The qualifications are expressed in terms of the type and amount of education, and/or the type and amount of work experience. A set of qualifications for the positions diagramed in Figure 13-1 might be as follows:

1. *Research director.* Holder of a doctoral degree in one of the social sciences *and* a Master's degree in a social policy area (such as public health, social welfare, education, urban planning) or comparable work experience in social policy; *or* a Master's degree in one of the social policy areas with a concentration in research methods or quantitative analysis *and* work experience conducting research
2. *Research associate.* Holder of a Master's degree with a concentration in research methods, quantitative analysis, or computer sciences, *or* comparable work experience
3. *Field supervisor.* Completion of a general high-school curriculum or demonstration of articulateness in written communication and the manipulation of abstract symbols; *plus* several years work experience in data collection, editing, and coding; *plus* skill in interpersonal relations
4. *Field workers.* Skill in verbal communication and sensitivity in interpersonal relations.

In some research designs it may be desirable, or required by the funding source, to specify procedures by which personnel are to be secured. When such personnel have already been secured, the individuals' names can be specified in the organizational chart, and their resumes attached to indicate the qualifica-

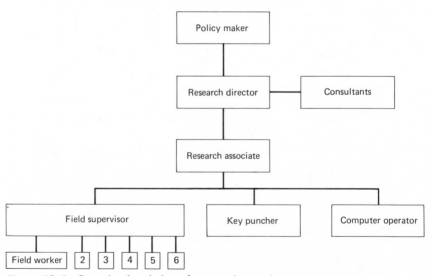

Figure 13-1 Organizational chart for a moderate size research project

tions they bring to their positions. In the absence of previously committed personnel, some discussion of their availability and steps to be taken in their recruitment should be part of the organizational plan.

MANAGEMENT PLAN

The second step in designing the administration of the proposed research is the preparation of a management plan. Such a plan entails listing the various activities to be carried out, determining their sequence and interdependence, and scheduling their execution to complete the research within relevant deadlines. This aspect of the research design borrows from techniques developed in business administration that have been applied to public administration. The management plan can be expressed most succinctly by use of the Program Evaluation and Review Technique (PERT) (Kueckeberg and Silvers 1974, pp. 231–255).

The basic process of PERT involves laying out the sequence of activities and their interrelationships that are necessary for the achievement of a stated objective. Beginning with the objective to be achieved, the analyst diagrams in reverse sequence those events that will lead to its attainment. PERT consists essentially of four steps: (1) identifying the major events, called milestones, that must be completed in order to reach the objective; (2) specifying the activities that lead to each event; (3) estimating the time that will lapse in completing each activity given the resources allocated to it; and (4) scheduling these events in relation to calendar time.

The first step can be easily accomplished. The various stages in research design correspond roughly to the milestones in completing a research project. With some modifications, these have been reproduced in Figure 13-2. It is assumed that the development of a research design is the first event. Four events

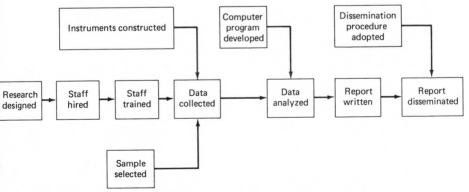

Figure 13-2 A milestone chart used in developing a PERT diagram

not directly reflected in the stages of research design have been added for greater realism: staff hired, staff trained, computer program developed, and dissemination procedure adopted. Notice that sequential events are located in a direct line running from left to right, and that those events which occur simultaneously with a milestone are located above or below that line with arrows leading to the events that are dependent on their occurrence.

The second step in applying PERT is the specification of those activities that are necessary to reach each event or milestone, a task that involves much greater detail and usually results in the identification of subevents. The tasks identified in connection with determining the personnel needs in the organizational plan constitute a listing of most of the relevant activities. These activities become the basis of a PERT chart (see Figure 13-3). In converting a list of activities into such a chart, the analyst must determine their proper sequence and interdependence. The following questions will help to establish that sequence.

1. What activity (activities) cannot start until this activity is completed?
2. What other activity (activities) can be done simultaneously with this activity?
3. What activity (activities) must be completed before this activity can start?

In making a PERT chart certain conventions are observed. Each activity links two events; the one preceding is called the *leading event,* and the one following is called the *following event.* Events are numbered and contained in circles. Activities are represented by arrows showing the sequence of events. Some events are milestones and thus correspond to the milestone chart. They are enclosed in boxes. Other events are terminal, that is, they do not precipitate activities which lead to other events, but rather feed directly into events that follow from other activities. Terminal events are connected to the events they feed into by a broken arrow, signifying a *dummy activity.* Each activity depicted in the PERT chart is described by the numbers of the lead event and the following event.

The third step in applying PERT is to estimate the time required to complete each activity. This step is essential, not only for estimating the length of time required for the overall project, but also for coordinating interdependent events through the scheduling of activities. Time is estimated on the basis of lapsed time rather than expended time. Lapsed time refers to the time that expires between the initiation of an activity and its completion. Lapsed time includes time during which project staff are idle, waiting for other persons to act or other services to be performed, for example, time between the mailing out of questionnaires and the receipt of responses, or time needed to run a computer program. By contrast, expended time refers to the time spent by the project

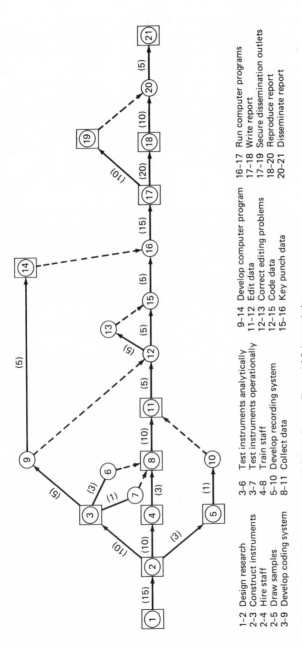

Figure 13-3 Activity-based PERT Chart, T_S = 103 lapsed days

1-2	Design research	3-6	Test instruments analytically
2-3	Construct instruments	3-7	Test instruments operationally
2-4	Hire staff	4-8	Train staff
2-5	Draw samples	5-10	Develop recording system
3-9	Develop coding system	8-11	Collect data

9-14	Develop computer program
11-12	Edit data
12-13	Correct editing problems
12-15	Code data
15-16	Key punch data

16-17	Run computer programs
17-18	Write report
17-19	Secure dissemination outlets
18-20	Reproduce report
20-21	Disseminate report

staff on the activity. Lapsed time is the basis for scheduling; expended time is the basis for estimating cost.

The estimation of lapsed time is illustrated in Figure 13-3, based on experience in a moderate-sized project. Because of the lack of precision involved, such estimates incorporate "positive slack," in order to assure that activities can be completed within relevant deadlines. The critical path is the single chain of events that involves the longest time lapse. The critical path runs on a straight line. Simultaneous activities are situated above or below the critical path and must require less time to complete than those on the critical path. The total time, T_s, is derived by adding the time estimates for each activity on the critical path. When the estimate of T_s exceeds the time limits imposed by policy making, the initial time estimates for each activity may be reduced by allocating additional resources to them. As a consequence, T_s is brought in line with the given deadline.

The final step, scheduling, consists of assigning calendar dates to each event. Nonworking days, such as holidays and weekends, must be taken into consideration in estimating calendar time. This step is not required in all research designs, but is essential when the analyst must demonstrate that his/her design will meet a specific deadline. It is, however, a useful technique in the management or execution of any research design.

THE FINANCIAL PLAN

The final step in the administration stage of a research design is the preparation of a financial plan or budget. The financial plan is a statement of the amount and type of resources needed to execute the design, along with the monetary cost of those resources. Its preparation involves estimating the amount and type of personnel and nonpersonnel resources needed to carry out the activities listed in the management plan, and attaching realistic prices to these resources.

In the course of estimating the essential resources, the analyst may discover that the costs exceed the funding that realistically could be expected to be available for the research. The discovery of such constraints may force the analyst to return to an earlier stage and to alter or eliminate certain aspects of the design to bring them into line with financial realities. For this reason, it is helpful for the analyst to have a rough idea at the outset of the design how much money is available. In discussing the budgeting process we will assume that financial constraints are a secondary problem, that the research as designed falls within a reasonable expectation of available resources.

When funds for conducting the research are to be solicited from a source outside the sponsoring agency, it is obvious that a budget must be prepared and submitted. When the research is to be carried out with existing resources of the sponsoring agency, however, this step may not seem so obvious.

Yet the fact that no new monies are to be spent does not mean that no cost is incurred in carrying out the research. The cost of a given research project is expressed in terms of the loss of alternative activities that could have been conducted with the same resources. Good management practice encourages the budgeting of any activity, even though monies for it already exist, so that efficient choices can be made between alternative ways of spending that money.

It will be helpful to our discussion of the tasks involved in preparing a financial plan if we begin with a brief description of the outcome of those tasks, a *line-item budget*. A line-item budget specifies the amount of money to be spent on each item to be purchased in connection with carrying out the research. It is the standard form used in accounting for organizational expenditures. In our illustration of a line-item budget, we will utilize a process known as functional or program budgeting; that is, budgeting based on estimating the cost of each activity by pricing the goods or services to be expended on it. Thus, a direct connection exists between the research design and the development of a functional budget. We can take each activity listed in the PERT chart and estimate the kinds and amounts of goods and services necessary to accomplish that activity. Once these goods and services have been priced they can be entered as the line items in the budget. We will begin, therefore, by briefly describing a standard line-item budget, and then go on to discuss procedures for estimating the cost of personnel and nonpersonnel items that make up such a budget.

Line-item Budget

The major items in a standard line-item research budget involve personnel (see Figure 13-4). The kinds of personnel typically employed in a moderate-sized study have been indicated in the organizational plan in Figure 13-1. Such a study will have a research director or principal investigator. If the project is large enough, or if the director has other commitments a research associate may be employed to handle many of the technical operations. When extensive data collection is involved, field workers will be hired. If their number exceeds that which can be supervised by the research associate, a field supervisor is necessary. Every study will require some secretarial assistance. In smaller proposals, the kinds of personnel needed can be reduced to a director and a secretary; or a director, field workers, and a secretary.

Two items in the budget are related to the salary and wages to be paid to personnel. One is the fringe benefits to be paid by the sponsoring agency. At a 1977 rate of payment, Social Security, retirement plans, and standard hospital-medical insurance fringe benefits can be estimated at approximately 17 percent of the total estimated salary and wages. The second item attached to salary and wages is overhead or indirect costs. Indirect costs cover items that will not be paid for out of the study's budget, such as office space, use of existing equipment, and supportive services (maintenance, general administration, accounting). For inside studies that are carried out as part of the operations of an established

Figure 13-4 Example of a line-item budget

ITEM		ESTIMATED COST
Personnel (see Fig. 13-5)		
Salaries and wages		
director		$_____
research associate		_____
field work supervisor		_____
secretary		_____
field workers (see Fig. 13-6)		_____
	Subtotal	$_____
Fringe benefits (on above)		_____
Indirect costs (on salaries and wages)		_____
Key punching		_____
Computer analysis		_____
Equipment, supplies, and related services (see Fig. 13-7)		
stationery and office supplies		_____
equipment		_____
telephone		_____
travel		_____
reproduction		_____
postage		_____
	Total	$_____

organization, they are included in that organization's budget. In studies funded by the federal government, this figure is calculated on the basis of actual operating costs of the sponsoring organization. For nonprofit organizations the rate varies between 50 and 100 percent of salaries and wages.

The remaining items in the budget are nonpersonnel. Consultation is considered a service and not a personnel item subject to fringe benefits and indirect costs. Computer services include key punching and verifying, as well as computer time necessary for data analysis. Additional nonpersonnel items found in most budgets are stationery and other office supplies; equipment, which may be either rented or purchased; telephone services; travel; reproduction services, such as mimeographing, commercial printing and xeroxing; and postage.

ESTIMATING PERSONNEL COSTS

Estimating personnel costs begins by estimating the total amount to be paid in salaries and wages in conducting the research. These costs can be derived by two separate procedures. One involves estimating the amount of time expended on each activity listed in the management plan by personnel who are employed for major portions of time, usually the duration of the study. This time is estimated in person-days and accorded a monetary value on the basis of an annual or monthly rate of pay. The other procedure is to estimate the per unit cost of completing discrete tasks, such as conducting or coding interviews, in personnel services that are employed on an hourly basis for those tasks. This estimated per unit cost is then multiplied by the number of times the task is to be performed to arrive at an estimate of the total wages to be paid such personnel.

Estimating Salaries by Expended Time

As an example of estimating salaries by person-days expended, we have prepared Supplemental Budget A (see Figure 13-5), based on our moderate-sized research project depicted in the PERT chart in Figure 13-3. To simplify the example we have selected six major activities involving salaried personnel. Although the design of research is not always included in estimates of personnel costs, it may be on the assumption that the analyst wishes to recover costs associated therewith, or that resources are required to prepare a more detailed design. Running across the top of Figure 13-5 are the activities on which personnel time is to be expended in this example: design, instrument construction, data collection, data analysis, report writing, and report dissemination. Running down the figure are four types of personnel whose services are to be costed by this procedure: research director, research associate, field supervisor, and secretary.

The first task is to assign reasonable per annum prices to each class of personnel service, based on salaries prevailing at the time of the study. The second task is to fill out the matrix with the amount of time to be expended by each type of personnel on each activity. Expended time is measured in standard units, in this case person-days, regardless of the number of persons assigned to the activity. Person-days refers to the number of days it would take one person to complete the activity. In estimating expended person-days we will assume that the various personnel do not have to be paid out of this budget for lapsed time, that is, time when they are not actively engaged in the research. We assume that they will be hired on a temporary basis, or that they will be employed on other projects during such periods. If such assumptions cannot be made, lapsed time must be used in estimating the cost of their services.

A sizable study will involve at least 25 person-days to design. This activity is usually shared between the director and his/her associate, since their collaboration is necessary if the associate is to have a major role in executing the design. Thus in column (1) we list 10 person-days beside the director and 10 person-days beside the associate. Approximately 5 days of secretarial time will be expended on this activity. The construction and pretesting of instruments (2) can be expected to take another 26 person-days of effort. In this activity the research associate can carry most of the responsibility, 10 person-days, with

Figure 13-5 Supplemental Budget A: Estimating salaries and wages by person-days to be expanded

Personnel	Design (1)	Instrument construction (2)	Collecting, editing, coding data (3)	Data analysis (4)	Report writing (5)	Report dissemination (6)	Total person-days (7)	Daily rate* (8)	Estimated cost (9)
Director/ senior researcher $___ per annum	10	4	0	5	10	5	34	$___	$___
Research associate $___ per annum	10	10	5	15	5	5	50	$___	$___
Field supervisor $___ per annum	0	7	20	8	2	0	37	$___	$___
Secretary $___ per annum	5	5	0	10	10	5	35	$___	$___

*Daily rate is figured by dividing annual salary by 261, since salaried personnel are paid on the basis of calendar time, which includes weekends, rather than person-days worked (expended time).

supervision from the director amounting to 4 person-days. The field work supervisor should participate for 7 person-days since his or her knowledge of the development of instruments will be useful in supervising their use. Again, approximately 5 person-days of secretarial time can be anticipated. It is assumed that the field supervisor will work full time during the collection, editing, and coding of data (3), which is to last 20 person-days, and that the research associate will expend 5 person-days on supervision. As for data analysis (4), the research associate can assume primary responsibility with 15 person-days, and the director will devote another 5 person-days of supervision. It is advisable to have the field supervisor assist in the analysis of data because of his or her intimate knowledge of conditions surrounding their collection, an expenditure we estimate at 8 person-days. The director will assume major responsibility for report writing (5), an activity that will take 10 person-days, with the assistance of 5 person-days of the associate and 2 of the field supervisor. The secretary will expend 10 person-days in its preparation. Dissemination and interpretation of the study findings (6) may involve the preparation of news releases, commercial publications, or speaking engagements before client groups. We will assume a fairly simple effort in this regard and allocate approximately 5 person-days each to the director, the associate, and the secretary.

It is now possible to complete Supplemental Budget A. The number of person-days in each row are summed in column (7). The daily rate of pay is computed in column (8). An estimate of the cost of each personnel item, column (9), is obtained by multiplying (7) by (8) for each row. These estimates of salaries can now be transferred to their respective lines in the research budget.

Estimating Wages by Per Unit Costs

It will be observed that the wages to be paid field workers were not estimated by the above procedure. Since such personnel often work sporadically and in large numbers relative to other personnel, it is difficult to estimate with sufficient accuracy the amount of time they will expend. When they are all engaged in the same activities involving a large number of standardized tasks—for example, conducting structured interviews and coding interview schedules—their wages can be estimated more reliably on the basis of the per unit cost of completing those tasks. It should be noted that this estimating procedure is useful primarily in survey-type studies in which structured instruments are used to observe a large study population or sample. In studies involving only a few units of observation such as a comparative case study, or in those using highly unstructured observational procedures (such as participant observation), the wages to be paid field workers can be more easily estimated with comparable precision on the basis of person-days expended using Supplemental Budget A.

The trick in estimating per unit costs is finding an appropriate basis or standard on which to estimate the cost of the tasks to be carried out in the proposed research. These standards can be derived from previous studies of a comparable nature (Dillman 1978). Most survey research centers of large universities, private consulting firms, or government bureaus have a good basis for estimating the costs of conducting surveys. By subtracting the costs of salaried personnel and of data analysis and report dissemination, one is left with the actual costs of collecting and preparing data for analysis in a given survey. Dividing this figure by the number of units of observation (the number of times a given task was repeated), one arrives at a per unit cost of collecting, editing, and coding data. This per unit figure must be broken down into personnel and nonpersonnel costs (which usually consist of travel) in order to enter the resulting estimates in the appropriate line of the research budget. Per unit cost standards can be prepared for different types of data collection procedures—for example, household interviewing, telephone surveys, and mailed questionnaires.

In using a per unit cost standard, one must know the relevant conditions on which the standard is based in order to adjust it to the conditions that will prevail in the study being designed. Conditions which should be considered are: (1) the data collection procedure used, (2) the construction of a sampling frame as part of the collection of data, (3) the length of the interview or questionnaire, (4) the amount of travel required per interview, (5) the amount of time required for coding a schedule, and (4) the rate of pay. For example, in a statewide household survey in 1970, the average length of an interview was 1.5 hours, the average time for coding was 3.0 hours, the average distance traveled was 60 miles, and the rate of pay was $3 an hour. Listing of the sampling frame cost $9, interviewing (which included time spent in an interview, in transit between interviews, in making call backs, in reviewing work with the supervisor, and in editing) cost $12, and coding cost $9 per interview. Travel expenses paid at the rate of 10¢ a mile were $6 per interview.

We have used these per unit costs as standards by which to estimate the corresponding per unit costs of our hypothetical study in Supplemental Budget B (see Figure 13-6). Down the left side of Budget B we list each of the personnel tasks and nonpersonnel items for which we have standard per unit costs. In column (1) we list the size of each standard task or item. In column (2) we list the estimated size of the corresponding task or item in the study being designed. For example, the listing of the sampling frame took 3.0 hours per interview in the standard study which involved a statewide, multistage cluster sample. Our hypothetical study, let us assume, will take place in a metropolitan area. Therefore we can anticipate that the time required to list our sampling frame will be about one-half that of the standard. Consequently we enter 1.5 hours in column (2). Let us further assume that on the basis of pretesting we have determined that our interview has an average length of 1.0 hour, which we also enter in column (2). Since our interview is shorter and requires much less coding than the standard, we will estimate our per unit coding time to be 1.0 hour.

Once the average sizes of personnel tasks and nonpersonnel items have

Figure 13-6 Supplemental Budget B: Estimating data collection costs by per unit costs

Task	Standard unit size (1)	Estimated unit size (2)	Adjustment factor [(2)/(1)] (3)	Standard unit cost (4)	Estimated per unit cost [(3)/(4)] (5)
Sampling frame	3.0 hrs.	1.5 hrs.	.50	$9	$4.50
Interview length	1.5 hrs.	1.0 hrs.	.66	$12	$8.00
Coding	3.0 hrs.	1.0 hrs.	.33	$9	$3.00
Total					$15.50
Nonpersonnel travel	60 min.	20 min.	.33	$6	$2.00

been estimated, an adjustment factor for each task and item is computed. It represents the ratio of the size of the estimated task to the size of the standard task, and is entered in column (3). The standard per unit costs for each task and item are entered in column (4). The corresponding per unit costs for the study being designed are then estimated by multiplying the figures in column (3) by those in column (4).

The final step in estimating wages involves summing the estimated per unit costs for all personnel tasks. In our example this amounts to $15.50. If the analyst anticipates a higher rate of pay, the per unit cost of personnel should be corrected by the percentage difference. The resulting figure is multiplied by the number of units of observation, and entered as the estimate of wages to be paid field workers in the line item budget. For example, let us assume we anticipate paying $4 an hour, a percentage increase of 33 over the standard. To correct for the rate of pay, our per unit cost for personnel tasks is $15.50 × 1.33 = $20.62. If we conduct 300 interviews, our estimate of wages to be paid field workers is $20.62 × 300 = $6186. Similarly, estimated per unit costs of nonpersonnel items are summed, corrected for any percentage change in the rate of pay, and multiplied by the number of units of observation. These estimates are then held for entry into Supplemental Budget C, the estimate of nonpersonnel items, which will be discussed in the following section.

The final step in estimating personnel costs is to sum all wages and salaries in the line-item budget. Fringe benefits are then computed on the basis of that subtotal and entered in the budget. At the same time, indirect costs can be computed and entered in the appropriate line. Since consultant services are not considered part of the direct operations of the project, they are added to the line-item budget *after* calculating fringe benefits and indirect costs.

ESTIMATING NONPERSONNEL COSTS

Estimating the cost of nonpersonnel items is an easier task. Nonpersonnel items constitute a relatively small portion of a research budget, so that imprecise estimates are less consequential. There are usually two categories of such items in a research budget: (1) computer services and (2) equipment, supplies, and related services.

Computer services can be estimated by a per unit cost procedure, as was described in the preceding section, on the basis of the documented cost of similar studies. With the per interview or questionnaire cost of key punching in the standard study, and the ratio of the length of the proposed interview to that of the standard, a per unit cost of key punching can be estimated. This estimated per unit cost can then be multiplied by any percentage difference in the rate of pay and by the number of interviews to be conducted to arrive at an estimate of the cost of key punching. Similarly, one can take the amount of computer time required for analysis in the standard study, adjust it for any difference in the amount of analysis anticipated in the proposed study, and multiply that estimated time by the prevailing rate of charges to arrive at an estimate of the cost of computer analysis.

Estimating the cost of equipment, supplies, and related services involves a two-step procedure. A certain amount of equipment, supplies, and related services are required to maintain any office, regardless of the level of research activities carried on. These can be estimated on the basis of the average monthly expenditures for such items as office equipment, paper, telephone service, and postage for an office with a comparable number of full-time, equivalent professional and clerical staff. These monthly figures can then be multiplied by the number of months the proposed study is expected to last to arrive at estimates of the basic cost of the respective items. The second step involves estimating the amount of equipment, supplies, and related services that will be required to carry out the procedures specified in the research design. For these estimates the analyst must return to the management plan and make an estimate of such items required to carry out each activity. The estimated cost of each item is summed for all activities and added to the estimated basic office cost, which sum is entered in the respective line of the research budget as the estimated total cost of that item.

We have demonstrated this procedure for our hypothetical study using Supplemental Budget C (see Figure 13-7). Down the left side of Budget C we list the equipment, supplies, and related services to be costed. In column (1) we enter the average cost of such items in an office of the size hypothesized in our example. In column (2) we enter the number of months the study is expected to last, based on lapsed time estimated in the management plan, which in this case is approximately four months (see Figure 13-3). The estimate of basic office costs in column (3) is arrived at by multiplying column (1) by column (2).

Figure 13-7 Supplemental Budget C: Estimating nonpersonnel costs

Item	Average monthly cost	No. of months	Estimated cost [(1) X (2)]	Estimated cost of research activities	Total estimated cost
	(1)	(2)	(3)	(4)	(5)
Stationery supplies	\$___ X	___	= \$___	+ \$___	= \$_____
Equipment	\$___ X	___	= \$___	+ \$___	= \$_____
Telephone	\$___ X	___	= \$___	+ \$___	= \$_____
Travel	\$___ X	___	= \$___	+ \$___	= \$_____
Reproduction	\$___ X	___	= \$___	+ \$___	= \$_____
Postage	\$___ X	___	= \$___	+ \$___	= \$_____

Next, the amount of equipment, supplies, and related services required to execute the activities of the management plan is listed, and their cost is entered in column (4). In our hypothetical study we anticipate extensive use of the telephone in supervising field workers during the collection of data. In Supplemental Budget B we estimated the amount of travel expenses connected with field work, and that figure is now entered in column (4). The final step is to add columns (3) and (4) and enter the sum in column (5). This last column of figures represents the estimated total cost for each item of equipment, supplies, and related services to be entered on the appropriate line of the research budget.

Before considering the research budget complete, the analyst should review the soundness of the assumptions upon which its estimates are based. The cost of research derives in large measure from professional services, the precise need for which is difficult to anticipate. Therefore, actual costs of research frequently exceed budgeted costs. Where the assumptions regarding the expended time of personnel seem questionable, the estimates should be increased to allow for unanticipated needs. In addition, multi-year budgets incur additional costs due to inflation, and to merit increases in salaries and the attendant fringe benefits. Such expected increases should also be incorporated in the final version of the budget.

SUMMARY

The design for the administration of the proposed research should consist of three components:

1. An organizational plan which specifies (a) the auspices of the study, (b) the type of personnel to be employed, expressed in terms of a

set of job descriptions, and (c) an organizational chart indicating the chain of accountability among personnel

2. A management plan which identifies the specific activities to be carried out, their sequence and interrelatedness, the lapsed time for their execution, and their date of completion

3. A financial plan (budget) which itemizes the type and amount of personnel and nonpersonnel expenditures anticipated.

REFERENCES

BERUBE, MAURICE R., and MARILYN GITTELL. *Confrontation at Ocean Hill-Brownsville.* New York: Frederick A. Praeger, Publishers, 1969.

CARO, FRANCIS G., ed. *Readings in Evaluation Research.* New York: Russell Sage Foundation, 1971.

DILLMAN, DON A., *Mail and Telephone Surveys.* New York: John Wiley and Sons, 1978.

KUECKEBERG, DONALD A., and ARTHUR L. SILVERS. *Urban Planning Analysis: Methods and Models.* New York: John Wiley and Sons, 1974.

MAYER, ROBERT R., *Social Science and Institutional Change.* Washington, D.C.: U.S. Department of Health, Education, and Welfare, 1978.

National Academy of Sciences and Social Science Research Council, *The Behavioral and Social Sciences, Outlook and Needs.* Washington, D.C.: The National Academy, 1969, p. 193.

PERT for CAA Planning, A Programmed Course of Instruction in PERT. Washington, D.C.: U.S. Office of Economic Opportunity, January 1969.

RIECKEN, HENRY W., and ROBERT F. BORUCH, eds. *Social Experimentation, A Method for Planning and Evaluating Social Intervention.* New York: Academic Press, 1974.

WEISS, CAROL H., ed. *Evaluating Action Programs.* Boston: Allyn and Bacon, 1972.

WEISS, CAROL H. *Evaluation Research.* Englewood Cliffs, N.J.: Prentice-Hall, Inc., 1972.

WHOLEY, J. S., et al. "Proper Organizational Relationships," in *Evaluating Action Programs,* ed. Carol H. Weiss. Boston: Allyn and Bacon, Inc., 1972, pp. 118–123.

index